EMPOWERING AND HEALING THE BATTERED WOMAN

A Model for Assessment and Intervention

Mary Ann Dutton, PhD, is a clinical psychologist specializing in family violence and other forms of victimization. She received her doctorate from the University of Utah and is Professor of Clinical Psychology at Nova University, where she also serves as the Director of Clinical Training.

Dr. Dutton's research and clinical interests in the area of victimization have come together in her specialty program within the Nova University Community Mental Health Center. She is the Founder and Director of the Family Violence Program, an applied clinical research program that offers services to victims and perpetrators of domestic violence, while also providing training to doctoral and post-doctoral students.

In addition to being the author of numerous articles and book chapters on battered women and post-traumatic stress responses, Dr. Dutton's expertise has provided her with many opportunities to become involved with the legal system. She frequently conducts forensic evaluations and provides expert witness testimony in criminal and civil cases involving domestic violence and other forms of intimate victimization.

EMPOWERING AND HEALING THE BATTERED WOMAN

A Model for Assessment and Intervention

Mary Ann Dutton, Ph.D.

SPRINGER PUBLISHING COMPANY
NEW YORK

Springer Publishing Company, Inc.
536 Broadway
New York, NY 10012

92 93 94 95 96 / 5 4 3 2 1

Library of Congress Cataloging-in-Publication Data
Dutton, Mary Ann, 1949-
Empowering and healing the battered woman : a model for assessment and intervention / Mary Ann Dutton
p. cm.
Includes bibliographical references and index.
ISBN 0-8261-7130-3
1. Abused women–Counseling of. 2. Abused women–United States–Psychology–Case studies. I. Title.
HV1444.D87 1992
362.82'9286–dc20 92-7826
CIP

Printed in the United States of America

To the women who have shared with me their experiences of victimization and their healing processes: I have tried to hear what you say with your words, your tears, your laughter, and your rage.

To the women who have not yet been able to share their experiences with anyone and to those for whom it is too late.

Contents

Foreword

The understanding of battered women has grown immeasurably among mental health professionals over the past 10 years. No longer is it permissible to blame women for their own victimization, although certainly some practitioners with a lack of knowledge about battering relationships may indeed continue to do so. *Empowering and Healing the Battered Woman: A Model for Assessment and Intervention* takes professionals who already have a knowledge base of battered women, as well as those who do not, through the steps of understanding and effectively intervening to assist the woman in increasing her safety, empowering her mentally, and helping her to heal from the abuse.

The cornerstone of effective intervention with abused women has been provided by the interaction of the feminist-political model of understanding battering behavior as a means of controlling a woman and the posttraumatic stress model of assuming that any normal person can have major psychological disruption from experiencing trauma such as the physical, sexual, and psychological abuse that make up the pattern of battering in relationships. Mary Ann Dutton has carefully detailed the research underlying both models, and then integrates them to draw a new paradigm. This paradigm broadens the concept of battering from a group of discrete or even connected violent incidents to a distinct pattern of abnormal power and control in a relationship. Dutton analyzes the seemingly infinite variety of psychological mechanisms that create the "glue" or context in which the violence pattern occurs.

Although battering behavior that occurs in relationships has been known to consist of a pattern of physical, sexual, and psychological abuse, less is known about the terrorist tactics that make up the psychological abuse. Yet these cues to potential danger often increases a woman's feeling of terror and have a major impact on her ability to function. Most battered women report certain recognizable signals that precede more serious abuse; a look in his eyes, a certain tone of voice, a particular type of nervous habit. By evaluating these reported signals in the context of the abnormal intent to control the woman's behavior, they are better defined as psychological mechanisms of terrorism, even though on appearance they do not appear abusive. Many of the more common scenarios are presented as case examples in this book.

The most common question asked of battered women is, "Why don't you leave?" However, research has demonstrated that leaving does not stop the violence. Rather, a woman is likely to be at greater risk for more serious violence or even death should she try to leave or employ other efforts to protect herself. Women develop a lack of faith in using escape as a means of stopping the violence through the many efforts they make that are unsuccessful. Keeping silent and protecting the batterer results in further abuse; telling the police may also result in further abuse and perhaps social ostracism too. Jobs may be lost if the woman stays home until the injuries are no longer visible; but she may also lose her job if she tells a boss who does not want to get involved. These "no-win" dilemmas are explored so that interventions can be planned to take the real lives of battered women into account. Lest readers think that such cautions are no longer necessary, Dutton tells of several cases in which therapists (or other helpers) have been known to tell women they will not take their cases unless they leave. When questioned about this behavior, they claim they are "rescuing" the women; the therapists do not understand the true coercive nature of their actions, which are not dissimilar to and are often an extension of the batterer's psychological abuse.

Goals of effective intervention for battered women can be broken down into three major components: (1) helping the woman find greater safety from violence, (2) empowering the woman to regain her own control and power, and (3) helping her heal from the effects of the abuse. Every action taken by a therapist must be scrutinized as to where it fits in this schema. Psychological interventions must address the negative psychological effects in three major areas: (A) cognition such as thinking processes, self-esteem and self-efficacy, memory deficits and intrusions, attributions, and perceptions of others and the world in general; (B) indicators of psychological distress and/or dysfunction such as high arousal and anxiety, fear, phobic responses, anger, high avoidance and depression, and drug and alcohol abuse; and (C) disturbance in interpersonal relationships, other than that with the abuser, such as difficulty trusting, fear of intimacy, numb feelings about people, feeling indifferent or like "spoiled goods," and avoidance as a result of shame.

Why women experience diverse levels of psychological impact from the same type of abusive incident has to do with mediating factors, such as the woman's personal strengths and internal resources, the presence of other simultaneous stressors, institutional responses, access to tangible resources and social support, family support, vulnerabilities, and the balance of positive and negative aspects of the relationship. These are further detailed within this book so that their measurement becomes a routine part of the practitioner's assessment. The social, cultural, political, and economic context within which the woman lives is another important factor in mediating the impact of the violence. Women who see themselves outside of the mainstream as well as those of a minority culture or ethnic group are more likely to have limited access to available resources, making healing even more difficult. Those groups who face other societal discrimination and oppression, such as lesbians, Blacks, Hispanics, Amerasians, and American Indian women, older women, poor women, and those with disabilities, are also at greater risk for serious impact.

The clinician's ability to make accurate assessments and develop appropriate treatment plans has been strengthened by the addition of new tests that are described and contained within this volume. The difficulties and benefits of using the Conflict Tactic Scale (CTS) to measure levels of physical abuse (it does not measure sexual abuse or psychological terrorism, nor does it measure the pattern of violence and escalation of abuse in context over time) are described; a new test is described, the Abusive Behavior Observation Checklist (ABOC), developed at Nova University, replaces the CTS in measuring frequency, severity, and types of violent acts and injuries. Other methods of assessment that have been developed from over more than ten years of experience at the Nova University Family Violence Program are also included in this book. Many of these assessment instruments have also been used to assist legal counsel in making decisions about defending battered women who kill, attempt to kill, or commit other serious criminal acts in defense of themselves or others.

Treatment to help women heal from the effects of repeated abuse follows both feminist principles of egalitarianism and the attention to the effects of gender and sociocultural oppression as well as the trauma model that begins with the assumption of normality prior to the trauma. Assessment to guide treatment planning must identify the strengths of the woman so that these can be rebuilt and used to help reempower her and strengthen her self-concept as well as restore her expectation of self-efficacy. Any psychological symptoms present are seen as coping strategies and not as a personality disorder. Specific suggestions for working with different issues that are common to abused women have been tested and found successful for many women. These are described in the final chapters and their relevance to the various psychotherapy theories explained. The practitioner has a veritable grab bag of techniques to go along with the careful analysis provided. In *Empowering and Healing the Battered Woman*, Dutton provides us with the next stage of development, which emanates from the expanding knowledge-base about woman battering.

LENORE E. A. WALKER, EdD, ABPP
Diplomate in Clinical Psychology
Denver, Colorado

Preface

This book is for those whose interest is in understanding battered women and assisting them in the process of reempowerment and healing. The work that helped to form the foundation for this book began in 1980 with the founding of the Family Violence Program in the School of Psychology at Nova University. I was then an Assistant Professor and was beginning to turn my professional attention from marital conflict in general, to domestic violence in particular. There was very little professional literature to guide the development of an applied clinical research program that was to provide clinical services to battered women in the community, to develop new knowledge about battering, and to provide training to doctoral clinical psychology graduate students working with battered women who were seeking help through mental-health services. For several years I struggled with conceptualizing a way to train students to provide clinical services to battered women without the pathologizing and victim blaming that the profession so readily encourages. The Family Violence Program has provided services to over 700 women. In 1985 the Program began to provide services to the perpetrators of domestic violence as well, although separately from the victims. The Family Violence Program continues to provide services to batterers, most of whom are court-mandated as a condition of probation after a domestic-violence arrest.

In 1984 I was asked to work on my first forensic case involving a battered woman charged with killing her boyfriend. I have since evaluated over 100 women and adolescents charged with a crime, usually murder or attempted murder, in which the violence they experienced from a family member (e.g., husband or parent) was at issue in the case. This work has had a profound influence on my understanding of the tremendous impact that chronic and severe abuse has on the whole person. It has also made me vividly aware of the secondary victimization that battered women routinely experience from the institutional systems (e.g., legal, medical, mental health) that are designed to protect them. At the point at which they fight back against their victimization, battered women are typically treated as criminals with little regard for their prior, and usually recent, history of abuse.

Working with students has also taught me much about understanding battering. It has provided a mirror for understanding my own reactions to this work, whether it be rage at the injustice of abuse, sadness about the many losses suffered when there has been abuse, fear related to actual danger of a vengeful abuser, vicarious victimization that results from witnessing the horrors of abuse or recognizing the shattered assumptions of my own invulnerability, the helplessness of being able to do just so much, or the joy of helping to ease someone's pain. My work with students has required that I continually examine my honesty and accountability. I have learned that I cannot hide behind the power and control typical of a traditional hierarchical teacher/student relationship and at the same time teach students about recognizing the misuse of power by the batterer toward the victim or by the therapist against the client. I have struggled with learning to responsibly use the inherently greater power of my position vis-à-vis students, without exploiting or retreating into it. I have attempted to teach my students the same.

This work has shown me repeatedly the pain and suffering that oppression and the abuse of power exacts on human life. The influence of my feminist colleagues and friends has been to help me understand that this pain is inextricably embedded in the social, cultural, and political context of a society riddled with sexism, racism, classism, ageism, and homophobia. The influence of a feminist perspective has also shown me how healing the pain can be accomplished through working to create a society in which all human life is valued equally. Working with other feminists has taught me to appreciate the emotional, spiritual, and vulnerable parts of myself and to recognize their importance in my work as a professional, along with the intellectual and rational parts.

This book is an attempt to fill a gap in the available literature on working with battered women. Clearly the first priority should always be safety; battered women's shelters and the battered women's movement have played an essential role in this regard. For some battered women, empowerment and healing from abuse requires more than finding safety. For others, a priority on safety may come only after enough healing has occurred to make it conceivable that one does not have to pay the high price of abuse in order to get one's emotional and physical needs met. This book is an effort to help mental health professionals address the broad spectrum of needs confronting the battered woman and to prioritize those needs accordingly.

The book is divided into two major parts. The first one addresses assessment issues relevant to understanding the battered woman. Chapter 1 provides a conceptual model for understanding the battered woman's response to abuse and the psychological effects that result from it. Chapter 2 addresses assessment of the violence and abuse experienced by the battered woman. Chapter 3 focuses on assessment of the battered woman's strategies to escape, avoid, and protect herself and her children from further violence and abuse. Chapter 4 covers assessment of the psychological effects of abuse, including posttraumatic effects, cognitive changes, and effects on relationships. The final chapter in this section, Chapter 5, focuses on assessing the various factors that mediate the battered woman's response to and the psychological effects of violence.

Part II addresses issues concerning intervention. Chapter 6 provides a general framework for understanding intervention by the professional from a mental-health perspective. The next three chapters address different components of the intervention process. Chapter 7 focuses on interventions geared toward protection of the battered woman, increasing her safety and her ability to respond to crises. Chapter 8 addresses the process of decision making and empowerment. Chapter 9 focuses on healing the psychic wounds of battering, work done primarily after danger is no longer imminent. Finally, Chapter 10 turns the attention to the professional by focusing on self-care and other therapist issues.

This book describes a process, not an end point. It is an attempt to understand how I, as a mental-health professional, and my students can be of help to battered women in their processes of reempowerment and healing. It is also an attempt to share the process of becoming a whole human being as I do this work. I invite you, the reader, to share in this process.

Acknowledgments

Most importantly of all I want to acknowledge each of the many women who have shared with me their experiences of violence and abuse, and the aftermath that followed; the revictimization by the institutions and professionals who should have helped instead, and, finally, their healing. It is from this connection—to the reality of women's lives—that I have been able to draw and write this book. To each one of you I extend my deepest thanks.

I want to thank Catherine Waltz, L.C.S.W., Clinical Coordinator of the Family Violence Program and friend, for helping me learn to share power and to receive support. I have lived in the trenches with her and feel honored for having done so. Former Clinical Coordinators, Dorothy Dionne, Psy.D.; Victoria Dellaporte, M.S.W.; and Janon Strom, Ph.D., have been remarkable in their support of the Family Violence Program and of me, and I want to thank them. I owe a great deal to the clinical and research students with whom I have worked closely during the past 10 years. In particular, I want to thank Ava Colantuono Land, Ph.D.; Sean Perrin, M.S.; Kelly Chrestman, M.S.; Pauline Halle, B.S.; Kim Burghardt, B.A.; Laura Hohnecker, M.A.; and Rada Strauss, M.A., for their dedication to the Family Violence Program research efforts. Other students who have devoted considerable time and effort to doctoral dissertation research and professional projects in the area of victimization and violence have facilitated my own learning as well. These students include Wendy Lader, Ph.D.; Sandra Rachley, Ph.D.; Ava Colantuono Land, Ph.D.; Susan Donnell, Ph.D.; Carol Williams, Ph.D.; Joy Doncaster Kenefick, M.S.; John Neil, Psy.D.; Joe Cimino, Psy.D.; Michael Borack, M.S.; Bonnie Larsen, M.S.; Charles Knecht, M.A.; Giselle Hass, B.A.; Andrew Bunce, M.S.; and Carol Adams, Psy.D. Lenore Walker, Ed.D., has been a mentor and a friend since 1980. Her prolific writing, her skillful guidance, and her personal support have greatly influenced my professional development in the area of battered women. To her I am deeply indebted. Anne Ganley, Ph.D., has been a continued source of inspiration and support. She has led me gently and clearly to understandings that seemed to originate from within me, but that were unmistakably harvested from her shared wisdom built on her remarkable years of work in the field of domestic violence. Her ability to construct a feminist analysis of a situation or problem has taught me a great deal. Her friendship has been healing and soothing. Christine Courtois, Ph.D.; Sherril Valdes, M.S.W.; Anne Ganley, Ph.D.; and Philinda Hutchings, Ph.D., provided valuable feedback on earlier drafts of the manuscript and have shared with me their life's work in the area of victimization and violence. Their input has been rich, and from them I learned a great deal. The process of sharing my work with them and with many other significant colleagues has been a privilege. Others I wish to thank include Daniel Saunders, Ph.D.; Kevin Hamberger, Ph.D.; Bob Geffner, Ph.D.; Alan Rosenbaum, Ph.D.; Marie Root, Ph.D.; Adrienne Smith, Ph.D.; and Elizabeth Rave, Ph.D.

I want to thank the many professional colleagues with whom I have had the privilege of working closely in the forensic and public policy arenas. I have learned a great deal working with them. In particular, I want to thank Sue Ostroff, Clearinghouse for the Defense of Battered Women, Philadelphia; D. Jean Veta, J.D., and Jennifer S. Divine, J.D., of Covington & Burling, Washington, DC; Ellen Leesfield, J.D., of Ellen L. Leesfield, P.A., Miami, Florida; Margaret Rosenbaum, J.D., Chief Prosecutor, Domestic Crimes Unit, State Attorney's Office, Metropolitan-Dade County, Florida; Dan Lilley, J.D., Mary Davis, J.D., and Robin MacDonald of Daniel G. Lilley, P.A., Portland, Maine; Bruce Lyons, J.D., of Lyon & Sanders, Ft. Lauderdale, Florida; Tim Day, J.D., and others from the Broward County Public Defender's Office; and Howard Greenstein, M.A., M.B.A., and Sarah Lennett, Office of Victim Services, Metropolitan-Dade County, Florida.

I want to thank Barbara Watkins, former Vice-President and Senior Editor of Springer Publishing Co., who provided me with much support and encouragement throughout the process of creating this book and from whose thoughtful editorial comments I have learned a great deal.

I am indebted to Frank DePiano, Ph.D., Dean of the School of Psychology, for his continuing professional and personal support in the development of the Family Violence Program, and for all the Nova University Community Mental Health Clinic staff who have contributed to its development. I appreciate the assistance of my graduate assistant, Linda Ludeke, M.S., as she skillfully helped me in the managing of many final details of this book. I also appreciate the technical assistance of Linda Lamb, Nancy Smith, and Diane Karol in the preparation of the manuscript.

I want to thank those of my local personal support network for their continuing support and encouragement, including Barbara Myrick, Estelle Fineberg, Stephanie Jordan, Mary Padlak, Christine Price, Sherril Valdes, Carol Davis, Marlene Schneider, Lillian Buchanan, Suellyn Winkle, Carol Peachee, Ruth Strokland, Kathy Peres, Judith Steward, and Barbara Windham. My family has always been available, including my sister, Martha Dutton Blackman, my parents, Norma and Edgar Dutton, my aunt, Betty Dutton, and my cousin, Wes Dutton.

PART I
Conceptual Framework and Assessment

1

Women's Response to Battering: A Psychological Model

Concern has been voiced about studying the psychological characteristics of battered women (Yllo, 1988) when these are used to explain why abuse occurs or why particular women are abuse victims. Characteristics such as problem-solving deficits, unassertiveness, emotional dependency, and traditional sex-role attitudes have been used to blame battered women for, among other things, allowing the abuse to occur, for not stopping the abuse, or for seeking out abusive relationships in the first place. But more recently, the psychological characteristics of battered women have been studied as effects, rather than as causes, of violence, abuse, and control (cf., Douglas, 1987; Walker, 1979, 1984). This focus on the effects of abuse in battered women parallels similar developments in work with other trauma groups such as childhood sexual abuse (Briere, 1989; Browne & Finkelhor, 1986, Courtois, 1988; Sgroi, 1988), crime victims of rape and other assault (Saunders, Arata, & Kilpatrick, 1990; Steketee & Foa, 1987), and sexual exploitation by professionals (Bates & Brodsky, 1989; Pope & Bouhoutsos, 1986).

The present chapter outlines a conceptual framework for understanding the battered-woman's response to violence, abuse, and control. That framework then provides the foundation for guiding both assessment and intervention as described throughout the rest of this book. Accordingly, psychological assessment of battered women will focus on (1) understanding the battered woman's behavior within the context of the violence, abuse, and control, and (2) understanding the psychological trauma and other sequelae of having experienced violence, abuse, and control from an intimate partner. Psychological intervention with battered women, which is necessarily based on an adequate understanding of the battered woman's response to violence, can be framed within three goals: (1) increasing the battered woman's safety, (2) helping to re-empower her through decisionmaking, and (3) healing the psychological trauma of abuse.

WOMEN'S RESPONSE TO BATTERING: THE MODEL

Various terms have been used to refer to violence, abuse, and control, such as wife beating, domestic violence, spouse abuse, marital violence, battering, and aggression. These terms may intentionally or unintentionally obscure issues of gender, responsibility, and the marital nature of the relationship (Ganley, 1989). In this book, I use the terms violence, abuse, and control in order first to include abuse that occurs in relationships other than heterosexual marriage, for example, cohabitating, dating (Pirog-Good & Stets, 1989), and lesbian (Lobel, 1986; Renzetti, 1988, 1989) relationships. Second, I wish to accurately reflect the fact that the battered woman is exposed to more than discrete violent episodes; rather, the abuse is characterized by continual occurrences of various behaviors by her partner that function to exert power and control over her, often for an extended period of months or years. I use the term abuse generally to refer to the acts of physical violence, sexual violence and coercion, psychological torture, and all other forms of power and control exercised against the woman.

The overall model presented here to explain the battered woman's response to violence, abuse, and control includes careful examination of the following components: (1) the nature and pattern of violence, abuse, and control, (2) the psychological effects of abuse, (3) the battered woman's survival strategies and other efforts to respond to the abuse, and (4) factors that mediate both the effects of abuse and the survival strategies used to respond to it (see Figure 1.1). All of these components must be examined within the cultural, racial, ethnic, political, and economic context within which the battered woman and her family live. Each of the components is described in detail in Chapters 2 to 5. Below is a brief overview of each component of the model followed by an example that illustrates the interrelationships among them.

The Nature and Pattern of Abuse

Understanding the psychological effects of abuse on the battered woman requires an examination of the nature and pattern of abuse directed at her (see Chapter 2). The function of the batterer's behavior is to control and exert power over the victim; this has been emphasized as essential to the

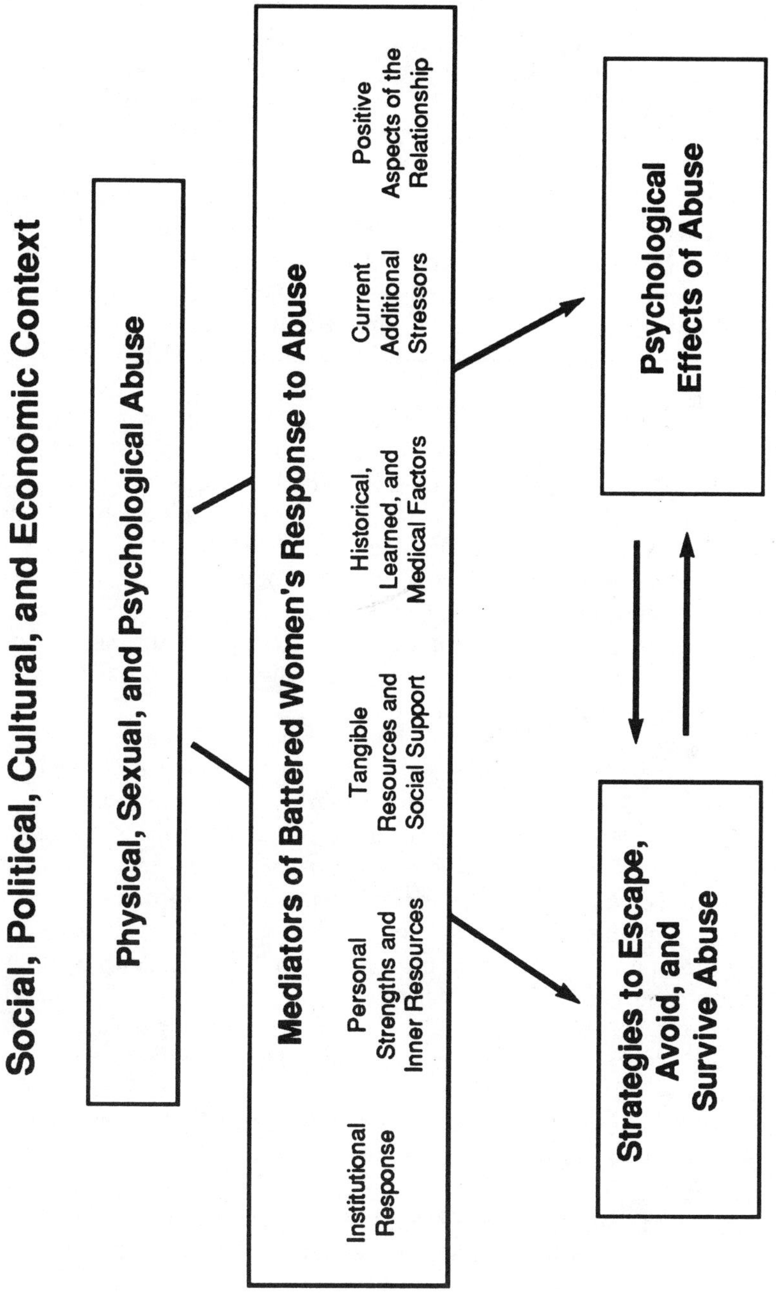

Figure 1.1 Model of battered women's response to abuse.

definition of abuse (Ganley, 1981, 1989; Pence & Paymar, 1986). Nonviolent behaviors may take on the same property as violent behaviors when their function is to control a victim by means of threats or prior patterning of behavior. For example, a husband's loud voice or a raised fist may signal danger when these behaviors have been associated with his actual use of violence in the past or the reasonable expectation that he might use violence in the future. Thus, subsequent to the initial occurrence of violence, many seemingly nonviolent behaviors of the batterer (e.g., angry voice, threatening gestures, extreme calmness, a particular look in the eye, excess use of alcohol, staying out late at night) may acquire similarly controlling properties. This may be explained by their prior association with actual violence through a process of chaining in a classical conditioning paradigm. Thus, the meaning of any particular behavior by the batterer must be considered in the context of his prior violence and behaviors intended to control his partner.

Many women describe a certain "look in the eye" that signals extreme danger. For a number of women, it was that look that triggered a self-defensive reaction. They had come to know that the look meant violence was inevitable and imminent. Unless one were to understand the patterning within previous incidents, when "that look" preceded the violent rape, the choking to unconsciousness, or the severe beating, it would make little sense why a woman might respond with such terror at simply "a look in the eye." When learned with precision, the cues given by the batterer that signal danger to the battered woman comprise a language whose subtlety defies meaning for those not familiar with it.

Defining the nature of abuse to which the battered woman is exposed, involves far more than describing simply the acts of violence or even the sequence of events that led to the acute battering. Understanding the battered woman's experience also requires understanding the meaning associated with the abusive context, whether or not, at any particular point in time, the battered woman herself is entirely aware of that meaning on a conscious level. For example, for one battered woman, the sound of her boyfriend's motorcycle gliding into the driveway in the early morning hours with the motor turned off was sufficient to elicit terror beyond the fear she already felt. The meaning to her, although perhaps undiscernable to someone else, was to greatly increase the certainty that he was going to kill, or seriously injure, her.

For another battered woman, a series of uncommon, and seemingly insignificant, behaviors by her boyfriend led her to feel even greater fear than usual: attempting to force her to eat some food he had brought when she repeatedly stated that she was not hungry, stating that his mother had commented on how he was acting strangely when he visited her earlier that day, and showing her a pair of brass knuckles in an intimidating manner. Taken together, this woman felt fear and apprehension; the context was one of unfamiliarity and uncertainty. Later, he began to beat her and she could feel his hands around her throat; the difference was that this time she could feel herself not able to breath. She reached for a knife on the dresser and repeatedly stabbed him. For some, it was difficult to understand how the overall context of meaning contributed to her perception of lethality in this versus previous incidents.

Strategies to Escape, Avoid, and Protect

Battered women engage in an impressively wide range of behaviors in responding to the abuse against them by their batterers (Bowker, 1983; Frieze, Knoble, Washburn, & Zomnir, 1980; Gondolf, 1988; Pagelow, 1981) (see Chapter 3). These efforts to escape, avoid, and protect themselves and their children from continued violence, abuse, and control may include legal strategies (e.g., calling the police, filing criminal charges, seeking protective injunction, filing a civil suit against the batterer); seeking help from a variety of sources (e.g., shelter, an attorney, a mental-health professional, a physician, clergyman, social-service provider, friends, family); leaving, separating, and/or divorcing; and compliance with and/or anticipation of the batterer's requests or desires.

Simply determining what efforts the battered woman has made to escape, avoid, or protect herself and her children is not adequate. It is also necessary to determine the effectiveness of those strategies for increasing the battered woman's safety. Although not commonly understood, even among professionals, many apparently reasonable and effective strategies such as calling the police, separating from an abusive relationship, telling family or friends about the abuse, are not effective in keeping the battered woman safe; sometimes those efforts may even increase the danger presented by the batterer.

In addition to examining the effectiveness of a battered woman's strategies with regard to safety, it is important to look at other consequences that may result from her efforts. For example, a battered woman's choice to call the police may result in a neighbors' social ostracism, perhaps preventing their children from playing with hers. Staying home from work in order to hide injuries received in a battering may be a woman's effort to protect herself by keeping the abuse a secret; it may cost her her job. Finally, a battered woman's decision to remain quiet about the abuse in order not to risk embarrassing or further enraging her batterer may well result in increased social isolation in that she may be even less protected as few people may know of her situation.

Previous institutional response to abuse is an important factor in understanding the context in which battered women live. For example, if a battered woman has called the police, what was their response? An arrest followed by prosecution may communicate to her that the police will intervene and do what they can within the limits of the law to protect her. Alternatively, the police may arrive only to minimize the seriousness of the danger to her, or perhaps arrest her if she appears too emotional ("hysterical" or angry) or if she threatens to defend herself if her partner continues to abuse her. One battered woman was told that her husband was a big man (he was 6 ft. 6 in. and weighed 250 lbs.) and that they were not going in after him after he had locked his wife out of the house. When one battered woman requested, after having separated from her batterer, that police escort her to her house to get her belongings, the response was that if it took longer than 10 minutes they had "better things to do."

A battered woman may seek help through a mental health professional. Understanding the response with which she is met is important. She may have been asked, "What do you get out of the abuse in this relationship" or "What have you done to help him with his problem?" This implies that the focus of intervention is on her deficits, not on her safety. One therapist bragged that he had helped a battered woman client by telling her that if she did not get out of her marriage that he would not continue seeing her. He believed that he had "rescued" her and did not see that his use of coercion was actually parallel to that of her batterer. More appropriately, a mental health professional may encourage a battered woman to examine the dimensions of her safety, validate her concerns for herself and her children, provide her with information and resources to increase her safety (e.g., shelter and legal information), and support her in acting in ways that re-empower her. Even when the battered woman desires to remain in her relationship, her safety must remain the initial focus.

Further, it is important to understand the outcome of fighting back as a strategy. For example, some battered women have threatened current or previously abusive partners with lethal weapons to find that this strategy worked, at least temporarily, to protect themselves. One battered woman was arrested and charged with first-degree murder after having shot her second husband during an ongoing assault. Unknown to prosecutors, she had successfully defended herself against her first husband's assault with a gun by using another gun against him. She had never been criminally charged in the first incident. Her experience taught her that there was one way in which she had been able to protect herself; however, she was eventually considered a criminal for doing so. Another woman had successfully defended herself using a kitchen knife against her husband in a prior assault in which he was injured; she was not charged. She later used a knife again to defend herself, only this time the stab wound was fatal and she was charged with homicide.

Alternatively, some battered women have physically fought back against the violence, only to find that the violence against them escalated. One woman stated that any effort to defend herself, including covering her head with her hands, resulted in even greater abuse. For another woman, when she pushed her husband away from her face after he had taunted her and violated her personal space for hours, the batterer used her push as rationale for a beating, arguing that she had "started it."

Knowing the consequences of the battered woman's past use of specific strategies to protect herself and her children provides a context for understanding the likelihood of using specific strategies in the future. If a particular strategy worked even one time in the past, she may be more likely to use it in the future than one that had failed or for which she was seriously punished. Most strategies of protection become very understandable when the prior context has been articulated.

Psychological Effects of Abuse

The psychological effects of violence, abuse, and control can be considered within three subcategories: (1) changes in cognition, (e.g., cognitive schemas, self-esteem, expectations, self-efficacy, attributions, perceptions), (2) indicators of psychological distress and/or dysfunction (e.g., anger, fear, depression, alcohol or drug abuse), and (3) relational disturbances in other than the abusive relationship (e.g., difficulty trusting, fear of intimacy) (see Chapter 4).

It is worth repeating that there is justifiable concern in examining the psychological characteristics of a battered woman because the information can be misused in a victim-blaming manner (Schechter, 1987). Ochberg (1989) proposed a model of posttraumatic therapy that starts with an assumption of psychological health. Regardless of whether this assumption eventually proves to be true in a specific case, a useful initial hypothesis is to attribute evidence of psychological distress or dysfunction to the trauma itself.

Given the relatively high prevalence of childhood sexual (Russell, 1983) and physical (Stets & Straus, 1990) abuse, rape (Koss, 1990), dating violence (Pirog-Good & Stets, 1989), as well as sexual exploitation by professionals (Brodsky, 1977; Pope & Bohoustous, 1986), many women experience battering not as the first, but as a repeated, exposure to intimate violence. Thus, apparent psychopathology that predates the onset of the most recent battering experience may actually be evidence of prior psychological trauma. Regardless, without a detailed psychological and social history predating the occurrence of any form of victimization, including but not limited to abuse in the current or most recent intimate relationship, indicators of psychological trauma and other effects cannot be reasonably attributed to other, nonabuse factors.

Mediating Factors

Several categories of variables influence or mediate both the psychological effects of abuse, and the battered woman's efforts to escape, avoid abuse, and protect herself and her children (see Chapter 5). Mediating factors do not provide an explanation of why abuse occurs. They are, however, hypothesized to help explain differences in the psychological effects of abuse among battered women, beyond that which appears to be explained by knowing the nature and extent of the abuse alone. Some women exhibit severe psychological trauma; others do not. Some women who have suffered extreme abuse call the police or seek help through formal channels, whereas others do not. Differences are not readily explained by the severity of violence alone.

Beyond effects explained by he nature of abuse itself, the following factors are hypothesized to mediate both the level of psychological trauma and the strategies used to protect the woman from abuse: (1) tangible resources and social support, (2) institutional response, (3) personal strengths/inner resources, (4) other current stressors in addition to the abuse, (5) vulnerability factors, and (6) positive and negative aspects of the relationship in which the abuse occurs. For example, a battered woman who has little money or no current employment may experience greater hopelessness or other forms of psychological distress than a woman with more financial resources. The former would have more difficulty seeking a new residence, paying for child care while she is working, or providing for the everyday needs of herself and her children. The battered woman who has little social support available to her may have nowhere to live for a few weeks while she makes a transition away from her residence with the batterer or no place to go in the early morning hours when she needs to leave with the children in order to stay safe. As a result, her (perceived and actual) viable options may be limited, her level of fear may be greater because she may experience herself as entrapped; she may feel depressed or suicidal.

One battered woman decided to request that the state attorney's office press charges against her boyfriend who had kidnapped and repeatedly raped and beaten her. But her decision was made only after a victim's advocate from the police department followed up the police report with a call to her home. After a previous incident in which charges were dropped, the boyfriend had gone to the woman's house upon release from jail, and beaten her as punishment for calling the police. The victim advocate's support is an example of how one sort of institutional response clearly had an impact on the battered woman's use of the legal system as a strategy to protect herself. After the battered woman's decision to request that charges be brought, the man was eventually charged and convicted after having been held in jail with no bond.

The personal strength of the battered woman may trap her in an abusive situation as well as be a resource for her to get out of and survive the effects of it. As long as she is committed to the relationship, the battered woman may rely on her personal strength in an attempt to endure long enough for the batterer to change, to accommodate to his increasing demands, or to determine what needs to happen for the abuse to stop. Some women believe that they must be able to endure anything in order to maintain the feeling of being "in control." Alternatively, once a battered woman has effectively escaped an abusive relationship, her inner resources may help her to "do what she needs to do" in order to establish a new life away from the batterer. Finally, a battered woman's apparent personal strength may interfere with her ability to allow herself the feelings of vulnerability, grief, anger, and fear to which she may need access in order to heal from the trauma of abuse.

Some battered women must not only cope with the abuse but also with other major life stressors. One battered woman had to deal with the reality of breast cancer and her batterer's psychologically abusive response to it in addition to his physical abuse of her. Other stressors can both exacerbate the level of psychological distress otherwise experienced and alter the battered woman's response to the abuse against her. This woman believed that she would be even more unlikely to find another man to love her after her breast surgery.

The vulnerability created by the trauma of childhood sexual abuse or other uncontrollable life events (Walker, 1984) may exacerbate the psychological distress associated with battering. The resulting compounded trauma may thus be even greater than it might otherwise have been, and the process of healing may be more complicated and lengthy.

One battered woman experienced her relationship as positive during the periods of time when her husband was not drinking and when they were getting along well. For her, these periods were generally in the morning, before getting out of bed, and while drinking coffee and getting ready for the day. During this time, the battered woman felt hope and other positive feelings; she described it as being "like it used to be." These feelings influenced this battered woman's efforts to leave the relationship by making it more difficult.

Social, Political, and Economic Context

The racial, cultural, ethnic, political, and economic context in which the battered woman lives plays an essential role in understanding both the battered woman's efforts to respond to the abuse against her and the psychological trauma resulting from that abuse. Dutton (1988) described these variables as the macrosystem in his nested ecological model used to describe wife assault.

A woman whose social, political, and cultural context has provided the experience of having control over her life, may respond one way when abuse occurs; a woman who lives in a context in which neither she, nor other women like her (including her own mother), have experienced very much control over their own lives may respond differently.

For example, a lesbian battered woman may be more reluctant to use police protection, fearing the stigmatized response if the police officers discover the abusing partner is another woman. A wealthy Anglo woman may be reluctant to utilize shelter services or the police due to the lower-class stigma she associates with them. A poor woman with several children may lack the transportation, social support, and economic resources to consider living apart from her husband, the economic provider of the household. A minority woman may believe that a predominantly white jury would consider abuse normal or expected in "those" families and thus fail to hold her batterer responsible for his assaulting her. Alternatively, the minority woman may be all too aware of the oppression of the majority culture against both herself and her male partner and protect him from that system, even when it means failing to protect herself. She may struggle with the dilemma of balancing the oppression based on gender inherent in the battering, and the oppression based on race or ethnicity inherent in the institutional systems available to help her.

CASE ILLUSTRATIONS

Lisa

A Caucasian woman, for whom I shall use the pseudonym Lisa, was 35 years old at the time I met her. She had been married to her husband for 15 years; they had two children, one of whom was a preschooler. Both Lisa and her husband were professionally trained and lived an upper middle-class lifestyle. Each had been born into upper middle-class Jewish families. For 14 years of the marriage, the husband had used power and control tactics of psychological abuse, especially intimidation (e.g., destroying property), emotional abuse (e.g., making degrading statements about her body, name calling), male privilege (e.g., expecting sex whenever he wanted it without regard for Lisa, expecting Lisa to take primary care of the children and the household and to run the household routine around his work and activity schedule), and sexual abuse (e.g., threatening to find other sexual partners if Lisa was not compliant with his sexual demands, responding to Lisa in a degrading way during sex). During the last year, the husband's abuse had escalated, on one occasion, to his use of physical violence when he slapped her. The severity of psychological abuse had also escalated.

Lisa exhibited psychological indicators of traumatic stress and other signs of distress that included fear, anxiety, or autonomic arousal when her husband arrived home, depression, minimization of the severity of his behavior and of her reaction to it, shame associated with having been treated as she had been, underexpressed anger, and suicidal thoughts. Lisa's tolerance for the cognitive inconsistency of love and abuse was considerable. She believed that she had few alternative responses that would not result in either her husband's leaving the relationship or his escalating the abusive behavior.

Lisa had attempted to protect herself from her husband's abuse by telling him how she felt about it, by attempting to avoid him, by talking with her mother and his mother about it, but primarily by complying with his demands, especially regarding sex. She had also left the relationship on several occasions suggesting that they divorce.

In Lisa's case, the psychological effects of the abuse were probably made worse by the messages in her mother's response to her: "You're too fat to get anyone else, he's a good husband; I put up with your father for 50 years, you should stay with your husband; it's not your place to leave him—he makes good money, etc." Lisa's depression and lowered self-esteem were compounded by a dysfunctional family of origin in which she had been ridiculed for being overweight as a child, been told that no boy would ever want to go out with her and experienced emotional deprivation from parental neglect. Although Lisa was professionally trained, she was unemployed at the time and working full-time as caretaker of her young child. She had few available economic resources on which immediately to rely in order to leave the relationship, although she had the job skills that created the potential for her to support herself in the future.

Lisa's efforts in threatening divorce and separation had a paradoxical effect. Initially, the abuse toward her escalated as her husband reacted to Lisa's exercising control over her own life. Following the separation, the abuse abated as Lisa's husband began to appeal to her to return to the relationship, stating how much he loved her and did not want to lose the family. His loving and gentle behavior repeatedly lead her back into the relationship where the cycle began over again. On one occasion following a separation, Lisa asked if her husband had practiced safe sex when he had been with other sexual partners during the separation. He indicated that he had, after which time Lisa agreed to have sex with him. She later found out that he had lied to her and had engaged in unprotected sex with other women on numerous occasions. When Lisa confronted her husband with his deception, he again became abusive. The cycle repeated itself.

The psychological effects of depression and low self-esteem also influenced Lisa's efforts to protect herself from her husband's continued abuse. It was only after she began to gain a sense of control over some decisions in her life, including economic ones, that she was able to take a firmer stand about the conditions under which she was willing to have her husband return home.

This case illustrates abuse which may commonly go unrecognized, that is, abuse that has not resulted in severe injuries or police action but which, nevertheless, functions to exert power and control over the woman. There is the pattern and a long history of psychological and sexual abuse that eventually also included physical violence.

Further, the case illustrates the multiple efforts the woman made to protect herself from the abuse, although these may often go unrecognized as such. Some of Lisa's efforts to protect against abuse, (e.g., leaving, threatening divorce), which may be considered reasonable or expected even by professionals, may actually have increased the danger to her.

The case shows how mediational factors can make the situation for the abused woman even more difficult. In Lisa's case, internalized messages from her mother affected her self-esteem; the caretaking responsibility for a preschooler, and the lack of support from others to which she turned for help also contributed to make her shame, anger, and depression even greater. Altogether, these factors helped to increase her perception that there were few alternatives to her situation.

Pat

The 58-year old, lower middle-class African-American woman, mother of eight grown children, was married to her alcoholic husband for 40 years before his death. She was physically, sexually, and psychologically abused by her husband for nearly their entire marriage. The psychological abuse included close monitoring of her behavior, such as allowing her only a limited amount of time to return from work at the end of the day or to go to the grocery store without fear of a beating. Pat's husband would bring home other women who he was dating. Sometimes she would feel relieved because that meant he would leave her alone sexually for awhile. Pat's husband would have sex with her whenever he wanted, usually after returning home drunk late at night. The physical beatings occurred regularly. When the children attempted to intervene to protect their mother, they too would be beaten or threatened with a weapon. Pat has permanent scars from the severe cuts her husband gave her during one beating. The beatings would often end by Pat's being locked out of the house for the duration of the night. If the children attempted to allow her back in, they would be beaten.

> Pat finally moved from her husband's home with the help of a grown son who provided physical protection. Nonetheless, Pat was abused again by her husband when he came to her new house. In prior years, Pat had called the police and her husband had been arrested numerous times. He had always returned. During the years, Pat complied with most of her husband's demands; she complained little.
>
> Pat is an angry, controlled woman who trusts few people but asserts herself infrequently. She speaks only when addressed and is then quite compliant; she appears depressed.

This is a case of quite severe and prolonged abuse of a woman whose efforts to protect herself against recurrent violence were essentially unsuccessful. It was the effort of her son that enabled her to leave the home of her abuser, but even that was not entirely effective in stopping the abuse against her. The pattern of abuse was prolonged, severe, and varied.

In particular, this case illustrates how the institutional response (e.g., police) to Pat's abuse, which was only intermittently and briefly effective, taught Pat that there was no long-term protection available to end the violence against her. The lack of economic resources functioned as a mediating factor to limit Pat's options, especially during the years when she had small children for whom to care.

The chronic psychological effects of extended abuse can undermine a battered woman's ability to act to escape from an abusive relationship. Although Pat was able to attempt to escape the abuse many years later, she remained realistically afraid of subsequent beatings until her husband's death. And the effects of her long-term abuse shaped characterological aspects of her personality.

The next four chapters present a more detailed discussion of each of the four components of the model of women's response to battering: abusive behavior; strategies to escape, avoid, and survive; psychological effects of abuse; and mediators of the battered woman's response to abuse. Each of these chapters discusses concrete strategies for assessing each factor's influence on the woman.

2

Understanding the Nature and Pattern of Abusive Behavior

According to Gelles (1974), the social definition of the family as nonviolent and nurturant results in a "perceptual blackout" of violence that goes on in "normal" families. In this chapter, an elaboration of the abusive behavior component of the conceptual model presented in Chapter 1 is discussed. More specifically, this chapter identifies the particular aspects of the abusive behavior that an adequate assessment with a battered woman must necessarily address. Traditional methods of psychological assessment do not adequately address victimization by violence (Koss, 1990). Obtaining specific information from the battered woman about the abusive incidents and the context in which they occur is an essential component of an adequate assessment.

Three basic types of information (see Table 2.1) are important for defining abuse toward the woman client: (1) description of the intimate partner's abusive behaviors, (2) cognitions about the partner's abuse by the battered woman, and (3) other forms of abuse both contemporaneous and historical. Prior violence and abuse is important to mention here but it will be addressed in more detail in Chapter 5 (Mediators of the Battered Woman's Response to Her Victimization).

DEFINING ABUSE

Describing the intimate partner's abusive behavior requires assessment of both specific violent or abusive episodes and the patterning of abuse across

TABLE 2.1 Overview of Target Areas for the Assessment of Violence and Abuse

Abuse by Intimate Partner
Specific abuse episodes
Type or nature of abusive acts
Severity of abusive behaior
Severity of injury
Frequency of occurrence of particular abusive behavior
Duration of specific abuse episode
Across abusive episodes
Total frequency of abusive episodes
Duration from first to most recent episode
Stage in relationship at onset of each type of abuse
Highest severity level of abusive behavior
Highest severity level of injury
Cycle of violence and other patterns of abuse
Battered Woman's Cognitions about the Abuse
Appraisal of severity of past abuse
Expectation of continued abuse
Expectation of potentially lethal violence
Attribution of causality of abuse, including attribution of batterer's motivation if the cause is attributed to the batterer.
Perceptions of self-efficacy regarding safety
Attribution of responsibility for battered woman's safety
Other Forms of Victimization
Previous victimization (e.g., prior rape, childhood abuse)
Contemporaneous victimization (e.g., sexual harassment from a current employer)

time. The relevant parameters of *specific episodes* that require assessment include the (1) type or nature of abusive acts from an intimate partner, (2) level of severity of abusive behavior based on potential for injury, (3) level of severity of actual resultant injury, (4) frequency of occurrences of a particular abusive behavior within a single abusive episode, and (5) duration of a specific episode. The *pattern of abuse* across episodes refers to the (1) total frequency of episodes in which some form of abuse (e.g., physical, sexual) or specific abusive behavior (e.g., slap, punch, rape) occurred, (2) duration of time from first to most recent episode, (3) stage in relationship at onset of each type of abuse, (4) highest severity level of abusive behavior based on potential for injury, (5) highest severity level of actual injury, and (6) cycle of violence and other specific patterns, including changes in the level of severity of both abusive behavior and injury over time.

The term "episode" is used to refer to specific occurrences of the abusive experience as if it is discrete when, in fact, it is not. An episode can be thought of as a period of time from the onset of a discrete occurrence of abusive behavior during which time the abuser actively maintains control over the victim, regardless of whether he continues to engage in discrete abusive behavior. For example, a batterer may beat his partner and then leave the house, but with the implication that he will return and continue his abuse. Or an abuser may intermittently hit a partner throughout the day, but within a "state of siege" such that the battered woman knows that it is not yet over. In some cases, the battered woman can define a point at which the abuse is "over for now," although other forms of control (e.g., kindnesses to win back affection) may be in effect. It is important to recognize that the abuser typically continues to maintain some level of control even when not actively engaging in abusive behavior.

Abuse within Specific Episodes

Ganley (1981) identified four types of abuse: physical, sexual, psychological, and abuse toward property and pets. More recently, identifying the function of abusive behavior (i.e., control of the victim) has been a central feature in defining behavior as abusive (Ganley, 1981, 1989; Pence & Paymar, 1986; Schechter, 1987). Thus, it is the context of meaning (i.e., identifying abuse as behavior that controls the victim) of a particular behavior in addition to its topology, which defines behavior as abusive. The Domestic Abuse Intervention Project in Duluth, Minnesota developed the Power and Control Wheel (Pence & Paymar, 1985) to assist in determing types of abuse by identifying eight different methods of using power and control in addition to physical and sexual violence. These include coercion and threats; economic abuse; intimidation; emotional abuse; using male privilege; using children; minimizing, denying, blaming; and isolation. These categories provide a further elaboration of the variety of methods by which psychological abuse may occur (see Table 2.2).

For example, a history of previous victimization by a partner or knowledge of a batterer's previous abuse toward another person helps create a context of meaning within which the use of a particular behavior (e.g., yelling, threatening) may easily function to control the victim's behavior. Control may not result from the typology of the batterer's behavior, per se, but rather from other past and present behaviors associated with it. That is, other behaviors associated with the specific abusive behavior may alter the meaning attached to it. The meaning of yelling, for example, is determined by what subsequent events it has come to cue. A battered woman who is now serving time in a federal prison for killing her batterer, experienced the first episode of physical abuse by her husband when he pulled the trigger of a handgun four times while the barrel was inserted in her vagina. The gun was loaded with only one bullet and it did not fire. Subsequent to that incident, however, which also included a severe physical beating, the mere raising of his voice was sufficient to terrify her. She knew exactly what he was capable of doing. His yelling signaled the potential for a recurrent violent episode.

TABLE 2.2 Categorization of Types of Abuse

Physical Abuse
- Threw something at you[a]
- Pushed, grabbed, or shoved you[a]
- Scratched you
- Slapped you[a]
- Kicked, bit, or hit you[b]
- Hit or tried to hit you with something[b]
- Wrestled you
- Punched you somewhere on the body (not face)
- Punched you on the face
- Beat you up[b]
- Threatened you with a knife or gun[b]
- Used a knife or fired a gun[b]
- Pinched you
- Pulled your hair
- Choked you with hands[b]
- Attempted to smother, strangle or hang you with an object
- Put dangerous substance (e.g., gasoline, acid) on your body
- Burned your body
- Threw you bodily
- Physically restrained you by holding
- Physically restrained by tying you up
- Dragged or pulled you
- Used force or threat of force to get you to eat/drink something
- Used force or threat of force to get you to take/ingest drugs/alcohol
- Used force or threat of force to restrict you from eating food/drinking
- Used force or threat of force to restrict you from using toilet, shower, bath or otherwise attending to hygiene
- Restricted you from taking prescribed medication
- Restricted you from obtaining needed medical treatment
- Threw hot liquid on you
- Used car to attempt to run over you
- Put excrement on your body

Injury
- Lost hair
- Minor cuts
- Severe cuts
- Minor burns
- Severe burns
- Minor bruises
- Severe bruises
- Black eye(s)
- Sprains/strains
- Lost teeth
- Human bite
- Broken eardrum
- Joint or spinal cord injury
- Broken nose or jaw
- Other broken bones, including ribs

(continued)

TABLE 2.2 ***Continued***

- Injury (*continued*)
  - Concussion
  - Internal injury
  - Permanent injury (blindness, loss of hearing, disfigurement, chronic pain)
- Severity of Injury
  - You required no medical treatment
  - You required medical treatment, but received none
  - You required medical treatment/outpatient or clinic
  - You required medical treatment/EMR
  - You required hospitalization
- Sexual Abuse
  - Type of unwanted sexual behavior
    - Vaginal intercourse
    - Fellatio
    - Cunnilingus
    - Anal intercourse
    - Sexual behavior with another adult (not partner)
    - Sexual behavior with a child (below 18 years)
    - Watched nudity or sexual behavior involving another
    - Viewed pornographic film, photographs
    - You were filmed during sexual activity
    - Others were allowed to watch while you engaged in sexual activity
    - Forced nudity
    - Required to dress in sexually provocative clothing
    - Unwanted objects were inserted into your vagina/rectum
    - You were required to be involved with an animal in a sexual way
  - Type of force coercion used to gain compliance
    - Actual physical force
    - Threat of physical force to you or another person
    - Threat of negative consequence (other than physical force)
    - Social pressure to comply sexually (expectations of self/others)
- Psychological Abuse[c]
  - Coercion and threats
    - Made or carried out threats to do something to hurt you or someone else
    - Threatened to kill you or someone else
    - Threatened to leave relationship
    - Threatened to commit suicide or made gestures
    - Made or carried out threats to report you to welfare, social services, police
    - Attempted to get you to drop charges against the abuser
    - Attempted to get you to engage in illegal activities
  - Intimidation
    - Instilled fear in you by looks, gestures, actions
    - Smashed objects
    - Destroyed your property
    - Abused pets
    - Displayed weapons
  - Emotional abuse
    - Insulted you or said "put downs"
    - Called you names

(*continued*)

TABLE 2.2 ***Continued***

Emotional abuse (*continued*)
Attempted to make you feel crazy
Humiliated you with words or gestures
Attempted to make you feel guilty
Verbally raged at you
Engaged in extramarital affairs
Withheld sex from you
Isolation
Attempted to control what you did
Attempted to control what you read
Attempts to limit your involvement with others
Used jealousy to justify actions against you
Restricted your use of the phone, transportation
Restricted your leaving the house
Minimization, denial, and blaming
Minimized abuse and did not take your concerns about it seriously
Denied that the abuse happened
Blamed you for the abuse
Shifted responsibility for abusive behavior onto you or someone else
Use of children to control you
Attempted to make you feel guilty about children
Used children to relay messages to you
Used visitation to harass you
Threatened to take children away (e.g., custody, kidnapping)
Threatened to abuse children
Use of male privilege
Treated you like a "servant"
Made major decisions without your equal participation
Acted like the "master of the castle"
Unilaterally defined male/female roles
Economic/resource abuse
Attempted to prevent you from getting/keeping job
Attempted to prevent you from going to school
Required you to ask for money
Controlled the money by giving you an allowance
Took money from you
Controlled your use of money
Withheld information about/access to family resources
Ejected you from car during travel
Restricted your access to transportation
Locked you out of house

[a]Overall Violence and [b]Severe Violence index items from the Conflict Tactics Scale (Straus, 1979). See Straus and Gelles (1990) for scoring instructions.

[c]Categories of psychological abuse are taken from the Power and Control Wheel (Pence & Paymar, 1986).

Physical abuse refers to any behavior that involves the intentional use of one's body against the body of another person in such a way that there is risk of physical injury, regardless of whether the behavior results in actual injury. Examples of physical abuse include hitting, pushing, shoving, punching, pounding, slapping, or use of a weapon or object to injure.

The severity level of physically abusive behavior varies, although no adequate measure of severity has yet been determined. Straus (1979), using the Conflict Tactics Scale (CTS), identified two levels of abuse (Minor Violence and Severe Violence indexes) based on the estimated potential for injury. New methods of scoring the CTS are presented in Straus and Gelles (1990), which may increase the adequacy of these measures for certain purposes. Generally, severity of action should be assessed separately from severity of the injury as they may not necessarily be the same. A particular action may not always result in a corresponding injury. For example, a push may result in a concussion if the victim is pushed against a sharp object, or death if one is pushed in front of a moving car, or it may result in no injury at all if one is pushed onto a soft bed.

The frequency of a specific abusive behavior may be determined by the total number of episodes in which there was an occurrence of that specific behavior. For example, on two separate occasions one woman's husband had used a weapon when beating her. Another means to assess frequency is to determine the number of occurrences of a particular action within a specific abusive episode. One woman reported that she was beaten twice by her husband during a three-hour long episode of abuse involving physical violence, threats to kill, emotional abuse, and rape. Duration of an episode of physical abuse describes the period of time from which the first physically abusive behavior occurred until the batterer ceases to maintain active control over the victim. For example, an abusive episode for one woman lasted only a few minutes, the amount of time it took for her husband to slap her three times in the face. Shortly afterwards, she left the house freely after her husband apologized and said he was wrong for having hit her. Although the woman may have been operating in fear even after having left the house, his active efforts to control her had ceased for the moment. For another woman, an abusive episode lasted 13 hours, from the time of the first physical blow until her husband allowed the daughter to call a cab and take her to the hospital where the husband's active behavior to control her stopped only temporarily. For other women the duration may be days, weeks, or months, during which time they are literally captive to their batterer's active efforts to control them.

Viewing the physical abuse across episodes provides an overall picture that is not as clearly available when looking at a single episode. The frequency of physically abusive episodes across a specified period of time provides a useful index of the pervasiveness of abuse the woman has experienced. One woman reported over 300 episodes in which she had been physically assaulted by her partner, beginning 12 years prior to the last incident of abuse when she used a gun to shoot him. The stage of the relationship when abuse began provides a context in which to understand the battered woman's experience. For one woman, the first episode of abuse in which her partner used physical violence was on the night of the honeymoon in their hotel room. For some women, the physical abuse begins years after the marriage ceremony, whereas for others the abuse begins during the dating relationship. Overall, the highest level of severity of abusive behavior for many women is considered "severe," based on the potential for physical injury; for example the item, "hit with something hard" from the CTS (Straus, 1990) is indicative of severe violence. The highest level of actual injury is a distinct measure of severity and should be considered separately from the level of abusive behavior. For example, a woman whose abuser hits her with a telephone may experience a wide array of injury ranging from pain but no physical injury, to bruises, to severe lacerations requiring sutures, to permanent closed head injury.

Finally, examining specific patterns of violence, including changes in severity over time and Walker's cycle of violence (1984), provides another context from which to evaluate the overall abuse. One woman's abuser rarely engaged in behaviors indicative of the contrite, loving phase of the cycle of violence. Rather, the acute battering behavior was followed merely by the absence of physical violence during which time the abuser ignored his partner. For many women, especially those seeking help or involved in the legal system, the severity of abuse has escalated over time. Empirical evidence is not yet available to determine if this is the norm for all women who have ever experienced physical violence in their relationships.

Physical abuse is measured not only by the behavior that defines it, but also by the resulting physical injury. Specific types of injuries and an estimate of the level of severity should be assessed. Determining not only the specific types of injury, but whether the victim's injuries required medical attention (whether or not she received it) is helpful in determining severity of injury.

Dimensions of injury may be evaluated by determining the (1) type of injury (e.g., lacerations, bruises, fractures/dislocation, internal injury, burn, poisoning, head trauma), (2) level and scope of impairment of functioning (physical, occupational, social), and (3) permanency of the injury. On one end of the continuum one has a broken bone that heals in a few weeks contrasted with minor bruises that require no medical attention; as compared to the other end of the continuum where one has a closed head injury that results in cognitive impairment and reduced ability to function. Finally, the most extreme level of injury results in death. Between 1980-1984, 10,521 women were killed by their abusive male partners (Browne & Williams, 1989).

Sexual abuse in intimate relationships appears to be underestimated, even more so than physical abuse. According to Shields, Resick, and Hanneke (1990), between 32% and 59% of women who have been battered are also victims of sexual abuse, the rate of marital rape in the general population is estimated to be between 6% and 14%. In Walker's study of battered women (1984), 59% of the women reported being forced to have sex with a battering partner, compared to 7% who reported forced sex with a previous nonbattering partner. George and Winfield-Laird (1986) found that among a sample of rape victims, 26% were victimized by husbands or lovers.

Sexual abuse has been defined in a number of ways; it is, of course, a form of physical abuse. Nevertheless, distinguishing it from other forms of physical abuse is useful. Clinically, sexual abuse refers to any unwanted sexual activity. Legal definitions of sexual assault against an adult vary from state to state, but generally include the notion of lack of consent, force or threat of force, and sexual penetration (Burgess, 1985). Recently, many states have changed their statutes so that there no longer exists a "spouse exception." Previously, it was legally impossible for sexual assault to occur in the context of marriage, simply by definition of the relationship of marriage. Russell (1982) included forced oral, anal, and digital penetration, in addition to vaginal intercourse, in her definition. Brownmiller's (1975) definition included any sexual intimacy forced on one person by another. This could refer to forcing a woman to remain nude, to engage in sexualized behaviors that may not necessarily involve physical contact (e.g., sexual dancing, dressing in particular ways), or to engage in sexual activity with children, animals, or objects.

Finkelhor and Yllo (1983) recognized four types of coercion used in marital rape. The threat of force may be used within the marriage to obtain sex. The threat may be implicit or explicit. Many women report that their partners communicate the implicit threat of force through their looks, gestures, or other behaviors that cue danger if compliance is not forthcoming. Other forms of coercion include the abuser's use of social coercion in which he pressures the woman to submit to sex by making reference to sex role expectations, for example. The remaining type of coercion used in marital rape is interpersonal coercion in which the abuser coerces the woman to engage in sex based on her fear of nonviolent, albeit negative, consequences that result from her partner's power or resource advantages (e.g., leaving the relationship, engaging in extramarital affairs, control of money).

As with physical abuse, the severity of sexual abuse should be assessed separately by examining (1) the sexually abusive action itself, (2) the physical sequelae that result from it. Although some women receive physical injuries during the course of sexual abuse, others do not. However, the medical consequences of sexual abuse may also include infections, sexually transmitted diseases, risk of human immunodeficiency virus (HIV) infection and acquired immunodeficiency syndrome (AIDS), unwanted pregnancy, risk to the fetus in a pregnant woman, and infertility.

The parameters of sexual abuse can be examined similarly to those of physical violence above-described. For one woman, the sexual abuse to her by her partner during a particular episode included oral, anal, and vaginal penetration during which the force used was his physical restraint of her through the weight of his own body. Physical injuries included bruises to her arms and legs where she was restrained. During the two-hour ordeal, the woman was raped vaginally twice and one time each via penetration of her mouth and rectum.

Evaluation of sexually abusive behaviors across the relationship is also an important dimension to assess. A young African-American woman had been raped by her boyfriend three times during the course of their year-long relationship. The sexual abuse began six months after the relationship began, following an abortion. The worst incident of sexual abuse involved a rape at knife point over a two-hour period during which time her body was bruised. Over time, the sexual abuse in this relationship involved a greater use of violence and occurred with growing frequency. Further, over time the sexual assault was followed less often by the abuser's acknowledgement of his abusive behavior.

Psychological Abuse. The definition of psychological abuse in intimate relationships is the least developed of the abuse categories. Skeptics may misunderstand psychological abuse as simply the negative verbal interaction commonly found in all couples, but particularly in distressed, nonviolent couples. Psychological abuse, however, is quite different from this, both in terms of its intensity and range of behavior. Ganley (1989) distinguished psychological battering from emotional abuse. She described psychological battering as occurring in the context of a spoken or unspoken threat and the actual occurrence of physical battering; emotional abuse occurs when there is "no credible threat of violence since the perpetrator has not been physically or sexually violent in the past" (p. 202).

Psychological abuse can be viewed similarly to torture of prisoners-of-war and hostages (Scrignar, 1988). Morgan (1982) sees the attitudes and behavior of the violent husband as bearing a remarkable resemblance to the political terrorist and describes the situation as "conjugal terrorism":

> Conjugal terrorism is the use or threatened use of violence in order to break down the resistance of the victim to the will of the terrorist. It is 'the use of coercive intimidation for political motive.' Ultimately the terrorist uses violence to further his political cause and for the conjugal terrorist, the violent husband, his political cause is the maintenance of his idealized self-image. (pp. 30-31)

Amnesty International's definition of psychological torture, which has helped to shape the current definition of psychological abuse (Walker, 1984), is divided into eight categories: (1) isolation of the victim, (2) induced debility, producing exhaustion, weakness, or fatigue (e.g., sleep or food deprivation), (3) monopolization of perception, including obsessiveness and possessiveness, (4) threats of harm to the victim or her family and friends and other forms of threat, (5) degradation, including humiliation, name calling and insults, and denial of privacy or personal hygiene, (6) forced drug or alcohol use, (7) altered states of consciousness produced through hypnotic states, and (8) occasional random and variable reinforcers or indulgences, partial reinforcers that keep alive the hope that the torture will cease (Walker, 1984).

Tolman (1989) empirically derived a two-factor model of psychological abuse in his development of the Psychological Maltreatment of Women Inventory (PMWI) that measures psychological abuse toward women by their male partners. One subscale of the PMWI, dominance-isolation, includes items dealing with isolation from resources, demands for subservience, and rigid observance of traditional sex roles. The second subscale, emotional-verbal abuse, includes items of verbal attack, behavior that demeans the woman, and withholding emotional resources.

As with assessment of physical and sexual abuse, assessment of psychological abuse requires identification of specific abusive behaviors; however, it is more difficult to determine the precise frequency of psychological abuse. This is caused in part by the ongoing nature of the behavior without discrete points of onset or termination. For example, a threat to kill may be spoken initially but intermittently reinforced by the use of gestures or subtle references to the earlier threat.

In clinical cases, psychological abuse frequently accompanies both physical and sexual abuse, but may occur in their absence as well. In one case, a woman was repeatedly physically battered over several days during which time her husband engaged in multiple forms of psychological abuse, including threats to burn her lips by igniting the lighter fluid he had put on her, monitoring her movement throughout the house, refusal to allow her to use the toilet when she requested, which resulted in her defecating in her clothing, refusal to allow her to shower or clean herself when she requested, and monitoring and regulating her intake of food, water, and access to sleep. Finally, he would intermittently indulge her with "kindnesses," including bandaging the burns he had inflicted on her arms, allowing her to bathe, sleep, eat, and drink at his discretion, and finally putting her in a cab and sending her to the hospital for treatment of multiple broken bones, burns, and head injury.

Other examples of psychological abuse include threats to the woman or her family and friends if she does not comply with particular requests. One woman was told that she would be killed if she did not perform "good" oral sex on her boyfriend, and that she would probably be killed afterward anyway. Another woman's abuser threatened that he would take away her son and give him up for adoption. Children are often the focus of psychological abuse toward the battered woman. For example, batterers threaten to or actually kidnap, sexually or physically abuse, and/or fail to provide support for their children as a means of controlling their partners.

A form of psychological abuse experienced by many battered women is the degradation and assault on the sense of self through name-calling or "put downs." One woman was told repeatedly by her husband that his frequent affairs with young, attractive women were due to her excess weight and unattractiveness. Comments such as "Look at you . . . you are a fat, ugly woman!" were common. Examples of psychological abuse using the framework of the Power and Control Wheel include use of a loud voice to demand that the women do what her batterer says (intimidation), pretending the morning after a rage that nothing happened (denial), telling her that when she starts "talking like that" she deserves what she gets (blaming), and refusal to allow her to make phone calls or to leave the house (isolation).

The function of control that some psychologically abusive behaviors are able to exert may be explained, in part, through their association with actual previous physical and/or sexual abuse by the woman's current or previous partner, or perhaps by having witnessed an abusive parent. The victim's belief that her partner would escalate his behavior in order to control or harm her is important to increasing the batterer's control over her. That is, the impact of a husband's degrading statement or threatening look may be attributed to the conditioned stimulus associated with previous abuse.

Destruction of Property and Pets. This is another component in an overall assessment of an abusive history. Important meaning often lies in the violence directed toward inanimate objects or pets. A batterer may very carefully select particular objects to destroy that have value to the victim. Alternatively, he may destroy his own prized possessions and then blame her with "look what you made me do" (Ganley, 1989). As a rule, the destruction of particularly valued items is fully intended, rather than random.

Torture or destruction of a loved pet may be an even more powerful abuse than personal abuse. One woman witnessed a succession of 12 kittens tortured and eventually killed by her batterer. This same man chronically tortured and eventually killed a cherished parrot because of his jealousy and attempts to control his wife; the parrot was responsive only to her. The woman's attempts to protect the animals were met with increased violence toward her. Another woman, who had been sexually and physically abused over a long period of time, shot her batterer at the point when he was attempting to steal her prized exotic pet bird. This act of psychological abuse toward the woman, through the abuse of her pet, went beyond the point of tolerability (Blackman, 1989).

Patterns of Abuse Across Episodes

In addition to information about individual abusive incidents, it is important to determine the overall patterns of behavior that characterize the abusive relationship. Walker (1984) identified the pattern referred to as the "cycle of violence" in which a tension-building phase precedes the acute battering incident, which is then followed by a loving-contrition phase. The cycle repeats itself when the tension-building begins again. Walker based her Cycle of Violence theory on social learning theory by suggesting that the behavior indicative of the contrite-loving phase reinforces the violence by virtue of its position in the chain of events. The contrite-loving phase includes gift giving, privileges, and warmth and attention by the batterer, which contrasts sharply with the previous abuse. This behavior may serve as the basis of hope for many battered women when their belief that this loving behavior represents the "real" person, not the abusive behavior for which she has been the target. It is during the contrite loving phase that some battered women also forgive or excuse the previous battering and thus do not hold their partners accountable.

In some cases, the behavior during the contrite-loving stage may not be loving at all, but simply the absence of violence, which by comparison, may be experienced as positive. This negative reinforcement (absence of violence or abuse) may function as powerfully to control the battered woman as the positive reinforcement resulting from gifts and her partner's loving attention.

In all phases of the cycle of violence the battered woman is being controlled by the perpetrator (Ganley, 1981, 1989). Although this is apparent in both the tension-building and acute battering phases, it is less obvious in the final, contrite-loving phase. In the final phase of the cycle of violence, the batterer's behavior functions to make it more likely that the victim will not leave the relationship, that she will forgive him and perhaps even recommit to the relationship more strongly now that he is remorseful for his abusive behavior. Athough some battered women are hopeful during the contrite-loving phase of the cycle of violence, they remain affected by the violence which has come before.

The Cycle of Violence theory (Walker, 1984) has contributed to an understanding of battering as a pattern of behavior, not as the perpetrator's discrete abusive behaviors (Ganley, 1981). However, the cycle theory fails to account for all stages of the cycle as different forms of controlling behavior. Labeling the third phase as contrite and loving may suggest that all is forgiven, that the relationship has resumed a normal status, and that the battered woman is happy and content, at least until the tension-building stage resumes as a precursor to another acute battering episode. Once physical or sexual violence occurs in a relationship, the relationship will never again be experienced by the battered woman in the same way, even when the violence ceases to recur. The cycle of violence is just that; it is a cycle in which the perpetrator's control of the battered woman takes on one form and then another, developing a pattern that often functions to keep a battered woman in an abusive relationship.

The sequence of physical, sexual, psychological, and property assaults by some perpetrators seem to deny a characteristic cycle of violence. Rather, several physically and sexually violent assaults may recur over a period of time with periods of psychological abuse interspersed between them. Fitting this pattern of abuse to the cycle of violence suggests that the acute battering phase may involve repeated occurrences of violence over an extended period of time, which are not separated by the other phases of the cycle. Still other patterns of abuse represent a variation in the Cycle of Violence theory described by Walker (1984). For example, in some cases the acute battering episode does not seem to follow a discernable period of tension building, but is described by the battered woman as coming "out of the blue." Some might argue that the tension-building phase was not recognized, but in fact was evident. The battered woman has undoubtedly the most expertise in detecting changes in the abuser's behavior pattern and it appears in some cases that an abusive episode is simply unpredictable.

Aside from the cycle of violence, other unique patterns of abuse are important to determine. Particular patterns may be defined when the abuse occurs within a clearly discriminanted context, for example, only when the batterer has been using alcohol or drugs, only when the couple is alone in the house away from other adults, or only at a particular time, such as during the evening or nighttime. Another common pattern reported by battered women involves the sequence of a physical beating followed by forced sexual behavior. It is important to remember that even with "typical" patterns, the occurrence of abuse is not perfectly predictable. Thus, the victim may never be quite sure when the next incident may occur nor be absolutely certain of her safety.

The cycle of violence is not intended to explain or justify why abuse occurs. The notion of a cycle of violence, or any other pattern of the abuse, is best understood as descriptive, not predictive. Patterns of abuse tell the abusive story more effectively than simply referring to discrete, isolated behaviors.

Battered Woman's Cognitions About the Abuse

The battered woman's cognitions about her partner's abuse form a context that provides an important adjunct to the assessment of the descriptions of the above-described abuse. Even when the descriptions of abuse are based on the battered woman's self-report (see Strategies for Assessment, later in this chapter), they differ from the cognitions that victims make about the abuse. The relevant cognitions about abuse include the victim's (1) appraisal of the severity of past abuse, (2) expectation of continued abuse, (3) expectation of potentially lethal violence, (4) attribution of causality of the abuse, including the perception of the batterer's motivation when the victim attributes the cause of the abuse to the batterer, (5) perceptions of self-efficacy regarding safety, and (6) attribution of responsibility for the battered woman's safety.

These cognitions provide the context in which to determine how the victim understands the meaning of the abuse she has experienced. Furthermore, it is useful to compare this framework of the abuse history to the one derived from the descriptive measures of abuse. As a coping response, some battered women may minimize or deny the severity of their victimization. Other women may report the abuse to be more severe or life-threatening than an outside observer might otherwise appreciate. My clinical experience suggests that few victims exaggerate the severity of their victimization; when their report appears to have been distorted, most often it is in the direction of underreporting. It has also been my experience that battered women often accurately perceive an increase in the level of impending danger, whether they are aware of it or not and, regardless of how an outside observer might appraise the situation. The most important point to emphasize is that understanding the battered woman's cognitions about the violence and abuse, which themselves are based on the actual occurrence of that abuse, provides a basis for comprehending her experience.

Other Forms of Violence and Abuse

In addition to the violence and abuse that battered women have experienced by their partners, some of these women have also experienced other forms of victimization. Knowledge of violence or abuse that has occurred in the battered woman's past (see Chapter 5 for a discussion of childhood victimization, previous rape or battering experiences) or which is occurring contemporaneously with the abuse by her partner is necessary in order to obtain an adequate picture of her overall victimization profile (Koss, 1990). Clinical reports indicate that women who are abused in their relationships with an intimate partner experience abuse in other ongoing relationships, for example, from adolescent or adult children, parents, adult siblings or other adult family members, employers, and lovers. One woman was involved simultaneously with her husband and a lover, both of whom were physically and psychologically abusive to her. Another woman experienced sexual harassment from her male employer during a relationship with her physically and sexually abusive husband. Finally, one young woman was being physically abused periodically by her parents with whom she lived, her older brother, and her boyfriend. Truesdell, McNeil, and Deschner (1986), found that in families in which a child had been subjected to incest, 73% of the mothers reported themselves to be the victims of at least one incident of prior physical abuse and 23% reported the severity level of the abuse to be life-threatening. Child incest victims also may have been victimized by witnessing abuse. When a woman reports the occurrence of abuse from her intimate partner, assessment of other forms of abuse toward her and other family members is essential.

STRATEGIES OF ASSESSMENT

Three primary strategies exist for the assessment of abusive behavior and of the battered woman's cognitions about the violence and abuse. These strategies as described below are the (1) open-ended interview, (2) structured interview or scenario methods (personal communication, A. Ganley, 1987), and (3) questionnaire methods, which may be administered via paper-and-pencil or interview format. It is suggested that all three methods may be used to obtain the most comprehensive assessment possible as the nature of the information obtained in each is somewhat different. Assessment strategies for obtaining information about other forms of recent and historical violence and abuse are also discussed.

These methods of assessment focus on obtaining information directly from the battered woman. In some circumstances, it may be useful to obtain information about the violence and abuse from additional sources as well. Other possible sources include police and hospital reports, court records, and interviews with others (e.g., family members, friends, co-workers); including the abuser depending, of course, on the circumstances. Of course, in all cases this information should be obtained with full and written consent from the battered woman.

Partner's Abusive Behavior

Open-Ended Interview. An open-ended interview is a useful tool to begin the assessment of violence and abuse, although it is typically not adequate to provide a complete picture. Prior to asking the victim to respond to more direct methods of assessment, it is very important to use an open-ended format in which the woman is free to tell her story, structured the way in which she most wants to tell it. Inviting the woman to "tell her story" about the abuse may be a sufficient prompt. Active listening, empathic responding, and providing validation are important to this method. For example, during one particular evaluation I conducted of a battered woman charged with attempted murder, the only point at which she shed any tears in the telling of 20 years of abuse beginning in childhood was when she mentioned that I not only seemed to want information, but that I cared how she felt about it as well.

Although the battered woman likely will not report every abusive act, nor provide every detail of the violence toward her, the therapeutic effect for the victim of simply telling her story can be powerful. It may also be very useful to compare the information provided in the open-ended format with that obtained in more structured methods. Further, through the open-ended interview the clinician can determine the level of abuse the victim is able to acknowledge prior to any particular attempt to assess it in detail. Finally, it is important to understand the abuse from the perspective of the victim before imposing a particular framework through the use of more structured methods.

Following the initial interview, the clinician is advised to complete one or both of the following assessment procedures in order to ensure an adequate assessment of the previous abuse. This is important in order to estimate the current level of risk of further abuse to the battered woman, her likely response to it, and/or any posttraumatic effects she may be experiencing.

Structured Interview: Scenario Method. The scenario method involves asking the client to describe a specific abusive interaction in detail, as if scripting a movie scene. Typically, it is useful to obtain descriptions of several specific abusive episodes, for example, the most recent, one of the worst, and the first (Walker, 1984). The therapist is required to be direct and specific in the questioning in order to reduce the use of minimization as much as possible. My clinical experience indicates that battered women may eventually recall abuse previously forgotten, perhaps because of the vast number of different incidents to remember or because of the extent of psychological trauma associated with them. By obtaining a moment-to-moment account of the abusive events, it appears more difficult to minimize or otherwise distort the level of abuse that actually occurred than when providing summary accounts.

A brief example of the use of a scenario method between client and therapist follows.

T: I would like to ask you in detail about what happened to you on the night you went to the hospital because of the violence. Do you recall the date?

C: Yes, it was June 4th, because it was the day before my birthday.

T: What time on that day did the fighting start?

C: It started about 5:00; I remember because I was fixing dinner.

T: Can you tell me, as specifically as possible, what happened from the beginning?

C: He just hit me a few times after we were arguing. I ended up with a black eye.

T: Where were you and where was he when the arguing started?

C: I was in the kitchen and he was in the living room, but he came into the kitchen.

T: What happened when he came into the kitchen?

C: He came in a couple of times, saying that I had better get into the bedroom if I knew what was good for me. When I didn't go with him, he walked out, but he came back. I knew that he wouldn't just drop it.

T: Let's start from the beginning when you were in the kitchen and he was in the living room. What first happened?

C: I was just making dinner and he said that he wanted us to go into the bedroom for a little while.

T: What did you think he meant when he said that?

C: I knew what he meant! He wanted me to have sex with him.

T: What did you say or do then?

C: I said something about needing to finish getting dinner ready because I knew that he must be hungry.

T: What happened next? What did he do or say?

C: That's when he came into the kitchen and said that he would tell me when he wanted to eat. He said that right now he wanted me to go into the bedroom with him.

T: What did you do or say then?

C: I just stood there, because I knew if I didn't it would upset him more.

T: Did you say anything?

C: I asked him why the hell was he doing this again; he had promised that he wouldn't act like this anymore.

T: What did he do then?

C: He left saying that when he came back that I had better know what was good for me.

T: What happened next? Where did he go?

C: I think he went into the bedroom or bathroom; I couldn't tell.

T: What did you do when he left?

C: I stayed in the kitchen trying to figure out what I should do.

T: What happened next?

C: He came back into the kitchen about 10 minutes later and that's when it all started.

T: During that 10 minutes, what was going through your mind?

C: I knew that I couldn't go through that one more time. He wasn't going to do that to me again.

T: When you say it all started, what happened first?

C: He grabbed me by the neck and started shoving me toward the bedroom.

T: What did you do when he grabbed your neck?

C: I started to hit him back. I was screaming at him to leave me alone, that I wasn't going to do it one more time.

T: How and where did you hit him?

C: I hit him on the chest with my fist.

T: How may times did you hit him?

C: Probably three or four times.

T: What happened next?

C: That's when he punched me in the face and I don't remember anything after that.

T: How many times did he punch you in the face?

C: Several times, probably four or five times.

T: Did he use an open hand or a closed fist?

C: A closed fist.

T: Do you remember where you were when he punched you in the face?

C: I was in the hallway going toward the bedroom.

T: What happened after he punched you in the face?

C: I think I fell down. I remember his boots kicking me in the back. I don't remember anything else until I woke up lying on the bed, bleeding and aching all over. He was gone, although I didn't know that at first.

T: What did you do then?

C: I could barely move, but I was able to reach the phone. I called my sister; she called the police and an ambulance took me to the hospital.

The clinician may pursue, moment to moment, the events that occurred. Recreating a specific abusive episode in the actual sequence in which it occurred often reduces any minimization. A clearer picture emerges of what the abuser actually did and what the battered woman did as well. What is also important to assess is the battered woman's cognitions about what the abuser was doing. For example, when he said, "Come with me," the battered woman believed that he was demanding sex and felt terrified. Understanding the battered woman's response to the violence against her is then placed in a "context of meaning" defined by the interactive sequence of the abuser's specific behaviors and the battered woman's behavioral, cognitive, and affective responses that followed.

In order to obtain an adequate understanding of the pattern of abuse, the evaluation needs to include the detailed account of several episodes of abuse. By obtaining an account of the first, the most recent, the worst, and several other abusive incidents, the clinician can gain an appreciation of the change in severity over time, consistency in the batterer's behavior, and patterns of the battered woman's response to the violence.

Questionnaire Methods. Another approach to the assessment of abuse is through the use of a questionnaire. Recognizing a particular abusive behavior from a list of items on a questionnaire may prompt the memory of a particular abusive incident, in which free recall of the same events may be inhibited by an attempt to avoid or deny its occurrence.

The Conflict Tactics Scale (CTS; Straus, 1979), an instrument developed for research purposes, is the most well known assessment questionnaire. It has been used in both telephone and face-to-face interviews in two major survey studies of the incidence and prevalence of abuse in American families (Straus & Gelles, 1989). Currently, three forms of the CTS have been developed; however, the CTS alone is inadequate for use in clinical settings as it does not include a sufficiently broad listing of possible abusive behaviors. It excludes sexually and psychologically abusive behaviors altogether, and includes no measure of injury. Further, it fails to assess the pattern of control, separate from discrete violent behaviors, inherent in the batterer's behavior. Saunders (1986) has recommended that the CTS not be ignored, but rather that it be supplemented by other measures that include type and severity of injury and that adequately handle the differences between men and women in the abusive context.

An informal survey of batterer programs found that most programs utilized some form of checklist or questionnaire, perhaps modeled on the CTS, but expanded. The Abusive Behavior Observation Checklist (ABOC), developed in the Family Violence Program, Nova University, is an example of such an instrument (see Appendix A). The ABOC includes a listing of psychologically abusive and controlling behaviors adopted from the Power and Control Wheel (Pence & Paymar, 1985), physically abusive, and sexually abusive behaviors, as well as a list of possible injuries and several questions concerning medical intervention. The ABOC incorporates the items from the CTS, so several CTS scores may be derived for comparative research purposes, if desired.

Few instruments, with one exception, have been developed to measure psychological abuse. Tolman's Psychological Maltreatment of Women Inventory (PMWI) is a 58-item inventory in which the relative pervasiveness of occurrence is indicated on a five-point scale ranging from "never" to "very frequently." The two subscales, dominance-isolation and emotional-verbal, were determined to have high internal consistency. Further work is needed in the development of this inventory, especially in determining its generalizability to ethnically and culturally diverse populations, but it is a promising step toward the systematic assessment of psychological abuse.

The combination of having the battered woman tell her own story as she chooses to frame it (open-ended interview), asking about specific incidents (structured interview or scenario method), and determining the extent of specific behaviors that have occurred over time and over episodes (questionnaire method) provides a sufficiently extensive array of information in order for the clinician to assess adequately the pattern of violence, abuse, and control.

Battered Woman's Cognitions about the Violence

Obtaining information about how and what the battered woman thinks about the violence and abuse can be obtained in three ways paralleling the above-described methods.

Open-ended Interview. In the context of an open-ended interview, the clinician can inquire generally about the battered woman's thoughts concerning the violence and abuse she has experienced. The battered woman may provide some useful information about her attribution of self-blame (e.g, "I guess I really deserved it") or attribution of responsibility for the violence to the batterer (e.g., "He doesn't know how to control his temper"), expectation of future violence and her ability to escape it (e.g, "I don't think there's any way to get away from him; he won't stop until he finds me"), or her appraisal of severity (e.g., "It's not as bad as what my Mom used to take"). These questions can be introduced as part of the open-ended interview asking about the violence and abuse described in the previous chapter.

Structured Interview: Scenario Method. Within the structured interview as the battered woman is describing the moment-by-moment course of events for each specific abuse episode, questions concerning her cognitions should be introduced. That is, not only should the clinician ask about the behavioral sequence of the batterer's and the battered woman's behavior, but also the battered woman's cognitions as they too occur simultaneously. The following example illustrates.

T: What were you thinking when he started to hit you with telephone?

C: I was thinking about the last time he did that. I had to go to the hospital to get 25 stitches in my head and I still have a scar from it.

T: Were you thinking anything else?

C: Yes, I was thinking that he's not going to do that to me again.

T: What did you do next?

C: I picked up the knife and pointed it at him.

Although the battered woman's behavior of picking up the knife to defend herself is understandable in light of her partner's violence with the telephone, it becomes clearer when not only the behavior, but also her thoughts, are identified. This is especially important as the observer can rarely, if ever, know the meaning of a particular violent or abusive behavior based solely on a description of its topography. Although a thorough assessment of history and context can contribute to the clinician's understanding of its meaning, the specific meaning to the battered woman is available only from her.

Questionnaire Method. Obtaining information on the battered woman's cognitions about the violence generally may be accomplished through administration of paper-and-pencil methods. Although there are instruments to assess attributional style and locus of control generally, these methods do not identify cognitions relevant to specific violent experiences. A brief questionnaire, modeled in part after the Attributional Style Questionnaire (Peterson, Semmel, von Baeyer, Abramson, Metalsky, & Seligman, 1982), which assesses the battered woman's attributions about the cause of violence and abuse, expectation of recurrent violence, expectation of lethal

Table 2.3 Types of Contemporaneous and Prior Forms of Violence and Abuse

Physical, sexual, psychological abuse of battered woman by someone other than her intimate partner, for example,
- adult sibling, parent, other family member, friend of family
- battered woman's adolescent or adult child
- battered woman's lover other than intimate partner

Physical, sexual, psychological abuse by former intimate partner

Rape by stranger

Sexual harassment by employer

Physical, sexual, psychological abuse or misconduct by
- helping professional (e.g., psychotherapist, physician, attorney)
- spiritual leader
- teacher or professor

Witnessing or knowing about physical, sexual, psychological abuse of someone else (e.g., sexual abuse of daughter by battered woman's perpetrator, observed physical abuse to mother or sexual abuse to sister during childhood)

Date rape

Childhood physical, sexual, psychological abuse or neglect

violence, attribution of responsibility for the battered woman's safety, appraisal of the severity of prior violent behavior, and expectations regarding controllability or the ability to be safe is presented in Appendix B.

Other Forms of Violence and Abuse

The most effective method of assessing the occurrence of other forms of violence and abuse experienced by the battered woman is through a structured interview that includes questions about specific forms of these behaviors. These forms of violence and abuse may be evaluated simultaneously with prior forms of violence and abuse. Types of contemporaneous and prior violence and abuse about which the clinician should ask are listed in Table 2.3. Throughout the interview when any of these forms of violence and abuse are endorsed, the clinician should inquire further about the details of each incident or each abusive relationship.

IMPACT OF ASSESSMENT PROCEDURES

The impact of the assessment process on the battered woman is as important a consideration as the procedures themselves. There are several possible effects that can be considered. A great deal of clarity often emerges when a battered woman systematically examines the nature of the abuse against her, the subsequent injuries, and its psychological impact. For some women, the added clarity regarding the abusive situation facilitates taking further action to protect themselves from the violence. For others, however, having such a clear view of the abuse history recreates the emotional climate associated with the abuse and is experienced as recurrent trauma. I have yet to observe a battered woman recite the events of her abuse without some level of emotional distress. For some women, recounting the abuse has the effect of providing some degree of emotional relief when the clinician responds with support, validation, and empathy.

It is important to titrate the emotional impact associated with recall of abusive incidents by regulating the timing or depth of assessment based on the client's response to it. This is especially important when considering the extent of prior victimization that some battered women have experienced, either as adults (e.g., previous intimate relationships, rape) or during childhood (e.g., sexual or physical abuse).

The clinician must be cautious not to allow curiosity or a voyeuristic stance to dictate pursuit of detail about abusive episodes beyond that which is necessary for an adequate assessment and beyond that which a woman can tolerate. Typically, it is not necessary to require the battered woman to recount every single incident, especially when there are many of them.

Assessment of victimization history must be completed within a therapeutic context. Assessment and intervention cannot be separated if either is to be effective. Further, standards of practice within the profession (APA, 1987) require that interventions be based on assessement information.

3

Victim Strategies to Escape, Avoid, and Survive Abuse

The determination of what efforts a particular battered woman has made to escape, avoid, or survive the abuse is an important component of a comprehensive assessment of her situation. Assessing why a battered woman has not used particular efforts is also useful as it distinguishes between her knowledge about specific strategies and her appraisal of these strategies, including her expectation of possible negative consequences for using them. Finally, evaluating the outcome of a battered woman's past efforts helps to predict the likelihood of her using particular strategies in the future.

Why battered women do not "just leave" the battering relationship is, no doubt, one of the most commonly asked questions among mental health professionals, law enforcement officers, judges, attorneys, and others involved in working with battered women (Mahoney, 1991). It and related questions (for example, why a battered woman might resist having her husband arrested) are often misunderstood as indicators that the battered woman is unwilling to do anything about protecting herself or her children, or worse that she "wants" to be abused. These interpretations fail to incorporate an understanding of the battered woman's experience or her motivation for protecting and ensuring the survival of herself and her children in the abusive situation.

The appropriate question is not what the battered woman has done to *stop* the abusive behavior, but rather what she has done to escape, avoid, or protect herself from it (Ganley, 1987). The former question implies that the battered woman has the ability to stop the abusive behavior. She does not.

Whatever her efforts (e.g., threats to divorce, calling police), it is ultimately the perpetrator who must choose to alter or end the abusive behavior, or perhaps be forcibly, though temporarily, stopped through incarceration from inflicting direct physical or sexual abuse. Even so, many perpetrators resist or get around most efforts of others (e.g., battered woman, criminal justice personnel) to stop the abuse. For example, even incarcerated batterers sometimes continue via telephone calls, or through others who act as proxies, to threaten or actually physically abuse the battered woman.

This chapter first reviews current literature pertaining to battered women's efforts to respond to the violence against them and the effectiveness of these efforts in preventing further abuse. Self-defense as a particular response to domestic violence is addressed specifically, in part because of the extenuating legal circumstances that surround its use. Factors that mediate a battered women's use of particular efforts are discussed. Finally, assessment methods and strategies are described.

ESCAPE AND SURVIVAL STRATEGIES

Battered women engage in an impressively wide range of behaviors in responding to the abuse against them. These efforts to escape, avoid, or to protect themselves and their children from the battering may be grouped within ten categories:

1. legal strategies,
2. formal help-seeking strategies,
3. informal help-seeking strategies,
4. escape behaviors,
5. separation or divorce,
6. hiding or disguising one's whereabouts, place of employment, or location of children's schools,
7. compliance with and/or anticipation of the batterer's requests or desires,
8. passive and active self-defense,
9. using children in efforts to seek help or protect against abuse, and
10. other unique escape, avoidance, or survival strategies.

Specific examples of efforts within each category are listed in Table 3.1.

In an interview study of battered women who were no longer involved in an abusive relationship, Bowker (1983) categorized their efforts to respond to the violence as: (1) personal strategies and techniques, (2) informal help-sources, and (3) formal help-sources. According to Bowker, among personal strategies, battered women's use of threats, aggressive defense, and avoid-

Table 3.1. Strategies Used by Battered Women to Escape, Avoid, and Protect Themselves Against Abuse

Category	Specific Strategy
Legal strategies	Calling police
	Initiating contact/cooperating with state attorney
	Seeking protective injunction
	Seeking divorce lawyer
Formal help-seeking strategies	Going to a shelter
	Seeking help–mental health professional
	Seeking help–clergy
	Seeking help–medical professional
	Seeking help–social service
	Seeking help–women's support group
	Seek help–other organized help group
Informal help-seeking strategies	Telling others about abuse (friend, family, in-laws, neighbors)
	Seeking help from child's school to protect child from being taken or the battered woman from being tracked
	Asking others to intervene
Escape behaviors	Walking away from threatening situation
	Leaving location of abuser
	Barricading oneself in locked room
Separation/divorce	Obtaining formal or legal separation
	Seeking temporary or permanent custody
	Filing divorce papers
	Obtaining final divorce
Hiding/disguising	Hiding or disguising place of residence
	Hiding or disguising place of employment
	Hiding or disguising children's school
	Disguising identify or appearance
Compliance	Compliance with batterer's explicit or implicit demands
	Anticipation of batterer's demands
Passive and active self-defense	Physically resisting or blocking
	Physically striking back against ongoing abuse
	Physically striking back at threats of abuse
	Use of weapon to resist or block abuse
	Use of weapon to strike back against ongoing abuse
	Use of weapon to strike back against threat of abuse
Using children	Asking children to call police
	Asking children to help fight back
	Asking children to leave to seek help
	Asking children to comply with abuser's demands in order to stop abuse or threat of abuse

ance were shown to increase over subsequent incidents of abuse. Seven different personal strategies were:

1. talking the partner out of the abuse,
2. attempting to get perpetrator to promise to end the abuse,
3. threatening abuser with nonviolent action, such as contacting the police or filing for divorce,
4. hiding from him,
5. using passive self-defense during the beatings to minimize the physical damage incurred,
6. relying on aggressive defense during the beatings by fighting back against the aggressor, and
7. avoidance (Bowker, 1983).

Informal help-sources were identified to include family members, in-laws, neighbors, friends, and shelter services. Formal help-sources included police, social-service agencies, lawyers and district attorneys, clergy, and women's groups. Bowker's data suggest that all types of informal and formal help-seeking strategies were used more frequently across subsequent violent incidents.

EFFECTIVENESS OF STRATEGIES

Empirical literature has focused on three types of outcome criteria as effectiveness measures of interventions used by battered women: (1) self-reported ratings of effectiveness (2) recurrence of victimization, and (3) decision to leave or actually leaving the abusive relationship (Dutton-Douglas & Dionne, 1991).

Self-Report of Effectiveness

Reports by battered women in a shelter indicated that no single strategy or help-source was rated clearly and consistently as the most effective in ending the battering (Bowker, 1983). However, among the strategies most frequently cited as most effective in their last incident of violence were talking to friends (14%), nonviolent threats (12%), aggressively defending self (10%), and contacting a women's group (10%). Among those strategies most cited as least effective included getting the husband to promise cessation (14%), calling the police (11%), and contacting a lawyer or district attorney (8%). Nearly a decade of community education concerning domestic violence might suggest differences in these findings were they obtained presently. Generally, women today may have access to a greater number of options to respond to the violence.

Bowker and Maurer (1986), in a study of respondents to a *Women's Day* questionnaire found that although women were more likely to receive help from counseling agencies (50%) or clergy (33%) than from women's groups (21%), the ratings of effectiveness were greatest for women's groups. Comparison of ratings for counseling, clergy, and women's groups showed that women's groups (60%) and counseling (47%) were more frequently rated as very or somewhat effective compared to clergy (34%) and less frequently rated as not effective or causing increased violence.

Relatively little data is currently available about battered women's ratings of effectiveness of the strategies that they have employed. The available data, however, may suggest that (a) there is no single best strategy for all battered women, (b) some strategies that theoretically might be considered useful (e.g., calling the police) may, in fact, be considered least useful by some battered women, and (c) the use of some strategies may actually result in an increase in violence. Further, researchers need to study the effectiveness of combinations of strategies battered women use to stop violence and abuse, as no strategy is typically used in isolation.

Recurrence of Violence

An important measure of the effectiveness of escaping, avoiding, or surviving abuse is a measure of the actual recurrence of violence and abuse. Few studies have examined this variable directly. Difficulty in maintaining contact with battered women after contact with police, mental health services, or shelter, for example, make such evaluation difficult.

Studies that have examined recurrent abuse following a stay at a shelter suggest that a significant number of battered women continue to be at risk. In two different studies, among women who returned to the relationship after leaving a shelter, 27% experienced recurrent violence or psychological abuse within six to 10 weeks (Snyder & Scheer, 1981) and 57% experienced a recurrence of violence within six months (Giles-Sims, 1983). In another study (Berk, Newton, & Berk, 1986), 19% of the sample of battered women had experienced a subsequent incident of violence six weeks following contact with a shelter or a prosecutor's office. For some of these women, the number of recurrent violent incidents ranged as high as six, with nearly 5 percent beaten again more than once within the six-week period. In some cases, the shelter experience may simply have had no effect on altering the pattern of violence and abuse. Berk et al. (1986) suggested that the battered women's use of shelter may even trigger retaliation.

The recurrence of violence when the battered woman returns home following a shelter stay is not particularly surprising. Although a shelter provides an opportunity for the battered woman to be safe from the violence, the question of recurrence is in the hands of the batterer. Thus, the question of effectiveness of a shelter stay on prevention of violence against women who return to the batterer is, in effect, a question of the effect of that shelter stay on the batterer's behavior, not the battered woman's.

For example, seeking help from a shelter allows the battered woman to communicate that she is capable of using the option to leave and that she no longer needs to remain in the abusive relationship. For some batterers, the threat of the battered woman leaving the relationship, based on her ability to have done so in the past (e.g., go to a shelter), serves as a deterrent to further abuse. For others, there is little threat because their batterers believe that they will inevitably return to the relationship. Finally, some batterers, as noted by Berk et al. (1986) may retaliate against the battered woman for her attempt to leave him.

Decision to Leave the Relationship

The decision to leave the abusive relationship has been used as a third criterion for evaluating the outcome of intervention, specifically shelter stay. Although leaving the relationship is itself an escape strategy, it has also been used as a measure of effectiveness for yet another escape strategy, namely, use of a women's shelter.

Identifying the decision to leave the relationship as an outcome measure implies that it necessarily represents an "effective" or "successful" outcome. This is not, however, true for all battered women in all circumstances. Some data suggest, for example, that the battered woman is in greater danger of being killed once she has left the abusive relationship. Bernard, Vera, Vera, and Newman (1982) reported that 57% of wives who were killed by their batterers were living apart from them at the time. Mahoney (1991) quite effectively redefines the issue of the battered woman's separation by referring to separation abuse.

As I write this chapter, a story of yet another homicide-suicide has appeared in the newspaper today, reporting a situation in which a 27-year-old woman was killed when she attempted to leave her live-in boyfriend. During this same week, a hearing was held in a local criminal trial in which the defendant was alleged to have killed his pregnant girlfriend by shooting her to death at her place of employment. During the hearing, testimony was provided by a police officer who indicated that the boyfriend had uttered the classic line, "If I can't have her, nobody can."

Studies have examined the decision either to leave a battering relationship (Schutte, Bouleige, and Malouff, 1986) or to seek a divorce (Stone, 1984) or the actual divorce or termination of the relationship (Synder & Scheer, 1981). Following separation, the rate of return to the relationship in which the woman had been previously battered has been reported to range from 60% within six to 10 weeks (Snyder & Fruchtman, 1981), to 42% at three

(Stone, 1984) and six (Giles-Sims, 1983) months. Greater length of relationship, previous separations, religious affiliation (Snyder & Scheer, 1981), economic dependence, and psychological commitment (Strube & Barbour, 1983) have been found to predict relationship status following the battered woman's separation from her abusive partner.

SELF-DEFENSE AS SURVIVAL RESPONSE

Even though self-defense is mentioned above as a strategy some battered women use for survival, its use has sufficiently important implications to warrant a separate discussion. Self-defense statutes allow a person to use force against someone who they believe is about to commit an act resulting in great bodily harm or death to themselves or to another person. Nevertheless, many battered women are charged criminally in the killing of their abusive partners each year. For battered women, the issue becomes how it is that she is to defend herself physically against a batterer, who often is taller, weighs more, and is physically stronger than she. Battered women who defend themselves using their own hands and fists may be successful, but the fight typically is not evenly matched. Sometimes battered women use nearby objects (e.g., lamp, vase) to defend themselves and some battered women use lethal weapons, or objects capable of causing death, to defend themselves against threatened or ongoing violence toward themselves or their children.

Clinical reports by battered women indicate that some batterers appear to respond with shock or surprise when their partners actually fight back against their abuse. For these batterers, their partner's physically fighting back may provide sufficient reality testing that they realize the danger involved were the violence to continue and/or to escalate. Bowker (1983) reported that 10% of women in a shelter reported that aggressively defending oneself worked best in ending battering in their last incident, although five percent reported that it worked least. The danger inherent in this strategy is readily apparent.

For many battered women, physically fighting back has actually resulted in increased violence. One battered woman reported that what made her partner the most angry were her attempts to resist his abuse or fight back. On those occasions, his violence escalated. For another battered woman, even a slight shove against her batterer after hours of his intimidation and psychological abuse toward her seemed to provide the justification to retaliate with severe violence. Once she touched him to defend herself, he behaved as though she had initiated the assault and he was now justified in using any level of physical force in response.

When considering the strategy of self-defense, one must examine the likely outcome. Unless a woman has the strength and ability to physically dominate her battering partner, he retains greater power and thus greater potential for inflicting injury even when she is capable of causing harm. The relative physical power between the two is imbalanced even when fighting back may decrease the batterer's violent behavior (and it may actually increase it).

Often, the only strategy for fighting back that provides the battered woman with an equal advantage is her use of a lethal weapon. If one considers a batterer's fist to be a lethal weapon, unlike his victim's, then a lethal weapon balances the power between the two. Obviously, the use of weapons is not a recommended strategy for responding to violence, but when violence is of life-threatening proportions, the use of a weapon in self-defense may be a woman's only viable alternative. In some circumstances, the only choice is the risk of being killed or fighting back with a lethal weapon. It is at this point that some battered women have considered or attempted to kill themselves as their only escape from the terror of the abuse. Thus, for some, the choices become to be killed, to kill oneself, or to fight back, potentially killing the batterer.

When a woman is successful in defending herself against the extreme violence of her batterer, she is often faced with criminal charges for having done so. Studies of women in prison convicted of homicide or attempted homicide of their intimate partners have shown that a substantial percentage of these women were previously abused by their partners (Browne, 1987; Ewing, 1987). For some battered women, their first significant attempt to defend against the abusive behavior of the batterer resulted in their incarceration. For example, after killing her boyfriend, one battered woman remained in jail 26 months waiting for trial, unable to seek sufficient funds to obtain bond. For this woman, this incident was the first time she allowed herself to fight back against battering that had been severe and prolonged. Her subsequent battle was to protect herself from secondary victimization by the legal system because she dared to fight back and defend herself. Even following a plea agreement, this woman is now in prison serving a 17-year sentence.

STRATEGIES OF ASSESSMENT

As with assessing the violence and abuse (see Chapter 2), the same three assessment strategies are useful when attempting to determine the efforts battered women have made to escape, avoid, or survive the violence toward them and their children. In the first assessment strategy, the open-ended interview, the battered woman is asked what she has done to escape, avoid, or protect herself from the violence or abuse; this approach may be most effectively introduced following the open-ended interview about the violence and abuse described in the previous chapter. The second assessment strategy, the structured interview or scenario method, focuses on particular abuse episodes. This approach to assessment also is best utilized by integrating it into the structured interview concerning the violence and abuse. Inquiry into the battered woman's responses to abuse can include questions about her specific efforts to escape, avoid, and protect herself (and others) from the violence and abuse. The third assessment strategy is the questionnaire method, which can be administered separately or in conjunction with the questionnaire concerning violent and abusive behavior described in the previous chapter.

Open-Ended Interview

It is useful to begin with an open-ended question, asking what overall efforts the battered woman has made in attempting to escape, avoid, or protect herself. This initial question allows the battered woman to respond based on what is most salient to her at that moment, providing the interviewer with important information not only about the particular strategies used but about the battered woman's attitude toward those strategies. The open-ended format allows the battered woman an opportunity to tell her story without the structure imposed by someone outside of her experience.

Structured Interview: Scenario Method

Following use of the open-ended format for assessing the battered woman's efforts to escape, avoid, or protect herself from violence and abuse, the interviewer may use the scenario method described earlier for assessing violent action and injury in particular abusive incidents (See Chapter 2). The interviewer asks about the violence; resulting injury; her efforts to escape, avoid, or protect herself; and the outcomes of those efforts. The specific incidents for which assessment occurs are selected for their significance, either for establishing a pattern of abuse or because of their special importance to the battered woman. The clinician, for example, may ask the battered woman to respond to the first, worst, or most recent incidents of abuse as well as to others (Walker, 1984).

As she describes the abusive incident, the clinician can ask specific questions about how the battered woman may have responded in an attempt to avoid, escape, or protect herself before, during, or after that particular incident. A caution is in order: The clinician must not imply that the battered woman should have engaged in any particular response to protect herself. The risk in doing so is that the victim may feel that she is to blame.

It is important to distinguish between efforts a battered woman makes during the course of an ongoing battering incident and those she makes after the acute violence has stopped. During the ongoing abusive episode, the battered woman is typically concerned with minimizing damage, that is, surviving and protecting herself; there is often little opportunity for escape or avoidance once the violence begins. That is, once the acute battering phase has begun, some options of avoidance and escape are no longer available in that particular moment. For example, leaving or using the telephone may not be possible because of the batterer's efforts to stop her from doing so. Without access to the telephone or to leaving, the battered woman is precluded from contacting police, shelter, family, or using any other strategy that requires contact with someone else. Once the acute episode is over, however, the battered woman may be able to consider a wider range of strategies than those available to her while the abuse was ongoing. Thus, clarity is enhanced by conceptually separating the assessment of protection efforts once a battering episode is imminent from assessment of efforts to escape or avoid anticipated future incidents.

After determining the battered woman's strategies to escape, avoid, and protect herself in particular battering episodes, it is important to assess the consequences of their use. That is, what happened as a result of using the strategy? Who did what? Further, it is important to know the battered woman's perception of the effectiveness of a particular strategy for the escape, avoidance, or protection both within a specific abuse episode and generally. For example, calling the police may have resulted in an arrest. The objective observer may consider that to be a desirable consequence. The battered woman, however, may consider the arrest to be an undesirable consequence since she may anticipate retaliation from the perpetrator when he is released, lack of economic support while he is incarcerated, or withdrawal of support from family and friends.

Finally, it is useful to inquire about the rationale for not using particular strategies within a specific incident. The reasons why a battered woman does not use a particular strategy are often as informative as the reasons she chooses to use others. For example, one battered woman explained that she did not physically fight back nor protect herself from the blows delivered by her husband. When asked why not, she explained that even to raise an arm to block a punch would result in an even worse beating. The goal of helping the battered woman protect herself from further violence and abuse requires understanding the experience from her perspective.

Questionnaire Method

Many efforts to avoid, escape, or stop the violence are not tied only to particular abusive episodes. That is, they may also occur between episodes. Even so, the clinician cannot possibly interview a battered woman about each and every abusive incident, nor can most remember each one. Thus, another approach to assessment is to ask a battered woman about the extent to which she has used specific efforts in her protection or attempts at safety. In order to ensure clarity, the clinician should attempt to elicit particular examples of each strategy. For example, when asking about compliance, the clinician should ask for specific examples of the battered woman's attempts to use compliance.

A striking example of the sophistication of battered women's efforts to comply involved a woman's response to her batterer's demand to prepare him a sandwich. She could not remember whether he had requested a half or a whole sandwich and she believed that she would be beaten if she did not produce the "correct" sandwich. Her strategy was to make both a half and a whole sandwich so that she could appear to have prepared the sandwich which he had requested, leaving the other one for herself.

The clinician should assess the effectiveness of each strategy in keeping the battered woman safe over time. The ultimate issue is whether she has been successful in protecting herself from abuse. Calling the police for protection does not imply that they will respond in a manner that ensures her safety once they arrive. For example, was an arrest made, or after arrest, was the batterer released on bond within a few hours, only to return and continue the violent assault? There are many examples of police failure to take measures that provide any protection once they leave the premises. Many women report being afraid to begin a process, which, if aborted in the middle, may result in increased danger. A suggested format for assessment of particular strategies, frequency of their use, self-ratings of effectiveness, consequences of their use, and reasons for not using the strategy can be found in Appendix C.

Generally, evaluation of a battered woman's efforts to escape, avoid, and protect herself from abuse include identifying the particular strategies used, the consequences that followed from those efforts, her self-evaluation of their effectiveness, and, for specific efforts not used, the rationale for not using them. Without all of this information, a full understanding of the battered woman's circumstances cannot be fully appreciated.

4

Psychological Effects of Abuse

This chapter presents current theoretical and conceptual models for understanding the psychology of a battered woman's traumatic response. It describes specific effect patterns, discusses assessment procedures, and addresses relevant diagnostic issues.

PSYCHOLOGY OF TRAUMATIC RESPONSE

Many different kinds of experience can cause a traumatic reaction, for example, natural disaster (e.g., earthquake, flood, hurricane), accidents (e.g., automobile, falls), combat experience, and criminal assault (e.g., mugging, rape, domestic violence, child sexual or physical abuse). Research and clinical attention to the phenomena of psychological trauma has tended to focus on one trauma group at a time, although there exist general theoretical models for understanding the nature of traumatic response. These models may have applicability across trauma groups. However, few of these theories have been adequately tested to determine the extent to which they apply equally across different forms of traumatic experience. For a historical perspective of concepts related to what is now termed Post-Traumatic Stress Disorder (DSM-III-R; APA, 1987) see Trimble (1985).

The study and recognition of psychological trauma specifically resulting from exposure to abuse by one's intimate partner is only recent. One reason for lack of previous recognition of any but the most severe forms of violence against women in the home is that it has been seen as normal. Victimization by "normative" violence was unrecognized as was the traumatic response that followed from it. Secondly, a focus on psychological distress or other clinically relevant phenomena in the population of battered women has been approached with caution, especially within the battered women's movement and among feminist scholars and clinicians. Mention of psychological symptoms has raised the concern that they may be used as justification for blaming the battered woman. By labeling her with personality deficits, she is falsely presumed to be responsible for having caused the abuse and certain actions (e.g., denying battered women custody of their children, mutual restraining orders against both the battered woman and the batterer) are assumed to be justified.

Theories explaining general stress responses to traumatic events may be categorized within two groups: (1) those that refer to what is known as Post-Traumatic Stress Disorder and (2) those that refer to other forms of psychological response or adaptation to traumatic events.

Post-Traumatic Stress Disorder

Post-Traumatic Stress Disorder is characterized by symptoms of intrusion, avoidance, and arousal (APA, 1987). The intrusion components refer to the survivor's reexperiencing the traumatic event through nightmares, distressing mental images, dissociative states, and distressing affective responses. The avoidance or denial components of Post-Traumatic Stress Disorder refer to the constriction of affect, avoidance, and psychic numbing. The intrusion and avoidance phases are assumed to coexist within an individual survivor, although the cycling of the phases may vary from individual to individual. A third category associated with autonomic arousal includes, for example, hyperalertness, anger and hostility, difficulty with concentration, and sleep disturbance.

Horowitz (1976, 1979, 1986) developed an information-processing model that relied heavily on psychodynamic theory to explain the biphasic aspects of Post-Traumatic Stress Disorder, intrusion, and denial. Horowitz explained the recurrence of intrusion experiences (e.g., nightmares, dissociative states, mental images) by the "completion principle" derived from Freud's concept of repetition compulsion, that is, a compulsive and involuntary tendency to repeat some aspect of the experience (Freud, 1958) through feelings, thoughts, images, and behavioral reenactments. Horowitz also referred to cognitive dissonance theory to explain the repetition of remembered traumatic events until inner cognitive models or schemata become congruent with the traumatic experience. Horowitz explained avoidance symptoms as inhibitory regulatory processes that function to slow down the assimilation of traumatic information, sometimes by psychic numbing, constricted affect, and denial. Clinical experience indicates that avoidance efforts enable the victim to avert the discomfort associated with having thoughts about the traumatic experience. The fear is sometimes expressed as "if I remember then I'll go crazy and thus couldn't protect myself." Although Horowitz's theory does not account for why some traumatized persons develop Post-Traumatic Stress Disorder and others do not, it is one of the most comprehensive theories to date (Jones & Barlow, 1990).

Mowrer's two-factor learning theory has been used to explain symptoms of Post-Traumatic Stress Disorder from a behavioral perspective (Keane, Zimmerling, & Caddell, 1985; Kilpatrick, Veronen, & Best, 1985). Application of the instrumental learning component of Mowrer's theory helps explain the avoidance behavior associated with Post-Traumatic Stress Disorder because of its negative reinforcing property of avoiding aversive events. Higher-order conditioning, the second component of Mowrer's theory, provides an explanation for how a broad array of nondangerous events can elicit memories and arousal responses in trauma survivors. This behavioral model accounts for the acquisition of fear, the avoidance of nondangerous situations, and the generalization of fear cues. It does not, however, adequately explain the symptoms characterized as reexperiencing the trauma (e.g., nightmares, flashbacks, and intrusive images) frequently associated with Post-Traumatic Stress Disorder (Foa, Stetekee, & Rothbaum, 1989). Jones and Barlow (1990) further note the limitations of a behavioral theory that fails to account for why fear and avoidance responses do not extinguish in synchrony (decreased fear with continued avoidance) as would be predicted by the theory.

Foa et al. (1989) proposed a behavioral/cognitive conceptualization of Post-Traumatic Stress Disorder based on previous work by Foa and Kozak (1986) that integrates behavioral theories described above with cognitive theories to account for the development of meaning for both the feared situation and possible responses to it. Their theoretical model describes fear structures within memory that provide information about both the feared stimulus and responses to it, as well as information about the meaning of these elements of the structure. The model incorporates both cognition and affect and derives from the work of Lang (1977, 1979). Based on this model, Foa et al. suggest that Post-Traumatic Stress Disorder is more likely to develop when the trauma occurs in a previously safe environment, which might be expected to be the case for many battered women. Prior to the onset of abuse, there is typically a period of time in the early stages of the relationship in which the battered woman experiences the relationship as positive and safe. For fear structures to change, Foa et al. suggest that the original fearful memory must be retrieved, new and incompatible information, which is at once both cognitive and affective, must be provided so that a new memory can be formed. This can be viewed as the "working through" of the trauma.

Jones and Barlow (1990) present a comprehensive and multidimensional model to explain Post-Traumatic Stress Disorder. Explained within the model are the role of complex interactions between biological and psychological predispositions; the occurrence of stressful events and subsequent "alarms" that trigger responses similar to those of the original trauma; and, the development of anxiety, coping, strategies, and social support. The advantage of this model is that it accounts for nontrauma-related variables that may mediate the development or course of Post-Traumatic Stress Disorder. For example, one battered woman's experience of a severe stress reaction in her physician's office was explained by her male physician's question of what he could do to "take care of" her; those words were a "trigger" for her reaction, explained by the perpetrator's use of those words prior to his severe physically violent behavior. Another woman's Post-Traumatic Stress Disorder appeared nonexistant due to her compulsive work behavior, a coping strategy that allowed her to effectively avoid feelings, thoughts, and memories of her husband's brutal attacks. When she was incarcerated for killing her husband during his attack on her and she could no longer spend so much time working, she experienced frequent and severe intrusion symptoms related to her husband's violence.

Van der Kolk (1987, 1988) described the biological response to trauma and its role in the development of Post-Traumatic Stress Disorder. According to van der Kolk, "the human response to trauma is relatively constant across traumatic stimuli: the central nervous system (CNS) seems to react to any overwhelming threatening and uncontrollable experience in a consistent pattern" (p. 64). He described two patterns, which may alternate within a single individual, in which victims tend to respond to the poor tolerance for physiological arousal in an all-or-nothing manner: unmodulated anxiety or social and emotional withdrawal. Further, many trauma victims use drugs and alcohol in an "ill-fated attempt to relieve these posttraumatic symptoms" (van der Kolk, 1987, p. 65).

Other Post-traumatic Responses

Ochberg (1988) suggested that a victim may suffer from a distinct subcategory of traumatic stress that may or may not reach the threshold for Post-Traumatic Stress Disorder. These include:

1. *Shame*: deep embarrassment, often characterized as humiliation or mortification.
2. *Self-Blame*: exaggerated feelings of responsibility for the traumatic events, with guilt and remorse, despite obvious evidence of innocence.
3. *Subjugation*: feeling belittled, dehumanized, lowered in dominance, powerless, as a direct result of the trauma.
4. *Morbid Hatred*: obsessions of vengeance and preoccupation with hurting or humiliating the perpetrator, with or without outbursts of anger or rage.

5. *Paradoxical Gratitude*: positive feelings toward the victimizer ranging from compassion to romantic love, including attachment but not necessarily identification. The feelings are usually experienced as ironic but profound gratitude for the gift of life from one who has demonstrated the will to kill. (Also known as pathological transference and "Stockholm syndrome.")
6. *Defilement*: feeling dirty, disgusted, tainted, "like spoiled goods," and in extreme cases, rotten and evil.
7. *Sexual Inhibition*: loss of libido, reduced capacity for intimacy, more frequently associated with sexual assault.
8. *Resignation*: a state of broken will or despair, often associated with repetitive victimization or prolonged exploitation, with markedly diminished interest in past or future.
9. *Second Injury or Wound*: revictimization through participation in the criminal justice, health, mental health, and other systems.
10. *Socioeconomic Status Downward Drift*: reduction of opportunity or lifestyle, and increased risk of repeat criminal victimization due to psychological, social, and vocational impairment. (pp. 8-9).

Anger, denial, sadness, and continued attachment to the batterer may be explained by theories of bereavement, grief, and mourning (Ochberg, 1988; Saunders, 1989). Battering may lead to many losses for a woman: loss of her partner to divorce or separation; her home when she flees for her safety; her children if they are taken from her or she is not able to support them; her positive self-image, employment when her employer no longer tolerates the disruption caused by the abuse; loss of contact with friends and family as her world is predominated by abuse and becomes more constricted; loss of income; and loss of a familiar standard of living, to name only a few.

Janoff-Bulman (1985) proposed that a victim's response is the result of the shattering of basic assumptions about self and the world. When assumptions of invulnerability, the world as meaningful, and positive self-perception are shattered by the experience of victimization, disorientation and distress result. McCann, Sakheim, and Abrahamson (1988) provided an information-processing model of psychological adaption that focuses on trauma-induced shifts in cognitive schemas, incorporating those described by Janoff-Bulman. Schemas are stable, cognitive structures that organize life experiences; they include beliefs about the self, others, and the world (Beck, 1967). Information that is discrepant with existing schemas (such as violence in a relationship that is expected to be loving and safe) is assimilated in one of three ways. The new and incongruent information is either (1) rejected or ignored, (2) interpreted within existing schemas, or (3) is the basis for altering existing schemas. For example, when a woman is told that her partner has been abusive in a prior relationship, she may choose not to believe the information (reject or ignore), understand the violence within a schema that would attribute the cause of the violence to the behavior of the victim (interpret the violence within existing schema), or come to see her partner as a batterer (alter existing schema).

Victimization may influence cognitive schemas about self and others in six areas: frame of reference, safety, trust/dependency, power, esteem, intimacy, and independence (McCann et al., 1988; McCann & Pearlman, 1990a, 1990b). Frame of reference is a concept similar to Janoff-Bulman's (1989, 1992) definition of schemas related to a meaningful world. Frame of reference schemas incorporate attribution of causality, hope, and locus of control. Schemas about safety refer to the illusion of invulnerability from harm. Trust/dependency schemas refer to the belief in one's ability to trust others to respond to one's needs for support and care and to trust oneself, one's own perceptions and judgments. Schemas of independence refer to the ability to control one's own behavior and destiny, to have control over one's own rewards and punishments. Schemas of power refer to one's ability (or inability) to control the environment or others, especially hurtful acts of other people. Self schemas about esteem refer to beliefs about one's personal worth, positive validation, and recognition. Finally, schemas about intimacy refer to beliefs about whether intimacy and emotional connection with others are possible or whether relationships with others are characterized by alienation and emotional distance.

Shifts in cognitive schemas are hypothesized to influence psychological adaptation to the traumatic experiences in five potential areas: emotional, cognitive, biological, behavioral, and interpersonal (McCann et al., 1988; McCann & Pearlman, 1990). Shifts in the cognitive schema may have profound effects on the lives of battered women. For example, disruption or shifts in certain cognitive schemas (e.g., intimacy, trust/dependency) may result in a battered woman avoiding further personal relationships. Change in other cognitive schemas (e.g., safety, independence) may result in a battered woman leading a narrowed and restricted lifestyle.

Applied to battering, the concept of learned helplessness (Peterson & Seligman, 1983; Walker, 1984) refers to the belief in the uncontrollability of future violence or abuse and the futility of the battered woman's responses aimed at stopping or escaping it. Unlike the laboratory animals in the original learned-helplessness experiment (Selgiman, 1975), battered women are not typically passive in their response to the violence against them. However, they may have learned that certain efforts (e.g., calling the police, fighting back, threats to divorce) were not effective in escaping or stopping the violence and thus were futile as future responses. In spite of this, many battered women are often quite resourceful in seeking continued alternatives to survive or to minimize the abuse (e.g., hiding, complying with demands, anticipating the batterer's needs), believing that escaping it is impossible.

For some, the only alternative that appears viable in avoiding further violence is action that results in the death of the batterer through homicide. For most, this conclusion appears to be reached when the battered woman believes that her failure to find another alternative to protect herself will certainly lead to her own death, or that of her children.

Blackman (1989) also has focused on cognitive changes that result from intimate violence. In addition to developing the belief that (certain) future responses may be futile in stopping or escaping further violence, she discusses three other cognitive changes: (1) tolerance of cognitive inconsistency, (2) diminished perception of alternatives, and (3) development of a continuum of tolerance. A tolerance of cognitive inconsistency refers to the battered woman's ability to simultaneously respond to two quite different realities: a partner whom she believes loves and cares about her and a partner who hurts her. The battered woman develops a diminished perception of alternatives to effectively respond to the violence from her direct learning experience with the abuse and her efforts to respond to it. She often has tried many alternatives (e.g., calling police, seeking help of friends or neighbors, separation) (Bowker, 1983; Gondolf, 1988; Pagelow, 1981), but without successfully escaping or stopping future violence toward her. Blackman (1989) suggested that the continuum of tolerance or "survivability" is developed through repeated exposures to the partner's violence. Certain behaviors, however, fall out of the range of tolerability and may precipitate new behaviors by the battered woman (e.g., self-defense, leaving). Determining the battered woman's particular response to violence that is beyond her tolerance must take into account the other cognitive changes previously described.

The battered woman's continued attachment and loyalty to the batterer has been explained by the theory of "traumatic bonding" (Dutton, 1988; Dutton & Painter, 1981). Two aspects of the battering facilitate the development of traumatic bonding: (1) the existence of a powerful imbalance between the woman and her batterer wherein she perceives herself to be dominated and (2) the intermittent nature of the abuse. The power imbalance between the woman and her batterer resulting from his use of physical force or other behaviors to intimidate or control her leads to negative self-appraisal. She experiences lowered self-esteem and increased dependency and may become socially isolated. The battered woman may come to experience herself as more and more dependent on the person who exerts so much control over her.

The intermittent nature of the abuse, which may include periods of positive and peaceful interaction between the battered woman and her partner, may lead to her belief that she has some control and that her partner will change his abusive ways. For example, following an acute battering episode in which the battered woman left the house for several days to stay with friends, the period of the batterer's calm and conciliatory behavior may fuel a sense of her ability to control his behavior. The contrite, loving behavior that often follows abuse in a cycle of violence (Walker, 1984) or simply the periodic absence of abuse serves to intermittently reinforce the battered woman's belief of hope for the future. The Stockholm Syndrome has been used to describe this phenomena among hostage survivors (Hilberman, 1980; Ochberg, 1980, 1988).

DISTINCTIONS BETWEEN DOMESTIC VIOLENCE AND OTHER TRAUMAS

There are a number of distinctions between battering and other forms of trauma (Stark & Flitcraft, 1988) that have direct implication for understanding the traumatic reaction of battering and for treatment decisions as well.

First, at the point when the battered woman initially seeks help from a mental health professional or a shelter, it is likely that she is currently involved in a relationship in which some form of violence, abuse, or controlling behavior continues to present a threat. Other forms of interpersonal abuse or violence, child sexual or physical abuse, for example, share this feature. Thus, unlike some forms of trauma such as combat experience or accidents in which the current affective experience may be of similar proportions to the original traumatic experience, the actual traumatic event for battered women is typically recent and the actual threat of its continuation is currently present and ongoing.

Second, the battered woman nearly always has multiple exposures to the violence and abuse, often over a long duration. Although repeated exposure is characteristic of some other forms of trauma (e.g., combat experience or childhood abuse), it is not of others (e.g., single-incident rape, accidents, or natural disasters).

Third, a woman battered by her intimate partner is victimized by someone with whom she has chosen to be involved. For most people, battered women included, the choice of a particular intimate partner is based on some positive aspects of the partner and of the relationship. Thus, when one's own partner, who is presumed to be safe, is the source of the trauma, a different psychological meaning is created than when the trauma originates from someone who can readily be identified as "the enemy" (e.g., an intruder, a stranger) (Foa et al., 1989).

Fourth, some battered women may have a history of exposure to other traumatic events that are similar to the battering experience. These may include other incidents in which personal boundaries have been violated in the context of a trusting interpersonal relationship, for example, childhood sexual or physical assault; abuse in a previous adult relationship; rape by someone other than a stranger; and/or sexual exploitation by a helping professional. Cumulatively, these victimization experiences may span the battered woman's entire life. As a consequence, the psychological effects are compounded by previous traumas that share similar features.

In summary, these dimensions, which distinguish battering from other traumatic experiences, provide an important framework within which to continue the investigation of posttraumatic reactions generally, as well as the traumatic reactions associated specifically with battering and abuse by an intimate partner. These dimensions include (1) the threat of ongoing traumatization, (2) repeated versus single exposure to the traumatic event, (3) prior history of exposure to similar traumas, and (4) the nature of the relationship with the perpetrator.

CLASSIFICATION OF TRAUMATIC EFFECTS

The psychological effects of battering as a traumatic experience include a broad range of cognitive, behavioral, emotional, interpersonal, and physiological responses (Dutton, in press). A classification of responses to trauma that integrates theoretical, empirical, and clinical work includes (1) indicators of psychological distress or dysfunction, (2) relational disturbances, and (3) changes in cognitive schema. All responses should be initially hypothesized as resulting from exposure to trauma alone, without assuming preexisting psychopathology. Testing this hypothesis should occur throughout the course of intervention.

Indicators of Psychological Distress/Dysfunction

Fear/Terror. It is, of course, expected that the battered woman may fear her abusive partner, especially if she perceives that he still continues to be a danger. For many battered women, the threat of continued abuse remains indefinitely, regardless of divorce, separation, or criminal prosecution of the abuser. The knowledge that further abuse is likely, or at least possible, understandably creates fear. An extreme form of fear, terror, may exist when the battered woman believes correctly not only that the likelihood of continued violence is high, but also that the violence may be lethal.

Even when a battered woman states that she no longer believes her partner will be violent towards her, she may behave as though she is afraid of him (e.g., avoid being alone with him, engage in compliant behavior) or she may experience the autonomic arousal associated with a fear reaction when she is near him or has contact with him. Other specific stimuli, especially those events or situations that have been associated with abuse or violence toward her in the past (e.g., weapons, other objects of abuse) are likely to be feared. The fear may be accompanied by intrusive reexperiencing of past violence, avoidance symptoms, or indicators of autonomic arousal.

Intrusion Symptoms. Intrusion symptoms refer to reexperiencing the phenomenona of the traumatic experience, for example, through nightmares, flashbacks, images, body sensations, and intrusive thoughts. Intrusive symptoms experienced by battered women may occur, for example, when talking about the abuse to another person; when seeing a car similar to that of the partner's; when the abusive partner (or perhaps an employer or new partner) raises his voice; when watching violence on television or movies that depict violence or conflict; or, when required to testify about the violence in a courtroom or to discuss the violence with an attorney, investigator, or other professional. The battered woman may well know that the abuse is not recurring, but her phenomenological experience at re-exposure to events that symbolize the abuse resemble those of the actual abuse.

Avoidance Responses. Avoidance responses, which include behavioral, cognitive, affective, and physiological components, function to minimize or deny awareness of the traumatic experience or its aftermath. Avoidance responses may include loss of memory for important aspects of abusive episodes (psychogenic amnesia), denial or minimization of the abuse experience, avoidance of situations in which the battered woman may be asked about the abuse (e.g., by professional helpers, friends, or family), neglecting to report or omitting extreme examples of physical abuse or sexual abuse even when otherwise seeking help, or, avoiding men generally.

Psychic numbing, another avoidance response, refers to feelings of detachment or estrangement or the inability to have feelings as if feelings are frozen, blocked, or limited to a very narrow and restricted range. Examples of battered women's psychic numbing include restriction of feelings when talking about the abusive experience, as if there were no feelings associated with it or speaking about someone else's victimization. For other battered women the numbing occurs during sexual activity with the abusive partner or a new partner, even when abuse is not occurring and regardless of whether actual sexual abuse had previously occurred.

Anxiety. It has been generally established that women who are victims of violence experience persistent and generalized symptoms of anxiety (Ellis, 1983; Hilberman & Munson, 1978; Kilpatrick & Veronen, 1983; Sales, Baum, & Shore, 1984). Victims also experience anxiety in relation to cues that remind them of previous abusive or violent incidents. These phobic reactions result in considerable distress as these cues often include events and situations that are encountered daily. For example, hearing the raised voice of someone in anger, seeing a movie that depicts violence toward women or seeing a weapon, and even being in one's own home at night, may each trigger severe anxiety reactions in battered women. These symptoms of anxiety may include those associated with panic disorder (e.g., unsteady feelings, trembling or shaking, exaggerated startle response, choking, sweating, fear of going crazy or doing something uncontrolled), generalized anxiety disorder (e.g., nausea, diarrhea, or other abdominal distress, "mind going blank," dry mouth), or agoraphobia (Saunders, 1990).

Sleep Difficulty. Difficulty getting to sleep or staying asleep is common for trauma victims (Figley, 1986), in part, as a function of the autonomic arousal that competes with the sleep response (APA, 1987). Separate from the sleep deprivation that is often part of the abusive pattern, battered women experience sleep difficulties after they are no longer in the abusive relationship. One battered woman who no longer had contact with her abuser was unable to sleep for more than a couple of hours at a time due to the constant recurrence of nightmares each time she fell asleep. Chronic sleep difficulty may result in sleep deprivation that may then influence mood and ability to function (for example, in occupational and parental roles).

Difficulty Concentrating. Difficulty concentrating may also result from increased autonomic arousal (APA, 1987) and impact one's ability to function effectively, for example in employment settings or while doing household or leisure tasks (e.g., reading, watching television). Even after the abuse or violence ceases, difficulty with concentration may persist.

Hypervigilance, Suspiciousness. The autonomic arousal that underlies hypervigilance and the cognitive belief that there is reason to be afraid combine to mimic paranoid-like features and may be erroneously interpreted as such. However, unlike paranoia in which there is an unrealistic belief that danger exists, the battered woman's hypervigilance and suspiciousness may either be grounded in the reality of possible reoccurrence of abuse (even after divorce or separation) or in a conditioned reaction based on past abuse.

Physiological Reactivity. One hallmark of posttraumatic stress response has been physiological reactivity upon exposure to events that remind one of past traumatic experiences (APA, 1987). This has at its base a physiological abnormality, specifically the loss of ability to modulate arousal (van der Kolk, 1987). That is, when exposed to a situation or an event that represents the traumatic experience, the body's ability to handle the physiological stress is diminished; thus, the physical and affective reaction may be similar to that of the original traumatic situation even though there is little or no actual threat. The physiological studies have yet to be completed with battered women, but clinical reports support the notion of physiological reactivity in battered women as well as other trauma survivors.

Women who have been previously battered have reported intense anxiety symptoms (e.g., difficulty breathing, heart pounding) when hearing loud voices, hearing the telephone ring, seeing a weapon, seeing their abusive partner at a courtroom hearing, hearing footsteps outside the door, or observing whatever cue may resemble or symbolize some aspect of the prior abuse.

Anger/Rage. Anger is a common effect of traumatic exposure (Ochberg, 1988) and, like fear, has a physiological component of autonomic arousal. Expressions of anger may be overt, such as aggressive or hostile behavior, or covert, such as passive-aggressive or manipulative behavior; somaticized symptoms; or depression.

Some battered women express their anger by misdirecting it at targets safer than their batterers (e.g., children, coworkers, family, friends, helping professionals, other highway drivers, clerks), although some do express their anger directly toward their batterers. Those who are able to express anger may do so in public or in other situations (e.g., in the presence of others, while holding children) considered to be temporarily safe. The battered woman's willingness to directly express her anger toward her partner is not a predictable indication of her level of fear of him.

For other battered women, the anger is never expressed overtly nor is it even a conscious reality. The battered woman may believe that she has forgiven him, that she never was angry with him, or that she has simply gotten over it. Instead, the feelings of anger are out of her awareness and may take their toll physically in the form of somatic symptoms such as difficulty sleeping, stomach pain, headaches, muscle tension, and as chronic depression.

Grief/Depression/Suicide. Grief refers to the emotional component of the bereavement process (Ochberg, 1988) and includes sadness and feelings of emotional pain associated with loss. Losses often experienced by battered women include loss of hope about the future, loss of sense of self-identity including self-worth, loss of children and partners, loss of home, and loss of income. Grief is a major response, which in one way or another, plays a role for most battered women.

Subjective feelings of depression and sadness may result from the battered woman's social isolation and the restriction of rewarding activities with her abusive partner (Lewinsohn, 1975). The battered woman often gives up enjoyable or rewarding activities (e.g., being with friends or family, employment, dance classes) as an attempt to reduce the batterer's anger. However, these attempts typically do not work.

In extreme cases, battered women may consider suicide to be the only way to stop the intense emotional pain resulting from continued abuse and the betrayal it represents. Suicide gestures are not uncommon among battered women. Stark, Flitcraft, Zuckerman, Grey, Robison, and Frazier (1981) found that of women admitted to a hospital emergency room following suicide attempts, 29% were battered women, half of whom had been battered the same day and 75% of whom had been battered within the prior six months. Battering is a catalyst event for one of every four suicide attempts by all women and one in two attempts among black women (Stark & Flitcraft, 1988).

Shame. Shame refers to the affective component of inferiority (Kaufman, 1989) or deep embarrassment (Ochberg, 1988), the feeling associated with believing one is bad, less than, and not worthy. Ochberg (1988) described the victim's sense of defilement, as if she were spoiled or damaged goods. The abuse causes shame reactions in the victim. The battered woman may experience shame when reporting about the abuse to a therapist, counselor, law enforcement officer, prosecutor, or clergy. She may experience the shame even when she merely remembers the abusive experiences, regardless of whether she also speaks about it.

Lowered Self-Esteem. Self-esteem refers to cognitions about one's own value or worth (which may or may not be accompanied by feelings of shame) that result from exposure to battering. Some battered women demonstrate their lowered self-esteem by believing that they do not deserve or are not worthy of better treatment by their intimate partner or by the institutional systems (e.g., mental health, legal, medical) designed to help them. Other battered women believe themselves to be less worthy than other women who have not been battered, somehow believing that the abuse has diminished their value as human beings.

Morbid Hatred. Morbid hatred is apparent when the victim is preoccupied or obsessed with the wish that her perpetrator were dead or with ideas of harming or retaliating against him. It has been my experience that it is not unusual for battered women to state their desire for their abusive partner to "get run over by a car" or "have a heart attack and die," in order that he would "just be gone." However, few battered women actually plot actions to do serious harm or to kill their abusers and even fewer carry out any actions that they may have contemplated. Those who do typically feel powerless to prevent future victimization and assume the inevitability of continued abuse unless they take preventive action.

Somatic Complaints. Somatic complaints may result from actual physical injuries that produce prolonged pain or dysfunction. It is probably the case that many injuries actually go undetected, especially closed head injuries, muscle tears, and/or other injuries that do not demand immediate medical attention. It is not uncommon for a battered woman to have received serious blows to the head during the course of a violent episode. Banging her head against walls or floors, falls that result in hitting her head against an object, and punches or blows directly to her head are all common abusive behaviors for batterers engaged in severe violence. One battered woman reported the onset of epileptic seizures following head trauma incurred during an abusive incident by her husband. A small percentage of epileptic seizures are related to the occurrence of trauma (Slagle, 1990).

It is well recognized that stress is directly related to the cause or exacerbation of multiple physical ailments, including tension headaches, lower-back pain, stomach aches, nausea, heart disease, cancer, Krone's disease, and other stress-related disorders. Thus, for some people, stress associated with traumatic and otherwise difficult life events is expressed through physical sensations. It is these effects of trauma, rather than emotional distress, for which some battered women are most aware.

Addictive Behaviors. Substance abuse among battered women functions as a means of self-medicating the distress and dysfunction described above by reducing immediate anxiety and enhancing the numbing effect, thus blocking out the experience of distress and emotional pain. Some women learn to abuse substances prior to the onset of battering, sometimes in relation to previous or early childhood abuse, where others discover its effectiveness only after the onset of violence in the adulthood. Stark, Flitcraft, Zuckerman, Grey, Robison, and Frazier (1981) found that among women presenting at nontrauma medical sites alcohol abuse increased from 3% prior to the first identified occurrence of abuse to 15% following the first reported incident.

Although alcohol and substance abuse represent a distinctive class of addictive or compulsive behaviors, other behaviors exhibited in a compulsive and ritualistic manner can function similarly in their ability to numb and avoid painful feelings. These other behaviors may include compulsive or binge eating; anorexia and bulimia; self-mutilation; compulsive or ritualistic "busyness" which may or may not manifest as workaholism or compulsive housecleaning; and, compulsive spending, shopping, or gambling. Although many of these behaviors are perfectly normal and adaptive when done in moderation (and, in fact, are demanded by day-to-day existence, e.g., food consumption, working, spending money), they may function to numb feelings and avoid emotional pain when done in a compulsive or ritualistic manner.

Impaired Functioning. The distress of living in an abusive intimate relationship can result in impaired functioning in numerous roles, including occupational, social, and parental. Battered women often report that they are no longer able to engage in social interaction with friends because their feelings of depression, anger, and distress interfere. Work performance may suffer simply due to the level of emotional distress they are experiencing. In extreme circumstances, some battered women may even be unable to adequately function as nurturing and protective parental figures due to the severe level of their own psychological distress and cognitive distortions resulting from the abuse.

Changes in Cognitive Schema

Changes in cognitive schema, or basic core beliefs about the world, oneself, and others (Blackman, 1989; Janoff-Bulman, 1985, 1992; McCann & Pearlman, 1990b; McCann et al., 1988) may or may not be experienced directly as distressing. However, these changes in cognitive schema may immeasurably impact the battered woman's life by influencing the manner in which she lives her life such as the relationships she develops or avoids developing, the places she is or is not willing to go, how she perceives her environment, and the opportunities she is or is not willing to seek.

Loss of Assumption of Invulnerability/Safety. Following exposure to a traumatic event, changes in the assumptions of invulnerability (Janoff-Bulman, 1985, 1992) or safety (McCann & Pearlman, 1990b; McCann et al., 1988) are evident for the victim. The parameters within which the trauma victim no longer feels safe may be a function of the circumstances in which the original trauma occurred. For example, if a woman was raped on the street, in her car, or in her home, her assumptions of where she is safe may vary. For the battered woman, since the violence and abuse toward her occurs in the most intimate, and presumed safe, environments (e.g., in her own home, perhaps in her own bed), her assumptions of vulnerability likely may extend to all places where her abusive partner has access. For some battered women, the physical environments in which the presumption of physical safety may be reasonable to her include the office of a therapist, a shelter, or the home of a friend where the locations of each are unknown to the abusive partner. For the battered woman, the assumptions of safety do not necessarily resume once a separation, divorce, or location change has occurred, as these transitions often signal increased, not decreased, abuse, sometimes to the point of lethality.

Loss of View of World As Meaningful. A central cognitive schema around which most people are able to create stability in their life is the notion that the world and the events that occur are meaningful; things that happen make sense. When persons who are supposed to love and care for women are instead violent toward them, then the task of finding meaning in the situation becomes more difficult. Making sense of the violence, in the context of a presumed loving relationship, is the battered woman's struggle. Even women who were abused as children by parents or other caretakers may believe that their present relationship with an intimate partner is different. Prior to the onset of abuse, some women believe that they have finally found a relationship in which they will be safe and cared for. This is sometimes based on interpreting their partner's stance as "protective and powerful." When the "protective and powerful" becomes "controlling, violent, and powerful" (Goldberg, 1982), the relationship no longer makes sense.

The battered woman's knowledge of violence toward other women, and the naming of violence as a social problem, may help her to make sense of her individual circumstance. That is, explaining that violence in specific intimate relationships is reflective of oppression toward women on a social level can help the battered woman to feel not alone and to understand the problem as one for which she is not causally responsible.

Perception of Futility/Diminished Alternatives: Learned Helplessness. It is common for trauma victims to have a general sense of powerlessness including hopelessness about one's efforts to escape further abuse and the belief in the uncontrollability of the occurrence of future abuse. The concept of learned helplessness has at its core the perception of powerlessness or the belief that the individual in unable to control the outcome or occurrence of events (Seligman, 1975). Walker (1984) introduced the concept of learned helplessness as it applies to battered women. This application has received criticism, however, based on the fact that most battered women do not helplessly give up attempts to protect themselves even though their efforts are often not recognized by others. Blackman (1989) clarified the problem somewhat by suggesting that it is the battered woman's attempts to actually leave the violent intimate relationship that are specifically perceived as futile. Further, her perception of other alternatives to respond may be markedly diminished. However, short of leaving, most battered women are engaged in many efforts to protect themselves and to survive.

As the battered woman continues to attempt various strategies for responding to the abuse, she may perceive only a few strategies that, based on her experience, allow her to somewhat protect herself and her children. For example, some battered women find that compliance in the threatening situation is the most effective strategy for minimizing injury. Women who are victims of forced sexual abuse by their partners often "give in" both to reduce the physical injury resulting from the batterer's use of force and to terminate the abusive episode more readily. Killing their abusive partners or killing themselves is viewed by some battered women as the only effective methods in avoiding further victimization. Other women choose neither of these and endure what they believe to be the inevitable continuation of abuse; unfortunately some of these women are killed.

Negative Beliefs About Self. The *attribution of self-blame* for an action or its consequences refers to a belief that one is guilty or wrong. Causal attributions and cognitive appraisals of the victimization experience may be important in the understanding of battered women's reactions to their victimization (Peterson & Seligman, 1983) and in explaining why some victims develop more severe and chronic patterns of response than others (Koss & Burkhart, 1989).

There has been considerable discussion concerning battered women's causal attributions regarding the violence against them (Frieze, 1980; Miller & Porter, 1983; Walker, 1984). In a recent review of the empirical data, Holtzworth-Monroe (1988) concluded that the data do not support the conclusion that most women blame themselves for their husband's abuse, although some do. Clinical experience suggests that many women report believing that they are not to blame for their partner's violence, but nevertheless believe that they are guilty or feel shameful in some way, perhaps for not stopping the abuse or for not leaving.

Most research has examined the battered woman's causal attributions for the violence, although battered women also blame themselves for other aspects, of the violent situation. Brickman, Rabinowitz, Karuza, Coates, Cohen, and Kidder (1982) provided a theoretical model of coping and helping that aides in clarifying various forms of attribution. By clarifying whether one takes responsibility for the problem (e.g., violence), or the "solution" to the problem (e.g., escaping, avoiding, or protecting from the violence), the battered woman may blame herself in several ways. Miller and Porter (1983) distinguished among three types of self blame: (1) blame for causing violence or "occasioning" its occurrence, (2) blame for not being able to stop the violence or change the batterer's behavior, and (3) blame for not being able to tolerate the violence. Thus, even though the data seem not to support the notion that most battered women blame themselves for the occurrence of the violence, many battered women seem to blame themselves in some other way.

Other shifts in core beliefs about self that should be assessed include the battered woman's *belief that she cannot trust her own perceptions and judgment.* Many women become confused by what they define as their inability to have better judged the character of their partners who later became abusive. Helping a woman discover that she may have noticed certain signs indicative of potential problems, but ignored them, or that, based on her partner's charming and loving behavior, it was reasonable for her not to perceive his potential for violence, can help her to build trust in her own perceptions. The battered woman's belief in her *inability to comfort or nurture herself* may develop from the continued or prolonged exposure to abusive and controlling behavior and from her need to defend against prolonged and chronic stress.

Developing a Continuum of Tolerance. However implicit, most battered women hold beliefs about what is acceptable and what is not. When the battered woman is confronted with her tolerance of violence or abuse, at whatever level of severity, she may begin to examine that continuum and make changes in it. Other women acknowledge what is true for them at that moment, which may be a decision or willingness to tolerate the abuse for some particular purpose. Sometimes the tolerance of abuse is the cost that a battered woman pays for basic privileges such as staying in her own home; not losing her children; maintaining a current economic standard of living; or, having an intimate relationship or a co-parent for her children. It is important to determine with the client the actual parameters of her continuum of tolerance for abuse as well as the parameters she might prefer adopting.

Tolerance for Cognitive Inconsistency. Incorporating both the reality of abuse with the reality of caring behavior in an intimate relationship requires the battered woman to tolerate inherent inconsistency. Some battered women learn to tolerate such inconsistency in childhood when parents who are needed to provide basic nurturance, including emotional nurturance are also abusive. These women may bring to the intimate relationship in adulthood the ability to tolerate the presence of both abusive and caring behaviors. Other battered women acquire the tolerance for inconsistency for the first time within the abusive relationship.

Recognizing the battered woman's ability to tolerate the inconsistency of both abusive and loving behaviors from her intimate partner allows the professional to make sense of the situation, without attributing the woman's focus on her partner's caring behaviors or her attachment to him as masochistic, crazy, or as an indication that she "wants" the abuse. She may want the relationship and have developed a cognitive ability to tolerate the abuse in order to have it.

Tolerating the inconsistency of abuse in an intimate relationship is, of course, not adaptive for the battered woman's overall mental health, although it well may be adaptive in some ways. By understanding how it is that she may remain in an abusive relationship, the clinician can refrain from pathologizing her and help her to examine her choices about leaving or staying within it.

Relational Disturbances

Attachment/Dependency. Attachment and dependency by victims toward their perpetrators is a common response to trauma (Ochberg, 1988). The phenomena has been referred to as the Stockholm Syndrome (Graham, Rawlings, & Rimini, 1988). Dutton and Painter (1981) used the theory of traumatic bonding to explain the process for battered women.

Battered women's attachment to and dependency on their abusive partners must be considered from two perspectives. The first is the love and attachment that developed in the initial stages of the relationship, typically prior to the occurrence of any serious abuse. This attachment is, of course, normal and desired in intimate relationships. The problem for women's attachment to persons who abuse them is the increase in attachment and dependency that results from repeated violence and abuse in the relationship. According to the theory of traumatic bonding (Dutton, 1985; Dutton & Painter, 1981), the battered woman's decreased sense of her own worth and increased isolation resulting from the abuse creates a greater forced dependency upon her abuser as the violence escalates and continues over time (Pence, 1990).

Attachment to the batterer may manifest itself in not wanting to cause him harm or embarrassment by telling family, friends, or reporting violence to the police. Protecting the batterer and his feelings is a common response among battered women. Sometimes this is a function of the woman's wish to protect herself against further retaliation, which may occur for simply talking about the abuse, or attempting to retain economic security by not causing the abusive partner to lose his job or move out of the home. However, much of the protective behavior towards the batterer may be motivated by emotional attachment to the partner who is abusive. His coerced isolation of her increases the battered woman's dependency on her batterer for tangible resources (e.g., access to transportation, money), as well as emotional and social support.

Difficulty with Trust. The betrayal of trust inherent in violent and abusive relationships often creates a difficulty or an inability for the victim to trust that she will not be physically or emotionally hurt in other relationships. Women who choose to remain with their formerly abusive partners have particular difficulty feeling trust again, and for good reason, even once the violence and dominance have ceased. It is important to understand these difficulties with trust as reality-based responses to situations in which trust may be, in fact, unfounded. Typically, however, the difficulties with trust may extend far beyond the relationship with the abuser, or even with men, to relationships with new intimate partners, employers, friends, and helping professionals, as well. Difficulties trusting in these relationships may also be based in reality; some battered women develop a keen ability to detect subtle violations of trust.

Difficulty with Intimate Relationships. Relational disturbances, other than problems with trust, occur following abuse in an intimate relationship. Battered women who develop new intimate relationships often have difficulty setting appropriate boundaries or they may respond to new partners with anger or fear as though they were the old abusive partner. It is, of course, understandable why these difficulties arise, but nonetheless, they create problems in the development of new nonabusive relationships.

The battered woman who chooses not to leave her partner can be expected to experience continued difficulties in her relationship with him. Although the violent and severe forms of abuse may stop, many batterers may continue to use, unabated, controlling behavior and less obvious abuse. The exercise of power and control by the "formerly" abusive partner presents continuous and ongoing victimization of the battered woman and represents a threat of recurrent violence. The battered woman who remains in a previously abusive relationship can never be certain that the violence will not recur. When her previously abusive partner continues to raise his voice and call her names, focus the blame for his anger on her, or maintain control of the money or transportation, the previously battered woman is presented with cues that in the past may have signaled the escalation of abuse to levels of violence. It is only when both violent and nonviolent controlling behaviors cease that it is reasonable to believe that the battered women can have a chance to rebuild trust in the previously abusive relationship.

Sexual Difficulties. A common aftermath of sexual abuse is the decrease in sexual desire or sexual functioning in relationships other than with the abuser. Although sexuality is not solely a relationship issue, it is addressed here in the context of relationship. For battered women who have also been sexually abused by their partners, the impact on their sexuality seems obvious. Sexual abuse for battered women, however, does not have to refer to rape or the use of actual physical force to engage in sexual activity. It may mean the use of implicit intimidation that comes when a batterer wants to have sex following a physically abusive episode. Although he may not use physical force or actual threats, the preceding physical abuse often serves as an immediate and present indication of the danger that her partner demonstrates. In other cases, the sexual abuse occurs when the partner sexually harasses her by grabbing her breasts or buttocks as he passes her, making explicit and unwanted sexual comments, or engages in unwanted sexual contact while she sleeps. The association of sex with her abusive partner, whether he has actually used force or not, may be sufficient to impair the battered woman's sexual functioning in future relationships. The association of sex with a person who at other times is degrading and hurtful may be all that is required to affect sexual functioning. Finally, the depression and other affective responses associated with the aftermath of abuse may affect many previously enjoyable activities, including sex, such that the battered woman no longer has any interest in or desire for them.

DIAGNOSTIC ISSUES

PTSD is defined as a normal, albeit traumatic, reaction when an individual has experienced a severe stressor typically considered to be "outside the range of usual human experience . . . that would be markedly distressing to almost anyone" including abuse characteristic of battering relationships (DSM-III-R; APA, 1987, pp. 250-251). Criteria necessary in order to diagnose a battering victim's psychological reactions to abuse as Post-Traumatic Stress Disorder (PTSD) include the following:

A. The person has experienced an event that is outside the range of usual human experience and that would be markedly distressing to almost anyone. . . .
B. The traumatic event is persistently reexperienced in at least one of the following ways:
   (1) recurrent and intrusive distressing recollections of the event, . . .
   (2) recurrent distressing dreams of the event,
   (3) sudden acting or feeling as if the traumatic event were recurring (includes a sense of reliving the experience, illusions, hallucinations, and dissociative [flashback] episodes, even those that occur upon awakening or when intoxicated),
   (4) intense psychological distress at exposure to events that symbolize or resemble an aspect of the traumatic event, including anniversaries of the trauma.
C. Persistent avoidance of stimuli associated with the trauma or numbing of general responsiveness (not present before the trauma), as indicated by at least three of the following:
   (1) efforts to avoid thoughts or feelings associated with the trauma,
   (2) efforts to avoid activities or situations that arouse recollections of the trauma,
   (3) inability to recall an important aspect of the trauma, (psychogenic amnesia)
   (4) markedly diminished interest in significant activities, . . .
   (5) feelings of detachment or estrangement from others,
   (6) restricted range of affect, e.g., unable to have loving feelings,
   (7) sense of a foreshortened future, e.g., does not expect to have a career, marriage, or children, or a long life.
D. Persistent symptoms of increased arousal (not present before the trauma), as indicated by at least two of the following:
   (1) difficulty falling or staying asleep,
   (2) irritability or outbursts of anger,
   (3) difficulty concentrating,
   (4) hypervigilance,
   (5) exaggerated startle response,
   (6) physiologic reactivity upon exposure to events that symbolize or resemble an aspect of the traumatic event . . .
E. Duration of the disturbance (symptoms in B, C, D) of at least one month.

Problems exist with the PTSD diagnosis for victims of battering and abuse in intimate relationships. First, the PTSD criteria are not sufficient to capture the breadth of symptoms typically exhibited by victims and thus fail to legitimize those reactions to abuse not explicitly named within it. This may lead to a problem when the aftereffects or sequelae to victimization for battered women do not fall within the diagnostic criteria, although she may be suffering considerable distress as a result of the battering. She may receive an alternative diagnosis (e.g., Major Depression; Generalized Anxiety Disorder; or, Borderline, Histrionic, or Dependent Personality Disorder) that fails to link explicitly her symptoms to the occurrence of abuse. Some of these diagnoses may serve to further victimize her.

Philosophically, a central issue in the diagnosis of traumatic reactions is the identification of effects as functionally linked to an external traumatic event, not to an aberrant psychic mechanism within the individual. From another perspective, posttraumatic reactions have been considered in the form of influence on personality development (Herman, Perry, & van der Kolk, 1989), especially when the trauma occurs during childhood. Chronic exposure to trauma in adulthood may also be considered to have pervasive effects on personality structure, especially when the traumatic experiences of abuse span many years.

The DSM-IV Task Force has proposed three different options for defining the characteristics of the stressor (APA, 1991). One option limits the scope of the stressor to "event or events that involve actual or threatened death or injury, or a threat to the physical integrity of oneself or others (p. H:16)." Another option includes the definition above, but adds a subjective component as a criteria for defining the stressor: "the person's response involved intense fear, helplessness, or horror (p. H:16)." The final option closely resembles the current DSM-III criteria, "exposure to an exceptional mental or physical stressor, either brief or prolonged (p. H:17)."

Other proposed changes make explicit the reference to "internal or external cues (p. H:17)" that trigger either intense psychological distress or physiological reactivity. The proposed requirement of avoidance symptoms has been reduced from three to two.

Although some of these changes suggest an improvement in addressing posttraumatic issues relevant to battered women (e.g., adding the focus to internal cues), even these revisions in diagnostic criteria for PTSD do not comprehensively define the aftermath of battering.

STRATEGIES OF ASSESSMENT

Similar to strategies for assessing violent or abusive behavior (Chapter 2) and battered women's response to it (Chapter 3), a multimethod assessment approach to the assessment of the psychological effects of battering is superior to a single-dimension approach. A comprehensive assessment of the psychological effects of exposure to physical, sexual, and psychological abuse includes both interview and psychological testing methods. Biological models of evaluations are also discussed.

Interview

The mental status examination should be included in a clinical interview for assessing psychological trauma in order to provide a global appraisal or overview of the client's level of functioning. The mental status examination relies on observations of the client's overt and verbal behavior as well as on her reported subjective experiences. Categories covered in the mental status examination include appearance and behavior; attitude toward the interviewer; psychomotor activity; affect and mood; speech and thought; perceptual disturbances; orientation; attention, concentration, and memory; intelligence; and reliability, judgment, and insight (Rosenthal & Akiskal, 1985). The mental status examination can provide information sufficient to assess whether or not the battered woman client is in a state of mental health crisis (e.g., extreme stress reaction involving hallucinations, delusions, or other psychotic-like symptoms; risk for suicidal or other self-injurious behavior; risk for homicide).

Beyond a mental status examination, the clinical interview is useful for obtaining information about the symptoms of distress and/or dysfunction presented by the battered woman. The behavioral interview (cf. Morganstern, 1988) is particularly well suited as a clinical interview method for clearly defining the problems presented, as well as for obtaining detailed information about relevant external (e.g., violence, stressors) and internal (e.g., cognitions, affective responses) events. Information obtained from the clinical interview provides the primary source of information from which a formulation (or functional analysis or clinical hypothesis) explaining a particular battered woman's unique set of responses to the violent situation and/or her distinctive constellation of posttraumatic effects can be derived.

Psychological Tests

Several specific instruments found in the literature and commonly used in clinical practice and research with battered women or other trauma victims are described below. For these measures, normative data derived from a sample of battered women seeking help within the Family Violence Program, a specialized family violence clinic within a community mental health center, are found in Appendix D.

Impact of Event Scale. The Impact of Event Scale (IES) was developed by Horowitz, Wilner, and Alverez (1979) to assess intrusive and avoidance symptoms of Post-Traumatic Stress Disorder. The instrument has been used widely in research with trauma survivors to assess symptoms of PTSD. The advantage of the IES is its brevity and ease of administration. A disadvantage is the inability of the IES to provide diagnostic decisions based on responses to the IES alone.

MMPI/MMPI-2. The Minnesota Multiphasic Personality Inventory (MMPI) has been used widely in research with combat veterans to assess traumatic reaction. Recently, Wilson and Walker (1990) proposed a trauma profile based on studies using the MMPI with veterans. Rosewater (1987) discussed the use of the MMPI specifically with battered women and makes the case for appropriately interpreting the MMPI as a reaction to trauma, not as indicators of long-standing personality patterns. Wilson and Walker (1990) provide a reinterpretation of the MMPI clinical scales from a trauma perspective.

The PTSD subscale (Keane, Malloy, & Fairbank, 1984), a 49-item scale derived from MMPI items has been used in research primarily with combat veterans (see Watson, 1990 for review). It now appears as a supplemental scale in the MMPI-2 as a 48-item scale with T-scores derived from combat veteran samples. Battered women's scores on this scale correlate at moderately high elevations with SCL-90-R PTSD subscale scores and with IES intrusion and avoidance scores (Dutton, Perrin, Chrestman, Hallo, & Burghardt, 1991), thus indicating the potential utility of this measure in the assessment of battered women.

All battered women do not experience the same posttraumatic reactions to violence and, accordingly, do not present a common MMPI trauma profile. A cluster analysis of MMPI clinical and validity scores produced five distinctively different MMPI profiles (Dutton, Perrin, Chrestman, & Halle, 1990); these data provide empirical support for the observation of variation in posttraumatic effect among battered women. More work is needed to determine what factors (e.g., nature or severity of violence, history of prior victimization, social support, economic resources) contribute to these differences in battered women's trauma profiles, as measured by the MMPI as well as other measures.

Symptom Checklist-90-R. The Symptom Checklist-90-R (SCL-90-R) was developed by Deragotis (1977) to assess unique symptom clusters (e.g., depression, anxiety, interpersonal sensitivity, somatic complaints, hostility) and, thus, can provide measures of indicators of specific types of posttraumatic reaction. The instrument provides T-scores for nine clinical subscales, as well as for three overall, global measures of distress. The instrument has been used widely in both clinical and research settings.

CR-PTSD Subscale. The crime-related PTSD subscale (CR-PTSD) was developed by Saunders et al., (1990) and is a 28-item measure derived from the SCL-90-R. Based on a raw cutoff score of 0.89, the scale correctly classified 89.3% of women as PTSD-positive or PTSD-negative following their exposure to violent crime (e.g., sexual assault, aggravated assault, robbery, and burglary). CR-PTSD scores obtained for a sample of battered women have been found to correlate at moderately high levels with MMPI-derived PTSD subscale scores and with both the intrusion and avoidance subscale scores of the IES (Dutton et al., 1991).

Biological Models of Assessment

Although biological models of PTSD assessment have been used with combat veterans, little or no attention has been given to their applicability in the assessment of PTSD among battered women. Theoretical models of biological alterations associated with traumatic experience (cf. van der Kolk, 1988) suggest that biological assessment may provide specific and useful information within a comprehensive PTSD assessment protocol. Empirical evidence has provided support for measures of psychophysiological arousal (e.g., heart rate, systolic blood pressure, electromyogram–EMG–responses) as useful for identifying PTSD among Vietnam combat veterans (Friedman, 1991), both as baseline levels of arousal and in response to trauma-specific stimuli. Exploration of the development of psychophysiological approaches to the assessment of PTSD among battered women is needed.

Little attention has been paid in the literature to the assessment of psychological dysfunction following head trauma specifically among battered women. However, several syndromes (e.g., posttraumatic seisures, postconcussional syndrome) recognized among persons with closed head injuries include symptoms that battered women also experience (Slagle, 1990).

5

Mediators of the Battered Woman's Response to Abuse

Physical, sexual, and psychological abuse are sufficient to produce negative effects in nearly any victim; however, some victims are affected more severely than others. There is considerable variation in victims' efforts to respond to the abuse against them. Mediating factors may help to account for variations in both the psychological effects of abuse and the victim's efforts to respond to it; they do not, however, explain why abuse has occurred. Understanding the role of mediating factors may be helpful for developing interventions directed toward both increasing the effectiveness of the battered woman's response to abuse and alleviating its traumatic impact.

This chapter addresses the differential influence of abuse by examining several factors that mediate its impact on battered women and influence their use of strategies to respond to it. Mediating factors that are examined in the present chapter include (1) institutional response both to the abuse and to the battered woman's efforts to protect herself from it, (2) personal strengths and inner resources, (3) tangible resources and social support, (4) personal historical factors, (5) additional life stressors, and (5) positive aspects of the relationship with the abuser.

THE DIFFERENTIAL IMPACT OF ABUSE

It is generally understood that the characteristics of abuse alone are not sufficient in themselves to explain differences in severity of psychological effects on the victim. This has been found in cases of childhood sexual abuse (Courtois, 1988; Browne & Finkelhor, 1986, Finkelhor, 1979), rape (Koss & Burkhart, 1989, Sales et al., 1984), and battering (Walker, 1984). Bowker and Maurer (1986) found that severity of violence toward battered women was not a predictor of use of three different sources of counseling, but that the frequency of both sexual and nonsexual assaults was. However, few if any studies have examined the effects of abuse in domestic relationships, defined broadly as power and control, on the psychological trauma of it victims. Although there is a general notion that more severe or more prolonged violence creates more severe aftereffects, it can be observed in applied settings that some women who have suffered less severe violence experience severe traumatic reactions to the abuse. Similarly, women who have endured the abuse for a relatively short period of time can suffer as extensively as those for whom the abuse has extended for years. With further research, it may be discovered that intimidation, control, and other types of power and control tactics may help explain serious traumatic responses not fully explained by the level, severity, or duration of physical or sexual abuse alone.

Finally, some women who have undergone exposure to very serious forms of abuse appear to be less affected than might otherwise be expected based solely on the nature of abuse alone. Thus, although the severity and chronicity of abuse may play an important role, these factors alone are not sufficient to account for the nature and extent of the detrimental aftermath of victimization. Other factors may help explain why some women may become less psychologically traumatized or less obstructed in their efforts to escape or protect themselves.

MEDIATING FACTORS

Institutional Response

One of the major factors that influence battered women's efforts to escape from the abuse is the response of institutions designed to provide protection. A positive institutional response can help facilitate a battered woman's success in avoiding further violence, for example, when police officers inform a battered woman of options available to protect and assist her (e.g., shelters, specialized family violence programs, civil protection orders, arrest). An effective victim's advocacy component of a prosecutor's office can provide support and education, thus, increasing the likelihood of successful criminal prosecution and potentially decreased risk for further violence.

Positive institutional responses can also potentially mediate the severity of traumatic effect of violence. The opportunity to tell her story of the abuse experience in the courtroom where a judge's management of the legal process validates and supports the battered woman can facilitate the healing process. A mental health professional who acknowledges the emotional pain of constant psychological abuse helps the battered woman to recover from psychological damage caused by it. Although a positive institutional response to battering cannot avert the psychological trauma associated with it, it can facilitate the healing process.

A negative institutional response may inflict additional traumatization or secondary victimization (Dutton-Douglas, 1988; Stark & Flitcraft, 1988). As a means of providing protection to battered women, law enforcement officers are often mandated to write reports of every domestic violence call (regardless of injury or level of severity), to arrest the abuser when probable cause to do so exists, and to provide information about battered women's shelters and other resources. Failure to conform to statutory requirements may result in secondary victimization of the battered woman. Occasionally, battered women are met with victim-blaming responses such as when a police officer asks her what she did to provoke her partner\abuser. Some women have reported being told that they "made their bed, now they had to lie in it." Other battered women have been arrested when they responded in a highly emotional manner when the police arrived. Such experiences teach battered women that law enforcement is unreliable, or worse, predictably useless as a means of protection and so they may be less likely to utilize law enforcement during subsequent incidents of violence. The failure of law enforcement to protect battered women may also add to the emotional trauma following the original abuse by her partner.

Institutional victimization can extend to the courts when battered women attempt to divorce their abusers. It has been recognized that batterers often attempt to use the legal system, primarily through manipulation of custody and economic issues, to perpetuate the control they exert over their partners (Report of the Florida Supreme Court Gender Bias Study Commission, 1990; The National Center on Women and Family Law, 1988; Walker & Edwall, 1987). The judges and divorce attorneys who collude with the batterer's attempts help continue the victimization of the battered woman and her children.

When battered women fight back in self-defense and are criminally charged, the legal system clearly fails them. The victim now becomes an alleged criminal offender and is treated accordingly (Dutton-Douglas, 1988). She is often isolated from her children and others in a jail cell. She often loses her job due to incarceration or the stigma of the criminal charges brought against her. She may await trial for many months, sometimes even years, before ever reaching the courtroom. And finally, she may receive a conviction, and a prison sentence, sometimes for life, which communicates that she had no right to fight back.

Recently, some battered women have successfully sued police departments in civil tort cases for failure to provide protection, pointing to lower arrest rates for domestic than nondomestic violence assaults (Watson v. Kansas City, 857 F.2d 690 10th Cir. 1988) and demonstrating failure to protect. In these kinds of cases, the battered woman can use the legal system to gain justice in relation to another part of the legal system that failed her. The legal system can provide considerable opportunity to help re-empower battered women and other victims, but when it fails to do so, the institutional victimization it perpetuates is often harsh.

Law enforcement and criminal justice are not the only sources of institutional victimization. The health care delivery systems have traditionally failed battered women by pathologizing their attempts to survive and protect themselves and their children from continued abuse. These failures include diagnoses that stigmatize and label (e.g., self-defeating or borderline personality disorder) and use of medication and psychotherapy that address only the symptoms of distress rather than the original problem of abuse. There is sometimes collusion with the batterer to blame the victim for her failure as a partner or mother (including her unwillingness to be controlled), her response to the abuse itself (e.g., anger), or her attempts to numb the physical and psychological pain of abuse through drugs and alcohol. Professionals also fail when proposing marital therapy as the solution to the violence as it tends not to recognize the inherent problem of power and control that underlie physical and sexual abuse. However, mental health professionals can have a particularly powerful positive role in re-empowering battered women to effectively escape, protect, or survive the abuse against them. Mental health professionals can also help them recover from the psychological trauma of not only the original abuse, but also from secondary victimization by institutions that have failed them.

Personal Strengths and Inner Resources

A woman's personal strengths and inner resources are important mediating factors in how she responds to the violence and abuse toward her. Personal strengths and inner resources may be considered primarily as aids to survival in a situation in which her life and her psychological well-being may have been continually threatened. Strengths observed in the battered woman may include confidence in her ability to find a solution to the problem of living with an abusive partner, belief in or sense of entitlement to live without violence, determination to accomplish personal goals, knowledge about abuse and its effects, perseverance and endurance in seeking solutions to problems or in accomplishing goals, and effective living skills (i.e., organizational, time-management, social/interpersonal, occupational, parenting). It is through tapping personal strengths and inner resources that many women, when battered, are able to respond in a way that leads to escape, avoidance, or protection from further abuse. Assessing for, validating, and encouraging these strengths can greatly facilitate the battered woman's attempts to protect herself and avoid further violence.

When a battered woman appears to lack personal strengths, it is important not to assume that this lack is the reason for her continued victimization. Regardless of the personal resources available to her, the level of threats or actual violence may make it impossible for any woman to effectively respond. Further, exposure to abuse impacts on the very resources that she may use to respond.

The process of battering is insidious and the same inner resources mentioned above may, in fact, keep a battered woman in the abusive situation, rather than help her to escape it. For example, she may keep attempting to change her husband's abusive behavior, to solve the problems (e.g., financial, family, social) she sees as the cause of the violence, or simply to endure as she adequately "copes" with the abuse by continuing to function at work, as a parent, and with friends. Over time, a woman with considerable inner resources and personal strengths will be effectively and significantly damaged and have fewer and fewer strengths on which to rely. Many adequately functioning women have been robbed of their inner strengths by experiences of abuse. Well-documented examples of high-functioning women for whom the abuse significantly damaged their lives include Hedda Nussbaum, an editor and author of children's books, whose criminal case involved the death of her daughter, and Charlotte Fedders, author of *Shattered Dreams*, an upper middle-class woman whose husband was the chief enforcement officer at the Security and Exchange Commission.

Tangible Resources and Social Support

The tangible assets and social support resources on which a battered woman may rely have a considerable impact on her ability to respond effectively to the violence against her. Demands on these resources must also be considered.

Educational, Occupational, and Economic Resources. The level of education, job skills, employment experience, and current employment are all important resources that may make a difference in a battered woman's ability to respond effectively to the violence against her. Kalmuss and Straus (1982) found a strong relationship between the wife's economic dependence and greater severity of domestic violence. These authors suggest that women who are highly economically (or emotionally) dependent on marriage are less able to discourage, avoid, or otherwise protect themselves from violence within the marriage. The greater the availability of educational and occupational resources, the greater the battered woman's access to the economic resources necessary for independent living for herself and her children. In addition, greater educational, occupational, and economic resources may provide a source of self-esteem and a sense of increased options.

The demand on economic resources must be weighed against their availability. For example, small children who require childcare present a different demand on resources than do adolescent children who can care for their basic needs themselves. The financial and emotional cost of caring for an ill child or elderly parent drains resources that a battered woman may otherwise be able to devote to herself. Excess debt or economic losses, perhaps accrued in her name by a psychologically controlling and manipulative partner, may absorb any financial resources to which she has access.

Not having sufficient resources to live independently provides a major obstacle to utilizing particular strategies for escaping abuse. Although battered women's shelters provide a safe place to live, food, and clothing for a limited period of time (usually 4 to 8 weeks), many women do not have the economic resources to continue on their own from the time they leave the shelter. The availability of low-cost transitional housing is typically quite scarce in most communities, if it is available at all. Many women are accurate in their assessment of the difficulty of their earning sufficient income to house, feed, and clothe themselves and their children, and to provide for adequate childcare, transportation, and medical/dental care. The possibility of having to return to the abuser after having once left may result in an escalation of violence and a greater feeling of being trapped.

Social Support. Social and emotional support from others may play a significant role, both in a battered woman's ability to respond to the violence against her and in terms of the psychological impact of the violence itself. The role of social support as a mediator in stress reactions has been well supported in the literature (Figley, 1988; Rachley, 1990; van der Kolk, 1988; Wilson, 1989). Social support may provide access to tangible resources (e.g., a place to stay, transportation), create a sense of belonging and affiliation, and provide someone to comfort and validate the victim's experience.

Social isolation, a common tactic used by batterers to control their partners, may result in the inaccessibility to available resources (e.g., shelter, police protection, friends). Social isolation may be particularly relevant for rural women, living in areas in which there is virtually no local police protection or shelters in close proximity. But social isolation may also present an obstacle for women living in urban areas where there is no community environment or neighbors on whom the battered woman can depend. Social support is sometimes limited because friends may also fear the batterer.

Social obstructionism (Gurly, 1989) should be considered alongside social support. Some battered women face other's attempts to thwart their efforts to respond to the abuse against them. For example, family members may encourage a woman to return to her batterer and "give him another chance" or may discourage her from leaving in the first place. More blatantly, some family members may testify for the batterer in a case of criminal prosecution against him, disregarding their knowledge of the previous abuse, at least in the courtroom. Sometimes a battered woman is threatened with physical violence, abandonment by the family, or other catastrophic events if she testifies against her husband, leaves him, or fights for custody of their children. Recently, in a divorce case a Florida judge dismissed a permanent injunction of protection obtained by a battered woman prior to her divorce proceedings.

Historical, Learned, and Medical Factors

Particular aspects of a battered woman's history may render her more vulnerable in her attempts to escape, avoid, or protect herself against the violence and abuse against her once it occurs. Walker (1984) terms these as susceptibility factors and suggested several that may play a significant role, including rigid sex-role socialization, early and/or repeated sexual molestation and assault, violence in the childhood home, and actual (or perceived) uncontrollable events in childhood (e.g., alcoholic parent, seriously mentally disordered or dysfunctional parent, serious illness or accident, critical losses). Additional historical factors may include physical or intellectual impairment. Virtually any factor that renders someone more vulnerable to the effects of trauma and less able to functionally respond to it might be considered a susceptibility factor.

Physical disability or limitations may result directly from abuse in the current relationship or may have existed prior to the onset of violence in this relationship. One woman had suffered permanent injury to her leg and back from her husband's violence, placing her at considerably greater risk during threatened or actual recurrent abuse from her husband. She was unable to run in order to get away during actual violence, and the pain from previous injuries had reduced her mobility so that she was less able to physically avoid potentially volatile situations. An older woman may have a diminished ability to escape or avoid violence due to physical ailments that may accompany her age.

Rigid sex-role socialization has not been shown to be a characteristic of battered women as a group (Walker, 1984), although women whose sex-role attitudes are more traditional may be at greater risk once the abuse occurs. Holding to the beliefs that a woman is responsible for her partner's happiness, that she is obligated to provide herself as a willing sexual partner at his demand, or that major decisions must be approved by the man who is head of household may reduce the battered woman's options for escape or avoidance of abuse. A traditional sex-role belief may even mandate that a woman tolerate physical and sexual force, if her husband chooses to use it. Beliefs, attitudes, and values that allow a woman to say no to the violence, call police to protect herself from it, tell family and friends about the abuse, and seek education and/or employment that allow her to be financially independent are generally not consistent with rigid traditional values about male and female relationships.

Prior victimization (i.e., childhood physical or sexual abuse, witnessing violence toward the mother, physical or sexual violence in dating relationships, rape by stranger, sexual harassment or sexual assault by someone in authority, assault by a stranger) or other forms of childhood trauma (i.e., loss of parent or sibling to major physical or mental illness, hospitalization, death, major illness or injury) may increase a woman's vulnerability to even greater negative effects of later victimization resulting from subsequent trauma (van der Kolk, 1987), including battering. The increased traumatic effects, or compounded trauma, result from the accumulation of victimization experiences that have not been addressed through effective intervention. The compounded traumatic response may occur with subsequent occurrences of the same type of victimization (i.e., repeated episodes of battering, repeated rapes) or occurrence of multiple forms of trauma (e.g., childhood sexual abuse, rape, battering). Ruch and Leon (1983) found that women with prior rape experiences had more severe reactions to a subsequent rape than first-time victims. Further, in that study, previously raped women were found to be especially at risk for delayed psychological responses to the later rape.

Stark and Flitcraft (1988) extend the notion of compounded trauma for battered women to include the original battering followed by victimization by the institutions that are designed to intervene (i.e., courts, law enforcement, therapists, counselors, physicians, nurses). One battered woman, in a divorce action, was required to answer questions concerning her childhood sexual abuse in response to allegations that the experience rendered her an unfit mother. There had been no allegations of sexual abuse by her toward the children. In an extended trial against a husband charged with attempted murder toward his wife, the tone of the trial, set by both the judge and the defense attorney, was one of blaming the wife for acts that her husband said "justified" his violence toward her. The newspaper coverage, which included a photograph of the victim on the witness stand, was not of a battered woman's suffering, but of the husband's allegations against her.

The mechanism by which prior victimization or trauma may exacerbate recurrent victimization may be explained through several processes. One, the effect of prior trauma may render the individual's biological and emotional systems more vulnerable, so that the subsequent trauma is responded to with a less intact system. For example, according to van der Kolk (1988, p. 64), "traumatized people continue to have a poor tolerance for arousal." Secondly, the effects of victimization may be considered to be cumulative so that the impact of subsequent trauma is simply added to the unremitting effects of previous trauma. Finally, subsequent traumatic events may not only produce their own effects, but may also trigger dormant responses from previous traumas. In such a case, the victim reexperiences the impact of a previous trauma, sometimes for the first time since the original event, simultaneously with experiencing the current trauma, creating a compounded traumatic response. For example, one battered woman who had left a previous relationship in which her husband was severely abusive was exposed to verbal abuse by a new partner in a subsequent relationship. This verbal abuse triggered a fear reaction that was probably far more severe than what might have been expected from the verbal abuse alone.

Few women in today's society have escaped victimization of some sort. Previous research has shown that 54% of girls under the age of 17 years were exposed to contact and noncontact forms of sexual abuse (Russell, 1983) and that 26% (Arias, Samios, & O'Leary, 1987) to 49% (Marshall & Rose, 1987) of women were victimized by physical violence in dating relationships. Further, 27.9% of women 14 years and older experienced attempted or completed rape in a dating relationship (Koss, 1989), and 44% of adult women had experienced rape or attempted rape (Russell, 1984). Thus, statistically speaking it is not unlikely for a battered woman to have been previously victimized by violence. When other forms of victimization are considered, for example, sexual harassment in the school system and in the work place and sexual objectification of women in the media and in entertainment, it is difficult to consider that any woman has not been victimized simply by living in this society.

Current Additional Stressors

Additional stressors can also mediate both the battered woman's psychological reaction to trauma and her efforts to respond to it. In addition to the violence, abuse, and their sequelae, most women experience other stressors that are currently affecting their lives. Children and parents with serious illness, psychologically distressed children, job stress, and legal problems unrelated to the violence are examples of the additional pressures some battered women face. Thus, in addition to the traumatic response to the victimization, the battered woman may be faced with the effects of other life stressors as well. These additional stressors may impact on her ability to devote economic and emotional resources to the problem of violence and abuse in her life.

Positive Aspects of the Relationship

Positive aspects of the battered woman's relationship with her abusive partner may have an impact on the victim's response, or they may mediate the effects of victimization either by reducing or exacerbating its negative effects. Positive aspects of the relationship for the woman might include (1) periods when her partner is friendly, calm, sociable, intimate, or fun-loving (the Dr. Jekyll and Mr. Hyde type), (2) positive and effective parental relationships with children, (3) a satisfying sexual relationship, and (4) financial security. The woman who has had significant positive experiences with her batterer may struggle with abuse issues in a somewhat different manner than the woman whose relationship has had fewer positive aspects.

When violence occurs in a relationship that includes many positive aspects there are two processes that may result. First, the psychological impact of the abuse may be even more serious because of its sharp contrast to the positive features of the relationship; the battered woman's trust is betrayed and her efforts to integrate the occurrence of the abuse with the positive aspects may create considerable difficulty. She may be particularly effected by the contrast following the first episode of abuse, as well as following periods when she believes that the abuse will never recur.

In the second process, the battered woman may minimize the seriousness of the abuse, when it occurs, and perhaps the aftermath as well (e.g., fear, anger) because of the cognitive dissonance it creates with her perception of a positive relationship. Blackman (1989) suggests that the battered woman develops an increased tolerance for cognitive dissonance as she remains in the relationship attempting to reconcile the disparity between the abusive and positive aspects of the relationship.

Without an awareness of the battered woman's perceptions of the positive qualities in her partner and of the relationship, her behavior in the abusive situation may be less easily understood. Attempting to develop an understanding of the parts of the relationship that the battered woman values and does not want to lose has important implications for intervention; this will be discussed in subsequent chapters. Further, the battered woman may feel more completely understood if the helping professional is interested in what she values in the relationship with the partner who abuses her, not just in its abusive aspects.

STRATEGIES OF ASSESSMENT

A thorough psychosocial history and face-to-face interview are needed to obtain the information described in this chapter. A genogram (McGoldrick & Gerson, 1985) is an effective method to identify intergenerational patterns of violence and other forms of dysfunction within the family of origin, as well as to record the information in an easily recognizable manner. Additionally, the development of a chronology of significant life events (e.g., marriages, separations, birth of child, geographic transitions, deaths) is a useful tool for mapping out potentially relevant mediators of battered women's response to violence and of its psychological impact.

Standardized questionnaire methods may be used in assessing some information, for example, sources of stress that may be otherwise missed by using a clinical interview alone. Life events scales, for example, the one developed by Holmes and Rahe (1967) are an example.

A complete assessment involving the battered woman includes information about the nature and pattern of abuse (Chapter 2), the battered woman's strategies to escape, avoid, and survive it (Chapter 3), the psychological effects of abuse (Chapter 4), and those factors that potentially mediate the later two categories (Chapter 5). This information is necessary for the development of hypotheses (or a formulation) to explain both the psychological impact of violence and abuse on the battered woman and her efforts to escape, avoid, and protect herself from it. Appendix E provides an example of a Psychological Evaluation Report that summarizes assessment information and provides a formulation and recommendations for intervention. The next section of this book describes a framework and specific strategies for intervening with victims of domestic violence.

PART II
Intervention

6

The Framework for Intervention with Victims and Survivors of Domestic Violence

Intervention with the victims of domestic violence requires an interdisciplinary approach for effective response to the variety of their needs. A battered woman may need assistance from any or all of several different helping systems: legal, medical, mental health, social service, self-help, and spiritual. The battered woman may initiate help-seeking from any one of these sources, although she may need assistance in gaining access to others. This chapter discusses the necessary principles for effective intervention with victims and survivors of domestic violence, goals and approaches to treatment by the mental health professional, and ethical and legal considerations.

GENERAL PHILOSOPHY OF TREATMENT

A core set of general philosophical principles is necessary for effective intervention with battered women. These ideas are adapted from Wilson (1989) and are based on "... our current collective knowledge about helping victimized individuals to heal" (Wilson, 1989, p. 212). Schechter's (1987) four tasks for empowering battered women are incorporated herein, as are the philosophical principles about intervention presented by others who work with victims of violence and abuse (cf. Courtois, 1988; Ochberg, 1988).

1. *Nonjudgemental acceptance and validation of the battered woman and her experience.* Battered women often feel overwhelmed and responsible for the abuse or some aspect of it. They are reluctant to disclose details of the violence and abuse, especially sexual abuse or other behaviors for which they may feel particularly shameful. Therapist nonjudgment comes from the basic assumption that the battered woman did not cause the violence and abuse toward her and that she is not responsible for the behavior of her batterer. A nonjudgmental framework avoids reinforcing the stigma and blame she may already feel.

2. *Providing immediate support and alliance.* When the battered woman seeks help, she needs support and alliance. This may begin to buffer the effects of the trauma while developing the trust and bonding needed in the therapeutic relationship. Attempts to expand the support network beyond the therapist increases the battered woman's available resources. Support might also come from other battered women who can understand her situation and from other people in the community. This reduces the risk of the therapist's inadvertent encouragement of excessive dependency through being the battered woman's sole source of support. This is a role few, if any, therapists can handle effectively.

3. *Advocating for safety and building options.* The woman's safety must be a primary consideration in all the work. The therapist may find her\himself advocating for the client's safety when she appears not to be. The therapist must recognize the battered woman's ability to perceive danger even when she masks her awareness of it. Building various options toward safety acknowledges the battered woman's central role of choice.

4. *Willingness to experience recounting and sequelae of the trauma.* When working with a trauma victim, secondary exposure or vicarious traumatization (McCann & Pearlman, 1990) of the therapist is inevitable. A therapist reluctant to hear the details of the battering and abusive incidents fails to provide a context where healing is possible. The message to the battered woman is that her experience must remain invisible through overgeneralizations, avoidance of details of abuse, and through the use of language which fails to accurately describe what happened.

5. *Assuming that posttraumatic stress responses are caused by the traumatic events.* Posttraumatic therapy with battered women assumes that the traumatic response is caused by the victimization, alone or in combination with previous traumatic experiences; it does not assume preexisting psychopathology unrelated to the exposure of trauma. Working with this initial hypothesis guards against pathologizing posttraumatic responses; it sees them as normal responses to trauma.

6. *Education about violence and abuse is therapeutic.* It is useful to educate battered women about what defines abuse and battering (Pence, 1987) as well as about common traumatic responses to it. Normalizing responses to victimization reduces the fear of mental illness and provides an increased

sense of control over specific posttraumatic reactions. For example, explaining that the feelings of anger and rage are common and normal as a response to victimization may be helpful when the battered woman believes that she is as "crazy," "bad," or "sick" as is her batterer. Normalizing intrusive flashbacks and nightmares may help the battered woman focus her energy and attention toward learning to cope with them, rather than worrying that she is "losing her mind" or "going crazy." Finally, normalizing a battered woman's fear of being touched by men, even in a handshake, may help to alleviate unnecessary distress caused by attributions about the fear as well as to provide a perspective to assist healing.

7. *Coping strategies are viewed as strengths, not pathology.* In order for battered women to cope with the trauma of battering, it is often necessary for them to use such cognitive and emotional coping strategies as denial, disavowal, dissociation, or alteration of personality style. Viewed as attempts to cope with the abuse or its aftereffects, not as indicators of unrelated pathological personality patterns, these coping strategies are recognized for their survival value. Nor should these coping strategies be seen as proof that the abuse is fabricated. When preexisting psychopathology or personality disorder is suggested, a hypothesis to seriously consider is that it is a chronic traumatic response, which may or may not have been identified previously, resulting from early childhood abuse or other previous traumas (Herman, Perry, & van der Kolk, 1989).

8. *In trauma victims, substance abuse is a common form of self-medication.* Due to the intensity of the posttraumatic response, some battered women use drugs, alcohol, food, activity, achievement, and/or sex to self-medicate against the pain. In some cases, adjunctive treatment for drug or alcohol abuse, eating disorders and other compulsive behaviors is necessary. Even when substances have been used prior to the onset of abuse, recognizing the role of the substance in numbing the pain associated with the trauma is essential. In all cases, the battered woman's substance abuse does not provide an appropriate explanation for the occurrence of violence toward the battered woman.

9. *Transformation of the trauma may result in positive changes.* The process of surviving, escaping, and transforming the trauma may lead battered women to positive outcomes: the development of personal growth and sense of personal empowerment, bonding and attachment to nurturing and supportive individuals, and a reclaimed future. Recognition of these as potential outcomes often helps to balance, although not compensate for, the losses associated with abuse and battering. In one example, a victim of battering determined that the abuse toward her helped her to recognize and become more involved in the world, seeing the injustice done to others through victimization.

10. *Prosocial action and self-disclosure facilitate the stress recovery process.* Prosocial action and self-disclosure are related to positive mental health and

recovery from trauma (Gleser, Green, & Winget, 1981; Kahana, Harel, & Kahana, 1988) and have formed one of the foundations of feminist therapy (Dutton-Douglas & Walker, 1989; Rosewater & Walker, 1985; Sturdivant, 1980) . For battered women, this may take the form of talking in support groups, volunteering in a battered woman's shelter, or becoming involved in political activities directed toward social and legal reform.

11. *Transformation of trauma is a lifelong process.* Traumatic experience, including battering and sexual abuse, leaves a "psychic legacy that may require years of transformation even after successful resolution and integration produced by therapy or other means of coping" (Wilson, 1989, p. 215). Normal life events may trigger a recurrence of the feeling of vulnerability once associated with previous trauma. Normalization of this process, along with the development of a life-long plan of healing and self-nurturance, may be necessary in working with battered women.

12. *The trauma of abuse and victimization results in noncompensable losses.* The losses experienced by victims of battering, sexual abuse by an intimate partner, or other forms of intimate victimization are not possible to replace; they are noncompensable (Courtois, 1988). What is possible is to grieve the losses in order to create an emotional space for "going on."

13. *Assumption of self-determination.* The assumption of self-determination for battered women, as with all other persons, provides the respect that is necessary in working effectively in the therapeutic context. Even when the battered woman makes decisions that seem contrary to the therapist's recommendation, it is important to communicate respect for the client's right to her own decisions. She is not responsible for pleasing the therapist with her decisions any more than she is responsible for pleasing her abuser.

14. *Therapist self-care is essential.* In order to be effective in working with battered women as trauma victims, therapists themselves need to be actively involved in an emotionally supportive environment and in routine self-care activities outside the therapeutic context. This is important not only as a way of bringing a mentally healthy perspective to the work, but also as a means of dealing effectively with the vicarious traumatization. Supportive supervision, peer support groups, personal therapy or personal growth experiences, time for adequate rest, relaxation, exercise, well-balanced nutrition, and private time are all means by which the therapist can and should provide self-care.

GOALS OF INTERVENTIONS

Mental health professionals may become involved with a battered woman in a variety of ways. The battered woman may seek help with the abuse as the target concern or she may present concerns etiologically related to the abuse, whether she recognizes them as such or not. She may not even disclose that she is a current or formerly battered woman.

Mental health interventions are usually aimed at one or more of the following main goals: (1) protection, in which interventions are focused on increasing safety, (2) enhanced choice making and problem-solving, such that interventions are focused on decisions about the relationship, relocation, and other transitional issues, and (3) healing posttraumatic reactions, for which interventions are focused on ameliorating the psychological effects of the trauma. Interventions directed toward these goals may be required within both crisis and noncrisis periods of treatment. However, safety must always remain a first priority. When the violence, abuse, control, or threat of abuse remains active, posttraumatic interventions focused on healing are not appropriate as the primary focus of intervention. Nonetheless, their concurrent use with the other interventions (e.g., protective and choicemaking) at these times may facilitate the battered woman's increased ability to respond effectively to the threat of violence, abuse, or controlling behavior.

Some women may not identify themselves as battered women, although they clearly have experienced a history of physical, sexual, and/or psychological victimization. For them, the preliminary goal of naming or labeling the abuse and recognizing that they may have been affected by it must precede the other three goals. One woman had undergone 22 years of physical abuse resulting in severe bruises, sexual abuse, and extreme psychological abuse without considering herself a battered woman. Although she knew that she had been very unhappy, it was only after she shot her husband and was required to examine her past experiences in greater detail that she began to label what had occurred to her as abusive.

Protection

Protective interventions are applied toward the goal of increasing the battered woman's safety (see Chapter 7). Protective interventions may include escape planning, protection planning, activation of sources of legal protection, and crisis mental health intervention. In this intervention component, it is essential to work in conjunction with other available community resources. Mental health intervention is often not sufficient, or even necessary, to keep a battered woman from further abuse. The battered woman seeking help through the mental health system should be afforded the benefit of other resources designed to protect battered women, such as legal protection and battered women's shelters.

Escape and protection planning is necessary when the battered woman is in a situation in which a threat of violence still remains. Of course, the immediacy of the crisis may vary depending on the level of threat, that is, both the likelihood of its occurrence and the level of its severity. Even in situations in which there is clear and convincing evidence of no further threat whatsoever (which is quite uncommon), escape and protection planning can serve a preventive function.

The threat of physical or sexual danger is but one situation that requires protection as a goal of intervention with the battered woman. Protection also becomes the goal when suicide is perceived by the battered woman as her one remaining option in ending the violence. When the stress of the situation exceeds the battered woman's level of tolerance and she experiences disorientation, dissociative symptoms, and acute psychotic symptoms immediate attention is needed to protect her. Other self-destructive behaviors (e.g., bulimia, self-mutilation, serious risk-taking behavior) may also require immediate intervention to protect the battered woman's physical safety.

Information and referral are important options when considering protective interventions. The mental health professional should not function as the only resource when others exist within the community to aid the battered woman in her effort to stay safe. For example, battered women's *shelters* provide safe residence for the battered woman and, usually, her children. Typically, shelters provide basic necessities such as food and clothing, information and referral to other social and legal services, advocacy, counseling and support groups, and an opportunity to listen to other women's stories about their own situations. Some shelters provide childcare, preschool, and counseling for children.

Referral to other *social services* that provide immediate assistance to battered women is important, including welfare and food stamps, crisis nurseries for children at risk for child abuse, housing and transportation services. Available *legal interventions* for the battered woman includes assistance from law enforcement, criminal justice, and civil court systems. Orders of protection, arrest, and criminal prosecution for domestic violence-related cases are mechanisms that may provide protection. Family law attorneys are in a position to provide important interventions in divorce and custody litigation for women involved with abusive husbands. Often, battered women injured during the violence and abuse do not seek *medical examination and treatment.* They are prevented from doing so by the influence of their batterers, financial constraints, personal shame and humiliation associated with acknowledging how the injuries occurred and denial of the severity of injury or of their right to care. In addition to the obvious importance of obtaining adequate medical care, accurate documentation of injuries and their cause are often essential pieces of evidence for subsequent criminal prosecution, divorce and custody proceedings, and civil action against a batterer.

Choice Making/Problem Solving

Many women seek help with deciding whether to leave or remain in the abusive relationship or to return to it once they have left (see Chapter 8). This issue often arises following an abusive episode, although it may occur at any time, for example, when the battered women senses that the abuse is about to recur. The goal of choice making is to facilitate decision making from a position of empowerment. That is, the battered woman must have viable options from which to make choices. Problem solving may be required in order to enable her to develop a list of options from which to select. Imbedded within the decision to leave the relationship may be many other decisions concerning employment, childcare, and relocation. The period of choice making may continue for variable lengths of time ranging from weeks to months to years.

The process of empowered choice making requires establishing or accessing a sense of entitlement to make choices about one's own life along with the development and/or use of problem-solving skills. The choice-making process may involve numerous attempts to separate, followed by periods of reconciliation, before the decision about continuation of the relationship becomes a stable one. Once a decision or choice has been made, for example, to leave the relationship, the battered woman still has the problem of putting her decision into action. The act of carrying out her decision may involve many other choices or decisions, including obtaining a job, arranging for alternative housing and childcare, and sometimes completely changing her identity in order to successfully escape.

Healing Posttraumatic Effects

Posttraumatic therapy includes the following components: (1) reduction of specific symptoms associated with exposure to trauma (e.g., anxiety, anger, depression), (2) integration of the traumatic experiences, (3) facilitation of the grief process associated with multiple losses related to the trauma of abuse, (4) reduction of shame associated with the trauma of abuse, and (5) rebuilding a life without violence (See Chapter 9).

Recovery from the psychological wounds incurred from victimization, whether short-term or over the course of a lifetime, requires healing of the whole person. The effects of victimization are neither unidimensional nor simple. Attention to the emotional, cognitive, behavioral, physical, and spiritual self is important if one is to heal the whole person.

The process of healing the psychological trauma associated with battering and abuse, or returning to wholeness, may begin even within the crisis management process or during the problem-solving processes. But primary attention to the healing from the posttraumatic response to violence is not appropriate when violence and abuse are imminent threats or when other life-threatening situations (e.g., active suicidal gesturing, severe bulimia, severe alcohol and drug abuse) are currently existing. A metaphor illustrates this point. Assume a house is being damaged by a fire that encircles it. Attempting to repair the damage to the house would not be wise until the immediate threat being presented by the fire is addressed. However, one might take certain action (e.g., douse the house with water) that could reduce the chances of the house becoming damaged even further. As with the house, one cannot begin to repair the damage of psychological trauma until the source of the damage–the violence and abuse–have been eliminated. Healing from the psychological trauma incurred from abuse is difficult, if not impossible, while the battered woman is continually faced with recurrent episodes of battering or threats of it. Most of her energy is needed to stay safe. The healing process requires an opportunity to experience one's vulnerability in a safe place where there is emotional and spiritual support. The possibility of creating a safe environment–for a period of time long enough to effectively complete the healing process–is difficult while living in the context of ongoing battering. Even the safety of a therapist's office for a relatively short period of time each week may not be sufficient. Further, the vulnerability that the battered woman may experience during the process of examining her wounds may make her even less able to effectively protect herself from further violence were it necessary to do so.

However, when a battered woman demonstrates difficulty in identifying her own safety, or that of her children, as a high priority, especially with making decisions to stay safe or difficulty carrying out decisions she has already made, she may benefit from some posttraumatic interventions. These interventions should be provided concurrent with, not instead of, protective interventions and only after protective interventions alone appear to be ineffective. The cumulative impact of abuse-related traumas may prevent a battered woman from acting in her own best interest. However, cessation of the threat of continued violence is a prerequisite for the healing process to be completed; otherwise, revictimization simply continues and the wounds never heal.

The posttraumatic reaction may be compounded by previous traumas, including childhood sexual and physical abuse, rape, or previous abusive relationships, for example. Depending on the extent of the psychological trauma incurred by the current and past victimization experiences, posttraumatic therapy may require many months or perhaps several years for its completion. Within a nurturing and supportive environment, much of the healing process can be facilitated outside of the psychotherapeutic relationship.

USEFUL TECHNIQUES FOR INTERVENTION

An eclectic approach to intervention best provides the clinician with the tools to adequately address the varied needs of the battered women. No one psychotherapy theory provides an adequate breadth of interventions. Battered women, as well as other trauma victims (Courtois, 1988) have a range of needs. Theoretical perspectives that have provided particularly useful intervention tools are divided into six groups: cognitive-behavioral, experiential, hypnotherapy, insight oriented, psychoeducational, and feminist. Use of specific techniques from each orientation may be appropriate in working toward each of the goals identified previously: protection, choicemaking or problem solving, and healing of posttraumatic responses.

Cognitive-Behavioral Approaches

Cognitive-behavioral interventions include stress reduction, relaxation, cognitive restructuring, role-playing, skills development, problem solving, and use of imagery (Freeman, Simon, Beutler, & Arkowitz, 1989; McMullin, 1986). These techniques may be applied toward developing escape plans for avoiding further violence, crisis intervention with suicide risk, developing assertiveness skills, making decisions about leaving or remaining in the relationship, and addressing cognitions that have been developed as a function of the abuse (e.g., self-blame, low self-esteem, tolerance of abuse, tolerance of the cognitive inconsistency inherent in the abusive intimate relationship) or cognitions that make responding to the abuse less effective (e.g., stereotypic and rigid sex-role beliefs) (Douglas & Strom, 1988).

An important caution with the use of cognitive restructuring techniques concerns the labeling of "maladaptive" cognitions as "irrational," or not based in reality, without recognizing the origin of the belief. Specific cognitions may have been developed within the abusive relationship as a means of avoiding further abuse. For example, as long as the battered woman believed that she must do everything her husband said, she may have avoided some conflict and the abuse that resulted from it, although typically not without considerable personal cost.

Other cognitions help to keep the battered woman in the abusive relationship, for example, "maladaptive" cognitions associated with tolerating abuse (e.g., "it's not that bad," "he didn't mean to hurt me," "it's not as bad as my previous husband"). These cognitions are, in fact, ineffective for avoiding further violence. However, the cognitions may function to maintain the relationship if that is the battered woman's primary goal.

The belief that "it is better to have an abusive relationship than no relationship at all" is a cognition that probably would be labeled "maladaptive" by most clinicians. However, "maladaptive" must be considered within the battered woman's framework of values and goals. A belief may be maladaptive for one goal but quite functional for another; it is the goal that may be the "problem." If a woman's highest priority is to be in a relationship, she may believe that it is worth it at almost any cost. However, that belief would be "maladaptive" if an equally high priority is to be safe. Cognitive interventions may extend directly to the examination of the battered woman's goals or to related beliefs (e.g., "if I don't remain in this relationship, I'm never going to be in another one," or "any cost is worth paying for a relationship").

Experiential Approaches

Experiential techniques in therapy, including gestalt therapy, psychodrama, movement therapies, use of art or music, and existential therapies offer the clinician techniques for focusing the battered woman's awareness to her present, here-and-now, moment-to-moment experience (cf. Korb, Gorrell, & Van De Riet, 1989; Perls, 1969). Because of the nature of psychological response to a traumatic event, battered women often are either numbed to or otherwise avoidant of their feelings (Horowitz, 1986). Experiential techniques allow for the battered woman to bring into focus her affective experience, just as the cognitive therapies allow her to focus on her thoughts and beliefs.

The use of experiential techniques is most suited to the goals of healing posttraumatic effects and choice making; it is less well suited to goals related to protection. However, in some cases, helping a battered woman become aware of her feelings (e.g., fear, anxiety) may facilitate action toward increasing her safety as well. Often, however, battered women are all too aware of their fear and increasing awareness of these feelings may only result in immobilization. Choice making is facilitated by experiential therapies that provide the battered woman with greater awareness of her feelings, and thus more information, on which she may rely to make choices. Healing posttraumatic reactions to violence is facilitated by an increased awareness and expression of feelings that can enable a battered woman to fully experience the emotional pain of the abuse, grieve the many losses she may have encountered, and integrate the whole of the traumatic experience, including the affect related to it.

Hypnotherapy

Hypnotherapy (Hammond, 1990) can be a quite useful tool for working with battered women. Useful applications are many including (1) ego-strengthening or confidence building, (2) use of metaphor to create methods for solving specific problems (e.g., self-nurturance as a method for addressing feelings of emptiness, asking for help from others when needing assistance to escape an abusive situation), (3) coping with overwhelming feelings (e.g., anxiety, panic) in order to mobilize the battered woman to some action (e.g., leaving the situation, calling the police, telling abuser that she is filing for divorce) which she may otherwise feel unable to accomplish, (4) retrieval of traumatic events in order to reduce posttraumatic stress responses and facilitate healing, (5) addressing compulsive behaviors (e.g., compulsive eating, smoking, shopping) which may be used as alternative coping mechanisms.

A caution should be given against using hypnotherapy in order to help the battered woman tolerate the abusive situation or the physical or psychological pain associated with it. Such use of hypnosis would be counterproductive to the battered woman's effort to increase her safety. Further, hypnosis which relies on confusional techniques or elaborate and subtle metaphor should be considered contraindicated for work with battered women since a focus on clarity and empowerment are a priority. Ultimate respect for the battered woman's experience and inclusion of her in the decision to and process of using hypnosis is quite consistent with the practice of hypnotherapy. Due to its powerful impact, hypnosis as well as other intervention methods should always be done based on the therapist's experience and the availability of competent supervision.

Insight-Oriented Approaches

Insight-oriented methods may include dynamic therapies that focus on examining the impact on the client of early or previous experience, including significant relationships. Both conscious and unconscious material are examined as well as the current therapeutic relationship. The latter is considered a repository of transference and countertransference material. Models of psychodynamic intervention that incorporate feminist theory (Chodorow, 1989; Daugherty & Lees, 1989) and newer theoretical models of female personality development (Gilligan, 1982; Jordan, 1984) embrace gender issues within the therapeutic framework, providing an opportunity to address those issues as they impact the client throughout the course of her lifespan.

Another method of helping the battered woman to gain insight about her situation is by use of family genograms (McGoldrick & Gerson, 1985). Although family therapy is not recommended for battered women in the initial stages of intervention, helping her to explore the dynamics of violence and abuse that have operated in her family across generations may be quite useful. The goal of such an intervention is not to justify the abuse, but to help her understand how the norms of violence, abuse, and control within her family may be negatively influencing her.

Psychoeducational Approaches

Psychoeducational interventions such as those developed in the Domestic Abuse Intervention Project (Pence, 1987, Pence & Paymar, 1986) in Duluth, Minnesota provide a mechanism by which the battered woman learns about the dynamics of abusive relationships, primarily the dynamics of social oppression of persons with lesser power by those with greater power. The Duluth model combines both a psychoeducational model with a feminist philosophical base. This base of knowledge is presumed important to assist the battered woman to make choices and take action to increase her safety. Psychoeducational methods may also be useful for addressing issues such as parenting skills, assertiveness, and anger management.

Feminist Approaches

The use of feminist approaches with battered women can be applied to the goals of protection, choice making, and healing posttraumatic effects alike. The primary contribution of feminist approaches is the analysis of battering within the context of the dynamics of oppression, based on gender, race or ethnicity, class, and age, among others. Domestic violence in heterosexual relationships is cast in a framework of male power and dominance over women. In this way, the violence, abuse, and control experienced by a woman is considered part of a social problem, not a problem unique to her. Feminist approaches to intervention emphasize validation of the battered woman's experience, empowerment, and self-determination (Brown & Root, 1990; Dutton-Douglas & Walker, 1988; Jones & Schechter, 1992; Schechter, 1987).

MODALITY OF INTERVENTION

Both group and individual methods are useful for working with battered women. Couples' therapy is not recommended as an initial intervention when issues of protection and choice making are primary. Couple's work exposes the battered woman to the potential for increased danger associated with openly expressing her feelings and thoughts to her batterer.

Group. Group methods include community support or education groups (Pence, 1987) that are often available through battered women's shelters or other domestic violence programs as well as therapy groups especially for battered women. Therapy groups may be short- or long-term and may focus on specific issues in a structured format or be open-ended. Because groups allow for contact with other battered women, they help break the isolation characteristic of many women caught in abusive situations. Although group members gain from the group process and from listening to other women, the amount of time available for each woman may not be sufficient to adequately address her needs. For that reason, individual treatment may be considered adjunctive to groups when the needs of the client dictate it (Brody, 1987; NiCarthy, Merriam, & Coffman, 1984).

Individual. Individual therapy methods allow the work to be tailored to a particular woman and her needs. This may be useful especially in crisis situations when the level of danger is extreme or when the battered woman is so severely distressed that her ability to function within a group environment is questionable. Individual methods may allow a woman the opportunity for a more in-depth exploration of her particular issues and they allow the therapist to provide more individualized attention to her.

Some women are more inclined to work individually with a therapist and are reluctant to join a women's group. In keeping with a philosophy of self-determination, providing the battered woman with an option between individual and group work allows her to select between the two modalities based on her own preferences.

Individual and group therapy alike can focus on protection, choice making, and posttraumatic healing as primary goals of intervention. Individual work simply allows a greater concentration of time and attention on a single battered woman than does group intervention.

Couple. Some authors suggest that conjoint treatment can be used with couples to reduce violence in the relationship (Mantooth, Geffner, Franks, & Patrick, 1987). Philosophically, there are problems with the use of couples therapy when the goal is to reduce violence. Furthermore, couples therapy may be dangerous to the physical and emotional welfare of the battered woman.

The first problem with the use of couples therapy to end violence is that it assumes the problem of violence is one that is etiologically based in the couple interaction where both partners hold equal responsibility (Bograd, 1984, 1986) or, at least, that the battered woman's presence is necessary in order to assist the batterer to cease violent behavior.

I recommend couples therapy only after several conditions have been met: (1) the threat of further abuse, including psychological as well as physical and sexual abuse, has been greatly reduced, (2) when there has been repetitive abuse, that the violent, abusive, and controlling behavior of the batterer has ceased for a period longer than the longest lapse between previous episodes of abuse, and (3) both the battered woman and her partner agree that they want to work at repairing the damage to the relationship caused by the abuse (Pressman, 1989). In many cases, in order to meet the first two criteria, the batterer must successfully complete a treatment program that fosters the cessation of violence and the acceptance of responsibility for his violent, abusive, and controlling behavior. When these conditions have been met, the goal of couples therapy is no longer to stop the violence; but rather to attempt reparation of the damage to the relationship that has occurred because of the violence, abuse, and controlling behavior.

Separating couple issues that may have existed prior to the onset of abuse from those that are contaminated by the occurrence of the abuse itself is an important therapy task. For example, the battered woman's anger toward her partner, withdrawal from sexual desire and activity, or difficulty with communication that may have resulted from the batterer's violence must be examined in light of the dynamics of power and abuse. Otherwise, the immediate situational influence on the couple's behavior may be attributed erroneously to individual factors, family-of-origin issues, or to relationship issues other than the imbalance of power inherent in the abusive relationship.

A dilemma for the therapist may arise when the battered woman and her partner specifically seek couple's therapy even though they do not meet the criteria stated above. Some clinicians might not regard the fact of two partners, both of whom state they want therapy, as an indication of a problem. However, in many cases, the battered woman may have finally convinced her partner to seek help for the abusive behavior, but finds that he is only willing to do so if she participates in the therapy. This dynamic in itself is controlling. The message of the batterer is that he will negotiate changing the abusive behavior only under certain circumstances, namely when his partner is also involved in the therapy process. All too often this provides the batterer with the opportunity to blame the victim for the behavior he cites as responsible for his use of violence. It is all too easy for the therapist to collude with this system and effectively, although perhaps inadvertently, support the batterer in blaming the victim for the abuse. The battered woman needs support for or modeling in, holding the batterer responsible for stopping the abusive behavior.

Even when the therapist is very clear about attribution of responsibility of violence to the perpetrator, the battered woman may still be at risk. When the therapist attempts to elicit information about past events or about feelings and thoughts, the battered woman is placed in a position to trust that the information will not be used by her partner as an excuse to further abuse her outside the therapist's view. Directly expressing her anger, placing responsibility for the violence on her partner, or "breaking the silence" of the physical, sexual, and psychological abuse may ultimately lead to even greater violence. The therapist is in no position to provide adequate protection to the battered woman. Behavioral contracts with the batterer may be useful for the individual who is committed to change; however, their use is likely not very effective for the batterer who is placating his partner, by agreeing to enter therapy, perhaps in order to keep her from leaving the relationship or who is otherwise unwilling or unable to control his behavior.

The battered woman may even believe that she is as responsible for the abuse as her partner. For this reason, couples therapy may make perfect sense to her. It is the position of the therapist to help the battered woman define what she is responsible for and what she is not. A therapist's attempts to work conjointly with both a batterer and his victim, both of whom share the belief that she is, partially or fully, responsible for the abuse would likely be met with great difficulty.

To reiterate, couple's therapy is useful after the abusive pattern has been successfully altered and the couple is committed to repairing their damaged relationship. This is an area in which the development of posttraumatic therapy with families and couples (Figley, 1989) is needed. The situation in which trauma has been perpetrated from within (e.g., battering, incest) represents a different clinical picture than the one in which the family has experienced a trauma from someone outside (e.g., murder of a child or rape by a stranger). In the later example the therapeutic task includes healing the traumatic wounds for each family member as a primary or secondary victim of some traumatic event. Nonetheless, some batterers change their behavior, beliefs, and attitudes and some battered women choose to remain with their formerly abusive partners. The focus of couple's intervention conducted following the cessation of the batterer's violent and abusive behavior should include establishing accountability and "justice-making" (Fortune, 1987) within the relationship; building trust; healing the wounds of betrayal; increasing the ability to communicate feelings, requests, and boundary setting in responsible ways; and realigning the distribution of power in a more equal manner.

ETHICAL AND LEGAL CONSIDERATIONS

Working with battered women raises some specific ethical and legal concerns about which the mental health professional must be aware. It is of course imperative to uphold the highest standards of practice established by ethical guidelines within the profession (e.g., APA, 1990). The Ethical Guidelines for Feminist Therapists (Lerman & Porter, 1990) offer further direction in proactively maintaining an ethical practice. Several points of ethics are essential when working with battered women, including (1) maintenance of the strictest level of confidentiality, (2) consideration of diversity issues (e.g., cultural, ethnic, class, sexual orientation), (3) attention to power differentials in the client's life and within the therapeutic relationship, and (4) involvement in social change.

A breach of confidentiality when working with a battered woman could place her at risk for serious physical injury or death. Awareness of the possibility of a batterer's deception or coercion in attempts to seek information about his partner is important. These may include efforts to seek information about a battered woman's involvement in therapy, about specific appointment times or her whereabouts, her disclosure of specific information about the batterer, or her plans for separation.

Beyond understanding the influence of diversity on a battered woman's situation (e.g., bias within a criminal justice system, differential access to resources), the therapist must attend to her\his own potential for bias based on diversity issues. For example, failing to recognize that violence occurs within gay or lesbian relationships, taking violence against a poor minority woman less seriously than against an upper-middle class Anglo woman, or overlooking the possibility of marital rape against an elderly woman are ways that bias may influence a therapist.

Recognition of the dynamics of power when working with a battered woman is not limited to an analysis of her abusive relationship. The therapist must develop the awareness and ability to monitor the power dynamics within the therapeutic relationship and to discuss these openly with the client. Even when done in subtle and unintentional ways, the abuse of power based on therapist status and expertise can compound the trauma of abuse resulting from the batterer's violence and control.

Involvement in social change is essential; noninvolvement means perpetuating the problem, actively or passively, intentionally or unintentionally. Social change may involve varying levels of time, energy, and social activism (e.g., working toward legislative reform, community organizing and education, or consciousness-raising with colleagues).

Legal issues when working with battered women include current and accurate knowledge of the local and state laws that influence the battered woman's ability to achieve safety (e.g., protective injunction orders; warrantless arrest; statutory definitions of domestic violence, sexual battery, assault, battery) and to retain access to her children (e.g., custody and visitation statutes, statutes that govern custody by a violent parent or property). Without such knowledge the therapist is in a handicapped position to facilitate protection for the battered woman and her children.

The statutory requirement of the therapist's duty to warn intended victims must be considered when a battered woman expresses her intent to do harm to her batterer. In considering this issue, separating the battered woman's feelings from actual intent is essential, as many battered women may feel angry and wish harm to their perpetrator. However, actual intent to do harm is much less common, although it should be taken seriously when encountered. Extreme caution should be used to protect the battered woman when exercising the duty to warn mandate, including informing her prior to taking such action and discussing her potential danger as a result of it.

7

Protective Interventions

Protective interventions are required when working with many battered women, especially those who remain in the abusive relationship. Because of the obvious danger inherent in an ongoing abusive relationship, there is a need for interventions that help protect the battered woman. When the danger is immediate or unpredictable, as it typically is, the problem should be considered a crisis. The goal of protective interventions is to increase the safety of the battered woman and her children or others around her. Crisis intervention is often required to stabilize the situation by reducing sources of immediate danger to the battered woman and others. Especially when the goal is one of protection, coordination of mental health services with shelter, law enforcement, criminal justice, and social service systems is needed to provide adequate services to the battered woman. This chapter defines several major potential issues for which protection is an immediate and predominate goal and discusses appropriate interventions for each.

RECURRENT ABUSE VICTIMIZATION

The Problem

Recurrent abuse victimization is one of the most frequently encountered issues facing battered women seeking help, especially for women from shelters and mental health clinics. The dangers facing the battered woman and her children are often quite serious and potentially lethal. Thus, mental health professionals' errors in minimizing the danger can lead to fatal consequences. Imminent danger of less serious injury also defines a crisis situation and requires similar protective interventions, thus making some form of crisis intervention a component of nearly all mental health work with battered women.

The danger of recurrent victimization facing battered women and their children consists of quite serious threats to safety, including further battering episodes, threats and attempts to kill, recurrent rape and other forms of sexual abuse, children's continued witnessing of abuse, physical and sexual abuse to children, and kidnapping of the children by the batterer. Some women seek help when they fear the occurrence of physical abuse for the first time. These women may have experienced abuse from a previous relationship, witnessed abuse toward their mother, or in some other way gained the awareness that "this could happen to me" and realistically believe the danger to be actual and impending.

Many other women seek help when the severity of abuse has escalated to a point where they no longer believe that they can cope with it. This may be due to increased feelings of fear, increased recognition of severity of recent injuries accompanied by realization of the danger the abusive relationship presents, or from an external source of information such as viewing a television show about battered women. Still other women seek help when they are planning a separation or divorce and fear retaliation or "separation abuse" (Mahoney, 1991) involving victimization toward themselves or their children. Finally, many battered women seek help immediately after a serious abusive incident, after recognizing that the violence is continuing and fearing its recurrence another time.

Intervention

Shelter/Safe Residence. Providing the battered woman with information about how to contact a local battered woman's shelter or how to access other safe residence is essential when there is risk of further abuse, immediately or at any point. A useful practice is routinely to provide the information to new clients, as both the clinician and the client may not have sufficient time to plan when the need for safe residence arises. Providing the information in concrete written form such as a brochure from the shelter or writing the telephone number on a card, is also especially useful when it appears that the woman may not require the information immediately.

Law Enforcement. Many battered women do not know the laws concerning arrest and domestic violence and hold the belief that a police officer must witness the battering to make an arrest. Explaining the state statutes concerning "probable cause arrests" may be useful when the battered woman encounters a police officer who resists arresting a batterer. Encouraging a battered woman to act assertively with a law enforcement officer by asking for her/his badge number and name and asking directly for what she wants may increase the likelihood of effective intervention. Discussing with the battered woman the possibility that the law enforcement officer may not be responsive to her needs, may blame her for the problem, and may even threaten her with arrest provides an opportunity to develop strategies ahead of time to deal with these possibilities.

Injunction for Protection. Injunctive orders for protection provide a court-ordered mandate intended to protect victims. The court order directs the named abuser not to engage in abusive behavior or it may also include other orders, such as restriction from property, from the battered woman's place of work, or from telephone or any other contact with the battered woman or her children. In some jurisdictions, judges automatically issue mutual restraining orders against both the victim and the offender as if assigning mutual and equal responsibility for the problem of domestic violence. A battered woman who violates such an order by "allowing" or initiating contact with her batterer is often viewed in a hostile manner by the courts.

Escape and Protection Plans. The battered woman is often not able, ready, or willing to leave the abusive situation at a given time. In those instances, an escape plan (a plan for the battered woman to escape or avoid abuse) and a protection plan (A. Ganley, personal communication, May 10, 1988) (a plan for minimizing injury once abuse is inevitable) can potentially increase her safety when an abusive situation arises. However, there are no guarantees that she will effectively escape and the risks of injury will remain quite high.

Developing an escape plan or protection plan requires the active participation of the battered woman, with the therapist providing the structure and emotional support. The initial step is to solicit the woman's participation in the process. Surprisingly, many battered women feel that an escape or protection plan is not necessary, believing that the violence will not recur or that they can "take care of themselves" if it does. Even though this level of denial is often shaken during and shortly after a recurrent episode involving actual battering or explicit threats to kill, denial is often used again to cope with the emotional aftermath and to avoid the cognitive dissonance involved in staying in the relationship. Most battered women eventually acknowledge the possible recurrence of battering that is generally accomplished by reviewing the cycle of past episodes of violence and the battered woman's hope that each was the last. The fallacy of her hope for her safety may become apparent to her through examining what makes this point in time different from all the previous times when the battered woman believed the violence to be over. The objective is not to discount the battered woman's trust in her own judgment, but to help her examine its basis in reality versus its basis in false hope.

If all else fails, the therapist can ask the client to participate in developing an escape plan or protection plan to help reassure the therapist. By the therapist's taking on the "responsibility" for needing to have the client develop a plan, the reluctant battered woman will often participate. Taking the issue of developing an escape or protection plan this far risks undermining the woman's trust in her own judgment. By conceding that perhaps the battered woman is correct in her appraisal that violence will not recur (and she may be), and asking her to develop the escape plan "for the therapist," the therapist takes on the concern as her/his own and leaves intact the woman's own beliefs. But having developed the plan, nonetheless, the woman has the benefit of it if or when she needs it.

Having solicited the battered woman's willingness to participate in developing the escape or protection plan, the second step is to identify the signals that are likely to cue the presence of impending danger. The woman may clearly know the typical pattern of events leading to an abusive incident, or she may identify indications of increased danger. However, when the violence is very unpredictable, an escape plan is likely to be only minimally, if at all, helpful. When identifying cues to danger, it is important to specify the chain of events as far from the actual occurrence of violence or abuse as possible, providing greater opportunity for escape. For example, one battered woman knew that her husband would most likely abuse her when he came home from work in a particularly angry mood. Although the abuse typically did not occur right away, she knew that such evenings were particularly high-risk times. Another woman identified her husband's stopping to have a few beers with the guys after work as high risk for later abuse. Both women learned to avoid or leave the "high potential" situations.

For other women, the abuse appears to "come out of the blue" without the slightest indication of anything wrong. In these instances, or when the escape plan has failed, the battered woman is left to protect herself during an episode of violence. With the ultimate priority being safety, the protection plan helps to identify those behaviors that may lead to greatest avoidance of violence and subsequent injury. Increasing the margin of safety becomes the focus. Protection plans involve behaviors in which the battered woman may otherwise prefer not to engage. Women protect themselves with an incredibly wide range of behaviors from compliance to threats with weapons. Of course, the development of any protection or escape plan should include a discussion of the possible escalation effect it may have on the batterers or legal ramifications it may have for the battered woman.

The solution to the problem of battering does not lie in the battered woman's ability to "read" her batterer and stay out of his way. Her use of an escape or protection plan merely helps, but in no way assures, her survival. The batterer remains accountable for his violent or abusive behavior even though the woman may attempt to protect herself by learning his behavior patterns.

Finally, escape and protection plans require a concrete plan of action, which the battered woman can implement when she identifies the risk of increased danger. It is important to emphasize that the battered woman does not have to be accurate in her prediction. Falsely believing the abuse is about to occur and taking action for safety is no doubt safer than a false negative judgment because of which the woman fails to act to protect herself from impending violence. The action plan may take many forms depending on the specific nature of the danger. Common escape plans include having an extra set of keys kept in a secret and safe place ready for easy access; keeping extra cash and a credit card available; storing a suitcase of clean clothes with a friend or relative; developing a signal with a neighbor indicating need for assistance such as calling the police; and teaching a child how to dial 911 or the telephone number of a neighbor or family member to call for help. Other plans have included always wearing shoes so that a sudden escape is easier to make, having an extra set of carburetor wires and spark plugs for the car, rigging a signal so that entry into a room during the night was audible, and parking a car in a particular location to facilitate quicker escape. Battered women should not be required to go to such lengths to protect themselves; however the reality is that often they need to.

As a way of coping with the consequences of extreme terror, some battered women have learned to numb themselves to the fear when certain cues of danger are apparent. These women subsequently learned to ignore or minimize signals of danger, not responding in a manner that would potentially increase their safety. Other women have not learned to ignore the cues of danger or numb themselves to the terror associated with the potential threat and thus feel overwhelmed by the terror they experience. This state of feeling overwhelmed can interfere with a woman's ability to think clearly about her options for a safe escape in the moment of greatest danger. Some battered women believe that escaping the violence literally is not an option. They believe that no matter what they attempt, the batterer will anticipate and interfere with their efforts to escape, overpower them, or otherwise "not allow" escape.

Any plan is a good plan as long as it is responsive to the battered woman's particular circumstances. However, a note of caution is in order. Not infrequently, battered women discuss plans that appear likely to increase, rather than decrease, their danger or, alternatively, which involve the likelihood of lethal action by one or the other party. For example, one battered woman stated that she would carry a pocket knife and cut her batterer's leg if he came toward her. Some battered women purchase guns or hide knives under the bed at night. The use of a potentially lethal weapon should be considered with great caution because it can result in a homicide, either of the batterer or the battered woman. Even though threatening with a gun or knife in self-defense may provide an opportunity to escape or avoid violence on a particular occasion, it is not likely to permanently solve the problem. At times, the physical risk to both parties can be extreme. It is incumbent on the helping professional to discuss other alternatives for safety while communicating to the battered woman that she has a right to protect herself.

In assessing the decision to use an escape plan, the battered woman must consider the consequences of doing so. For some women, any effort to protect themselves results in an escalation of violence. For these women, an escape plan can only be used once as there is no second chance to escape. When a battered woman chooses to use a lethal weapon in self-defense, she also faces major consequences. Although the defense of battered women who acted to defend themselves against their batterers and were then charged with homicide or attempted homicide now often incorporates expert testimony to explain their actions, many of these women are nonetheless convicted and sentenced to prison (Browne, 1987; Ewing, 1987; Walker, 1989).

Finally, for some battered women the act of developing an escape or protection plan clarifies the danger they confront. In these cases, not only has the development of the plan functioned to help the battered woman protect herself against individual abusive incidents, but it may also help her more clearly evaluate her overall situation.

SUICIDE RISK

The Problem

Some battered women reach a point at which they see their only options as continued abuse or suicide. Typically, these women have made many attempts to escape the violence, but without success. Suicide, for some, appears to be the only viable option for ending the pain and is born out of the perception of hopelessness and lack of other alternatives (Freeman & White, 1989).

The risk of suicide also may increase after a woman has separated from her batterer, regardless of whether the separation is due to his death; his leaving the relationship, perhaps for another woman; or even her decision to end the relationship. Coupled with a sense of hopelessness and low self-esteem resulting from the battering, the experience of abandonment or loss may be experienced as more painful than is tolerable.

Intervention

As with suicide risk for any population, it is important to thoroughly assess the level of risk among battered women. Evaluating the distinctions between feelings of hopelessness, suicidal ideation, and specific intent to act with plans to do so is extremely important in determining the level of risk.

Identifying, strengthening, or creating deterrents to acting on the suicidal ideation are first steps in the intervention. Creating the perception of options

(Freeman & White, 1989), that is, hope for change, protection, or escape, is essential. For example, following one battered woman's self-defensive killing of her abusive partner after 25 years of marriage, the hopelessness and grief she experienced was moderated only by her belief that she had some life purpose yet unfulfilled. At a basic level, creating a safe place for the battered woman is a step toward which the helping professional can immediately work. Developing rapport and support within the therapeutic relationship can facilitate the development of a trusting and safe environment. For some battered women who are separated from the support networks of family and friends by their isolation, the therapeutic relationship may initially provide the only source of support, caring, and trust. As well, it provides an immediately available bridge to other sources of hope for the future. The therapeutic relationship can link the battered woman to support groups and to other resources within the community. Developing a contract with the battered woman for alternative plans of action, other than suicide, from which she can choose helps to make more concrete the available options as well as generating some level of commitment for their use. When the battered woman is part of an ongoing therapy or support group, a contract between the suicidal woman and each member of the group can also be a powerful link to hope and to alternatives to death.

Reframing the consideration of suicide within the context of empowerment can assist the battered woman to access feelings other than hopelessness (Freeman & White, 1989). Many battered woman have struggled, fought, and schemed simply to save their own lives from their partner's violence. It is therefore rather ironic that these same women then consider taking their own lives. For some women, the act of suicide represents the only option for taking control and for reducing the pain and suffering. If the battered woman believes that she will be killed anyway, her taking control of that outcome may represent a rather extreme form of self-determination or empowerment. In such a situation, the existential choice to die is placed in a context of lack of options. Developing options for the successful avoidance or escape of the batterer's attempt to kill her becomes a crucial point of intervention.

Another intervention is cognitively reframing (Fodor, 1988) the idea of suicide. The battered woman's potential suicide can be reframed as giving away her power to the batterer, instead of taking her power back. This creates a new choice point: using her own power to continue the destruction her batterer has begun or using her power to find alternative ways of relieving the pain and healing, including escape.

It is essential to validate the battered woman's current reality (Jones & Schechter, 1992, Schechter, 1987; Sturdivant, 1980) whatever it is and in whatever way it has been influenced by her recent or chronic exposure to abuse. However, her expectations of the future may be unnecessarily limited by her perception of a single option, suicide, as the way out. Development of hope and creation of the expectation that the battered woman can choose to continue fighting for her life, and her children's, is of ultimate importance.

HOMICIDE RISK

The Problem

Occasionally, a battered woman may indicate that she wishes her batterer dead or that she had plans to kill him. Sometimes the threat is couched in the context of self-defense, such as "If he comes at me one more time, I'll kill him." At other times, the victim's statement may indicate a decision to rid herself of the batterer altogether as a result of the abuse that has already occurred. The proportion of all battered women who kill, or attempt to kill, their batterers is unknown. Between 1980-1984, 6,408 women killed their partners (Browne & Williams, 1989) although the numbers of male partners killed by women have decreased by over 25% from 1979 to 1984 (Browne & Flewelling, 1986). This reduction has been attributed, in part, to increased availability of legal and extralegal resources in some geographical areas (Browne & Williams, 1989). Among women who are convicted of homicide against an intimate partner, a large percentage killed following physical, sexual, and psychological abuse toward them by their partner (Lindsey, 1978; Sherman & Berk, 1984; Totman, 1978; Wolfgang, 1967).

Intervention

As with suicide risk, the first step in assessing homicide risk is to assess the level of intent to act. Any statement with reference to wishing the partner dead or to wanting him to be killed may reflect an emotional state of frustration or anger, but without the intent to actually kill. Many battered women say that they have had thoughts associated with their batterer's death. Mothers of battered women who have killed have understood their daughters' actions saying that they could easily have done or almost did the same thing to their own abusive husbands.

In my experience, it is quite rare for a battered woman to premeditate the murder of her abusive partner. She may, however, premeditate her self-defense strategy in the event of a recurrent threat of violence or abuse. Many domestic homicides by women occur in the midst of an abusive episode that has escalated to the point of imminent danger. During these times, a readily available weapon is used, often a gun or a knife. Alternatively, some battered women believe that they have tried everything in order to stop the violence against them. Because nothing has worked, seemingly their only option is to arm themselves with a lethal weapon for the purpose of stopping the violence of subsequent attacks.

Even though it occurs rarely, when the battered woman is actually considered at risk for homicidal behavior, several interventions are essential. Under both legal and ethical obligations, the therapist must notify the intended victim; informing the battered woman of the intent to do so can perhaps avert the intended homicide as well as the possible (and likely) threat to the battered woman's life as well. Helping the battered woman consider (even extreme) alternatives to homicide helps to create options for protection (e.g., relocation, witness protection plans, hospitalization) or for the expression of her rage. As justified as is her rage and her right to defend herself against violence, the risk of severe abuse or death to her children, the risk of death to herself as well as her likely experience of criminal charges, pretrial incarceration, the ordeal of trial, and possibly lengthy imprisonment, make almost any alternative more favorable than homicide. For the battered woman and, obviously, for her batterer as well, alternatives to homicide are important to discover.

ACUTE AND SEVERE STRESS REACTION

The Problem

Occasionally, the battered woman's response to the accumulation of actual and threatened violence against her may be an acute anxiety reaction, brief reactive psychosis, or other acute and severe posttraumatic response. This level of response is likely to interfere with routine functioning and can easily be misdiagnosed if the complete history of abuse and other traumatic experiences is not assessed.

Intervention

The most critical need of the battered woman in this emotional state is an environment in which she can begin to experience emotional and physical safety. Because battered women often do not have ready access to supportive friendship or family networks, such options are sometimes limited. Occasionally, hospitalization is the only option available that is sufficiently secure to adequately protect the woman during this acute phase of posttraumatic response when even battered women's shelters may exclude her based on her psychological condition. Safehouses where staff or volunteers are equipped to deal with such reactions avoid the stigma attached to hospitalization. They are, however, not readily available in most communities. The adjunctive use of psychotropic medication may be considered as a method of managing acute and severe symptoms, although the long-term use of medication may hinder the battered woman's ability to increase the safety of the environment around her. The use of medication, even for a relatively short period of time, should be carefully considered against the potential risks involved. Providing a safe environment may have considerably more impact on reducing an acute posttraumatic stress reaction than medication. Further, without considerable clarification, the use of medication may indicate to the battered woman that her distress can be addressed by something other than her effective escape from continued abuse. For some battered women, the use of medication implies that the solution to the problem of abuse rests in their ability to handle the stress of the abuse rather than in escaping the abuse itself.

It is most important for the therapist to respond to the battered woman in such a manner as to validate her extreme stress reaction as "normal" within the abusive context; to facilitate hope, not that her batterer will change but that she can find her own sense of power against the abuse; and to facilitate her experience of knowing that she is not alone. Although these therapeutic responses are essential for working with battered women at any stage, they are even more important at the critical point of severe stress reaction.

8

Making Choices

This chapter discusses interventions with the battered woman as she directly confronts the problem of abuse and violence by her intimate partner. Choice making is a means of empowerment. It includes a basic choice about leaving or remaining in the relationship that was and/or continues to be abusive. Further, there are many other choices the woman faces. Unlike work with many other trauma victims (e.g., combat veterans, those raped by strangers, victims of accident or natural disaster), a major component of the intervention is protecting the woman from ongoing victimization by actual or threatened violence and abuse. Although no battered woman has power to control her partner's violent behavior or threats, she can empower herself by joining with others to have control over her actions to reduce the risk of victimization.

The goal of intervention is to enable the battered woman to make choices about removing herself from ongoing violence and abuse and about leaving or remaining in the relationship. Whether or not she actually leaves permanently, without the option to do so, the battered woman remains in a one-down position of power in the abusive relationship. From this position, the battered woman cannot negotiate nonviolence as a condition for remaining in the relationship. Thus, whether the battered woman leaves the relationship, she necessarily needs to perceive leaving as an option in order to secure her own safety in or out of the relationship.

Women who consider the idea of leaving the relationship often face issues that make the decision a complicated and difficult one. Barriers to leaving may involve other people's response to her decision; difficulty earning sufficient income to support herself and her children, including providing adequate childcare; the likelihood of retaliation by the batterer for her leaving and/or taking the children; and the lack of employable skills, job training and/or employment experience. Finally, the posttraumatic effects of violence and abuse may also create barriers. There have been referred to as the Battered Woman Syndrome (Walker, 1984). (See Chapter 4 for a discussion of posttraumatic effects of abuse and Chapter 9 for intervention with posttraumatic effects).

COMPONENTS OF CHOICE MAKING

In order to have control over one's own life, several prerequisites are necessary. First, one must believe in the right to make personal choices, often a difficult task in its own right. Second, one must be aware of the choices that exist. Finally, one must have the resources (e.g., tools, skills) to engage in choice-making behavior.

The Right to Choose

The belief of the right to make choices directly contradicts the stereotyped sex-role notion that women require someone stronger than themselves, a parent or a husband, to take care of them. The battered woman's belief about her right to make choices about her own life is challenged by other people who attempt to control her. These attempts to control may be motivated by an intent to protect or rescue the battered woman (e.g., a parent who tells an adult daughter she must return home to live as a means of attempting to get her to leave the abusive partner, a therapist who insists that she call the police the next time the battering occurs) or by an intent to dominate her (e.g., the batterer who will not allow his partner to leave the house to see her friends, who forces sex on her, or who demands that she comply with his requests). In either case, she must confront another's assertion that she has no right or ability to make her own choices.

Awareness of Choices

Another prerequisite to making personal choices is the awareness that a choice exists. For some, engaging in certain behaviors seems automatic and not an issue of choice, for example, behavior to please other people or to comply with expectations or demands. Stereotypic female sex-role socialization encourages women to respond based primarily on the needs of others (e.g., husbands, children); the choice not to do so, even if acknowledged, is considered generally to be unacceptable.

Increasing awareness of choice for one's personal behavior leads to a recognition of responsibility for choices, and thus for behavior, as well. Resistance to acknowledge choice can result from a reluctance to own responsibility for the choices that are made. Along with the principle of self-determination (Schechter, 1987), advocated for in battered women, comes the responsibility of making choices.

Problem-Solving Skill: A Tool for Making Choices

To help the battered woman to make choices about her life and to increase her empowerment, a problem-solving model provides a useful framework (D'Zurilla, 1986; Nezu, Nezu, & Perri, 1989). Within this framework, a therapist may use specific intervention techniques and tools, that is, education, support, skill development, development of strategies for coping to reduce interference with routine functioning, and social and political activism to counter barriers to the battered woman's taking control of her own life. This framework incorporates cognitive, emotional, and behavioral mechanisms of change. Goals identified through problem solving may be problem-focused goals (i.e., changes in the problem itself) or emotion-focused goals (i.e., reducing impact of distress associated with the experience of a problem) (Nezu, Nezu, & Perri, 1989).

The general process of problem solving involves a sequence of several steps, including (1) identifying and describing the problem, (2) identifying and describing thoughts and feelings about the problem, (3) identifying alternative choices or responses to the problem, costs and benefits associated with each, and potential obstacles to each possible choice, (4) making a choice, (5) detailing the plan to implement the choice, (6) implementing the selected choice, and (7) evaluating the choice concerning its effectiveness in solving the problem. When the choice has been ineffective or otherwise problematic, a second viable choice must be selected. Thus, the process continues until the problem has been solved.

This model of problem solving places the locus of control within the battered woman, while the therapist assumes the role of educator, facilitator, and supporter. The process of problem solving can be empowering for the battered woman; she has controlled the direction of her own life by making a choice intended to solve a problem, resolve a dilemma, or chart a new direction and carry out a plan of action. The therapist is not seen as the problem solver or someone who has taken control of her life. An authoritarian therapist exacerbates the battered woman's problem of being controlled by others around her and may even lead her to discontinue therapy, possibly increasing her inclination to avoid seeking help with the abuse. In contrast, an empowering therapist helps the battered woman reestablish control of her own life. The battered woman is not in control of her batterer's violent behavior; thus, if her partner is unwilling to change the abusive behavior, her only choice for attaining safety may be to leave the relationship.

INTERVENTION STRATEGIES

When addressing issues of empowerment and choice making, the battered woman may enter or reenter a crisis period at some point. For example, when a battered women begins to take action to change her own response to the batterer's behavior, the abuser may escalate his attempts to control her. Throughout the course of intervention, the focus of the treatment process may shift back and forth between crisis management, choice making, and healing of posttraumatic effects. The next section presents specific strategies for intervention with choice-making behavior.

Encouraging Self-Nurturance

Self-nurturance is an issue for most women (and perhaps men) and it is particularly important for women who have been abused (Courtois, 1988; Malmo, 1990). Self-nurturance is taking care of basic physical and emotional needs. It is even more basic than addressing psychological effects resulting from trauma. Even without trauma or unusual stress events, self-nurturing is essential for healthy functioning.

An obvious beginning point for addressing the physical well-being of a battered woman is to identify residual injuries from the physical or sexual assaults. Referral for medical or neuropsychological examination may be necessary. The extent of closed head injury among battered woman who have experienced head trauma as a result of battering has yet to be estimated, although indicators of postconcussional syndrome (e.g., headache, fatigue, dizziness, insomnia, difficulty concentrating, memory problems) (Slagle, 1990); posttraumatic epilepsy (Bennett, 1987); and posttraumatic migraine headaches (Gordon, 1989) have been observed among battered women. Other forms of physical injury, for example, internal injuries or fractured or dislocated bones may also account for some of the physical discomfort expressed by the battered woman. Many of these injuries may have gone unidentified, especially if the battered woman has been reluctant to seek medical assistance following previous abusive incidents. Even when medical treatment is obtained, the battered woman's reluctance to report the extent of her battering, if at all, and the physician's reluctance to inquire about it may result in inadequate medical evaluation and referral for related examination (e.g., neuropsychological).

Helping the battered woman manage attention to her physical well-being also includes a focus on nutrition, exercise, and sleep. Especially during times of high stress, some women may fail to eat a proper nutritional diet by failing to eat adequate amounts, skipping meals or snacking on nonnutritious foods. Others overeat or use food as a way of reducing stress. It is important to help the battered woman recognize the detrimental effects of caffeine, sugar, and highly processed foods (Merwin & Smith-Kurtz, 1988) and the need for adequate nutritional care, especially while under stress.

The benefits of physical exercise on anxiety and depression have been reported consistently in the literature (Cotton, 1990). Encouraging moderate physical activity among trauma victims can aid in sounder sleep, more energy, and generally promote greater physical and emotional well-being (Scrignar, 1988). Women who have been physically inactive over a long period of time may require preliminary physical evaluation and education about the effects of inactivity to provide an explanation for muscle weakness, fatigue, and other indicators of poor muscle tone (Scrignar, 1988).

Sleep disturbance, a common aftermath of trauma (APA, 1987), can lead to chronic sleep deprivation. Intentionally processing the traumatic experience of a battering and abusive relationship toward the goal of healing requires a great deal of physical and emotional energy. Adequate sleep on a regular basis in order to maintain energy is an important component. Relaxation exercises may also be useful to facilitate sleep.

Attention to nurturing the emotional self is as important as nurturing the physical self. Helping the battered woman to identify her emotional needs, identify ways in which she can get them met, and accept that she has a basic human right to do so is the beginning of the nurturing process. Whether her needs are for someone to hold her, listen to her, or tell her that she is a worthwhile person, meeting basic emotional needs is important in strengthening the inner resources from which the healing occurs.

Increasing Knowledge about Battering and its Effects

Increasing the battered woman's knowledge about violence toward women in society is useful. Understanding that the "personal is political" provides a framework for seeing that her abusive situation is part of a widespread problem, not limited only to her. Education about the common effects of abuse is essential so that the battered woman can identify her distress and specific symptomatology within a context of what are considered normal posttraumatic stress reactions. Providing this information to the battered woman can go a long way in alleviating any fear that she may have that she is crazy. The healing effects of normalizing her posttraumatic stress reaction as a predictable response to violence (given her often chronic traumatic experiences within the abusive relationship) can be powerful.

Providing information about legal options available to protect the battered woman is essential. This includes information about protective orders, the process of criminal prosecution, and civil action available to compensate for medical and other costs associated with physical and psychological damage. The more a battered woman is prepared to deal with the legal system, the more she can demand an effective response. For example, it is suggested that battered woman be counseled to routinely ask for an officer's name, badge number, and case report number so that they may later obtain a written copy of their reports. When the battered woman is informed of state statutes that require an officer to file a written report on all domestic violence calls, she is in a better position to expect them to take such action.

Attempting to use the legal system to prevent an abusive partner from continuing acts of power and control can sometimes be viewed as evidence of retaliation and manipulation by others. The resulting effect can be detrimental to the battered woman. For example, in one court case a woman filed civil action against her abusive husband. The civil court questioned her own investigative efforts to uncover evidence of fraud in their previous divorce action and suggested that she was not in fact suffering from posttraumatic stress reaction. The logic here was that, otherwise, she would not have revisited the original traumatic experience by seeking evidence or by using litigation that would place her in contact with the batterer. In this case, the battered woman was confronted with the court's invalidation of her experience, which only added to her anger, frustration, and hurt. Nevertheless, the overall benefits gained by using the legal system in most cases outweigh the disadvantages of it.

Increasing Social Support

Social support is an essential component in intervention as a means of countering the battered woman's isolation. Support from well-intentioned professionals or family members sometimes cannot compare with the support that comes from knowing and hearing about other battered women and their stories (Jones & Schechter, 1992). An example comes from a battered woman who spent 26 months in jail awaiting trial for the killing of her abusive husband during which time a guard told her that she had been battered and offered her support. She had never previously talked to another woman who had experienced battering. The effect was profound in decreasing her feelings of isolation. Education and support groups for battered women provide similar support (NiCarthy, Merriam, & Coffman, 1984).

Increasing Economic Resources

For some battered women, leaving the relationship is difficult due to lack of sufficient economic resources. Some battered women have family and friends who may provide economic and other tangible support during a time of transition; however, many others have no one to help bridge the gap between the time when economic support is provided primarily by the abusive partner and when the battered woman can provide it for herself.

Battered women's shelters provide the bridge for some women, although many others are not willing to use them. Sometimes the six or eight weeks women are allowed to remain in most shelters is not sufficient for some to develop employable skills, obtain a job, and save sufficient money to establish a residence and cover the regular expenses incurred by her and her children.

Some battered women plan prior to leaving by developing job skills, obtaining employment, and acquiring sufficient economic resources. For some, the experience of periodic battering episodes is less difficult to face than the daily struggle of having sole financial responsibility for self and children. When a battered woman who has little or no economic resources leaves her abusive relationship, she may face homelessness, lack of transportation to job or schools, and continued sexual or physical victimization by others while living in an unsafe place. She may also lose her children to her abusive partner, to his family, or to a social service agency for lack of ability to provide for them. It is not uncommon for a battered woman to lose residential custody of her children because she is not able to financially support the family home, nor to provide a comparable lifestyle to the children prior to the divorce due to her economic situation. Helping the battered woman to obtain economic resources sufficient to escape and to gain the ability to provide for herself is necessary in order to maintain her ability to stay safe once she has left the batterer.

Challenging Cognitions

As discussed previously (Chapter 4), normal cognitive effects of exposure to battering include hopelessness, self-blame, restricted view of options, perception of helplessness or lack of control of the outcome of events, and minimization or denial of the occurrence or severity of abuse or its effects. These cognitions are important targets of change in their own right, but more significantly, they serve as internal barriers to the battered woman's effective action to escape or avoid the violence toward her.

The following interventions directly address the cognitive distortions and barriers to a woman's effective response to violence and abuse. Based on the premise that cognition, emotion, and behavior form a triple-response system in which the components are interrelated, cognitive intervention can be effective in impacting on both emotion and behavior as well as upon the cognition for which intervention is most directly focused. Intervention with one component may have an impact on the others.

Reframing. Reframing helps the client change the meaning of behavior by developing a new perspective on it (Goodrich, Rampage, Ellman, & Halstead, 1988). An important and useful positive reframing is to normalize or legitimize the battered woman's response to violence (i.e., her efforts in reaction to it as well as posttraumatic stress reactions). It is important to help remove the stigma and blame placed on victims, by themselves or others. For example, the woman may feel stigmatized or blamed when a judge or therapist points out that the woman failed to leave the battering situation. In that example, helping the battered woman understand her own reasons for remaining, in spite of the potential for further abuse, may help her to understand her behavior in the context of her own appraisal of danger and her priorities and values. Identifying the actual efforts to escape or avoid abuse (e.g., sleeping in separate bedrooms, inviting a relative to live in the house, obtaining a job that requires that she be away much of the time when the batterer is home), which the battered woman has made, in spite of remaining in the relationship, may further aide the battered woman in identifying her behavior as "normal" or adaptive given her circumstances. Although the therapist may want to increase the battered woman's options for staying safe, it is nevertheless important to recognize those efforts that she has already made, regardless of their past level of effectiveness.

Another example of reframing is to define the battered woman's decision about leaving or remaining in the relationship as a choice (Douglas, 1987). By so doing, the focus shifts solely from one of reaction against the abuse to one of empowerment. The battered woman actively takes control of her life by making choices about its future direction.

Challenging the Minimization and Denial. Labeling violent and controlling behavior as abusive challenges the minimization and denial the battered woman may be experiencing, and thus may enable her to respond more effectively to it. Correctly identifying behavior as abusive helps the woman to recognize its inherent oppressive function, which is to exert power and gain control over her. Labeling the partner's behavior as abusive requires that she move from a position of denial to one of acceptance.

For example, following a history of chronic and/or severe abuse a battered woman may respond with minimization and denial that the violence is nonthreatening or unlikely to recur. By failing to help the battered woman correctly label the abuse against her, the therapist supports her in avoiding recognition of the real danger that the situation may hold for her and her children. Helping the battered woman to accept the reality of her abuse requires considerable support by the therapist, as she often feels despairing and temporarily left without hope. A battered woman may fear what it means "if I'm really an abused woman" or "if the abuse is really that bad." It these are true, she may believe that she is a failure, her life is over, or she must leave her husband, none of which she wants.

In addition to correctly labeling behavior as abusive and helping the battered woman to recognize its function as dominance over her, it may be necessary to challenge the battered woman's denial by examining the detrimental effects of abuse on her and her children. Children's behavior problems, for example, may be a direct result of their witnessing violence in the home, of being co-victims of the batterer, and/or the indirect effect of their mother's posttraumatic reactions.

Reattribution of Responsibility for the Violence. It is important to help the battered woman to attribute correctly the responsibility of violence to the person who engages in violence. As discussed in Chapter 4, many battered women blame themselves for the abuse they experience. Even for women who do not make overt self-blaming statements, the underlying belief system may reflect this self-blame. Some battered women do not blame themselves for the occurrence of the violence, but hold themselves responsible for changing their partner's battering behavior. Challenging the attribution of responsibility for both the violence itself, and for stopping it, is an important intervention. Otherwise, much of the battered woman's energy is focused on how she can change the abusive situation, rather than on how she may avoid or escape the dangers of it or take care of herself.

Acceptance of Personal Responsibility. Some battered women attribute the responsibility for their own safety to others around them, including the batterer. Some may assume that no one, including themselves, is able to insure their safety and well-being. It is important to help the battered woman examine her goals (which may or may not include safety as primary) and take responsibility for acting to meet them. She is not always in absolute control over her safety, but she can take control of her actions in attempting to insure it.

Sometimes it only appears that battered women place other considerations before their own physical safety when they are in fact carefully behaving in a way to increase the safety of themselves and others (e.g., children, family, friends). For example, when a battered woman expects that leaving—without adequate protection (which is sometimes difficult or nearly impossible to arrange)—may result ultimately in her death by the batterer, the act of staying in the abusive relationship can appear, and sometimes actually is, the safer course, at least temporarily.

Some battered women stay in their abusive relationships even when they do not believe that leaving will result in their being killed. For these women, other considerations (e.g., trying to make the relationship work, not taking the children from their father, not being alone) are given primary emphasis over their own physical safety. Without an acceptance of responsibility for their own behavior, while simultaneously acknowledging the obstacles to their behavior, battered women cannot assume control of their own safety or any other aspect of their lives.

Increasing Perception of Viable Alternatives. If the battered woman perceives a limited number of alternatives to escape violence as a result of her learning experience with the abusive relationship (Blackman, 1989), she may feel trapped in a hopeless situation. In order to increase the perception of viable alternatives, other changes (e.g., behavioral or emotional) may be required. For example, acquiring a job to earn sufficient income to leave the abusive relationship may require skills or assertiveness training. Another example, calling a friend or a shelter in order to escape violence, may require overcoming the shame and embarrassment involved in identifying oneself as a battered woman.

Challenging Socialized Sex-Role Beliefs

Challenging socialized sex-role stereotypic beliefs is another use of cognitive techniques. Many socialized beliefs are "dysfunctional" for women generally (Sturdivant, 1980) and for battered women in particular. Further, chronic exposure to abuse helps to create and shape additional dysfunctional beliefs in its victims. Examples of beliefs that are dysfunctional for the battered woman in effectively dealing with her abusive situation include "I am unable to take care of myself," "I don't deserve anything better," "It is my responsibility to take care of other people's needs before my own," "It is my responsibility to make the relationship work for both of us," "Hitting me means you love me," and "I am helpless and have no control over my situation." Challenging socialized beliefs such as these helps the battered woman examine her own belief system, parts of which she may have adopted unwittingly.

Increasing Behavioral Skills

Even though a woman may desire to leave the abusive relationship, she may believe that she does not possess the skills necessary to successfully live away from her partner. Of course, it is important to determine whether the problem is one of ability or performance. The lack of ability is a different problem from lack of skills or problems with utilizing the skills. There may be many obstacles to the battered woman's use of skills that she may well have, such as lack of sufficient resources or the lack of self-confidence to use them.

Possible behavioral deficits may include inadequate income-producing skills, instrumental living skills (e.g., financial management, household or car maintenance), or social skills. Inadequate behavioral skills do not make it impossible to leave a battering situation; many women do so. Nonetheless, these behavioral barriers increase the difficulty some battered women have in doing so. After leaving an abusive relationship, many women learn that they are able to develop or engage in behaviors that they believed were previously unavailable to them. Many women simply leave and then learn whatever new behaviors are needed to live independently. Other women need or want to have an employable skill or an ability to make new friends before they can leave a relationship that is abusive.

Although the therapist should advocate for safety (Schechter, 1987), one should also be in a position to understand the reasons a battered woman has for remaining in the relationship and honor her right of self-determination (Schechter, 1987). It is important to help her distinguish between behavioral, emotional, and cognitive barriers to decision making. She may believe that it is the behavioral barrier that prevents her from leaving; but on closer examination, she may discover that it is her fear of, or her attachment to, her partner.

When the battered woman is certain that the lack of a job or social skills has created barriers to leaving the relationship, helping her increase her skills and experience, even while in the relationship, may be an option. However, for some battered women, the control exerted by the batterer may be so great as to prevent her from enrolling in classes, taking a job, or having control of income earned from her job. In this case, there may be very little to be gained by remaining in the relationship long enough to make successful leavetaking more possible given that her options are so limited.

Increasing Coping Strategies

Another focus of intervention is helping the battered woman develop strategies for coping with the aftereffects of victimization. Even though it is not expected that she recover from most or all effects while its threat remains, she can develop coping strategies that help reduce the interference of the symptoms while she focuses attention on increasing her control of her life. Developing some control over specific symptoms can effectively increase her experience of empowerment; however, it is unreasonable to expect that a battered woman could develop skills to remove the effects of victimization while she is still in the violent context.

An analogy may be useful here. If one were to find oneself unavoidably in the middle of an earthquake, it would be prudent to engage in certain coping strategies until escape was feasible or the earthquake had ceased. The coping strategies would not make the earthquake go away, but they could minimize injuries or keep fears from interrupting ongoing attempts to escape. Like the earthquake victim, the battered woman's coping strategies help her to continue in her efforts to escape, so that the effects of previous violence do not render her helpless or less effective in her efforts.

The range of specific symptoms for which coping strategies may be required include depressed mood, anxiety, and phobic reactions as well as agoraphobia, intrusive symptoms, panic attacks, sleep or eating disturbances, and many others. Brief therapies, including hypnosis, may be effective in addressing these problems.

Other concerns for which the development of new coping strategies are indicated include behaviors used in an attempt to cope with the distress, for example, drug or alcohol abuse and aggressive or violent behavior (other than self-defense) toward children or others. As with other symptoms, these problems interfere with the battered woman's attempts to gain control over her own life, may be dangerous to others (e.g., her children), or produce negative effects (e.g., drug or alcohol addiction, arrest, loss of children to social services).

Providing Advocacy

The response of those representing social institutions are chief among the external barriers to battered women's seeking safety. Helping the individual battered woman to activate institutional systems on her behalf or working generally to increase the responsiveness of institutional systems to help battered women is an advocacy role consistent with feminist therapy principles (Rosewater & Walker, 1985). Law enforcement officers have the power to protect a battering victim from life-threatening violence. However, some women still meet with a nonchalant or, worse, blaming attitude when they call for help. Even today, some women hear "You married him, I didn't" in response to their request for help. A young black woman, when asking for help with her battering boyfriend who was standing half a block away at the time, was told by police officers that there was nothing they could do. A few minutes later she shot him.

Though most law enforcement officers, lawyers, judges, physicians, and mental health professionals receive education and training about domestic violence, such training may be incomplete. Even training that is extensive may not be sufficient in preparing these professionals to adequately deal with domestic violence situations. As a result, some cities have provided special law enforcement units for responding to domestic violence cases, special prosecutors and judges to deal with these cases, specialized intervention programs for domestic violence victims and perpetrators, and specially trained medical professionals in emergency rooms.

The battered women's movement has been instrumental in calling attention to the need for training within law enforcement. Battered women have formed groups to pressure police departments to respond more effectively to domestic violence cases. Helping professionals can encourage individual battered women to file a report subsequent to a battering incident to activate the law enforcement efforts on her behalf.

Other components of the criminal justice system require broader change to respond more effectively to domestic violence. The judicial system has considerable power in determining the level of protection available to a victim through hearings for permanent protective orders, divorce, custody and visitation, as well as criminal proceedings involving the batterer. The more that judges are educated about the dynamics of domestic violence, especially as it applies to victims, the more likely their actions will serve to protect, rather than neglect, battered women. Social pressure from community groups and professionals advocating for the rights of battering victims also serves to challenge the judicial process.

State attorneys or prosecutors also have considerable power to influence the action taken when a batterer has been arrested or a case report made. Given the considerable latitude within which state prosecutors may operate, education about the impact of not prosecuting a domestic violence case is very important. For some time, a victim's refusal to cooperate with prosecution was sufficient to drop many cases. The fact that her uncooperativeness resulted from coercion or threats by the batterer or the batterer's family was ignored. Battered women are often understandably ambivalent about criminal prosecution if the result means that the source of economic support for themselves and their children is taken away. Following her batterer's arrest on domestic violence charges, one woman was routinely beaten each time her batterer was released from jail as retaliation for her calling the police. In some jurisdictions, policy changes within prosecutor's offices have meant that criminal prosecution proceeds regardless of the cooperation of the victim/witness. These are referred to as no-drop policies.

Prosecution of an individual case can be encouraged by an interested party, especially when there is strong community support for it. Likewise, policy changes within communities can occur due to the effort of individuals, groups of formerly battered women, or concerned professionals.

Recent research (Browne & Williams, 1989) suggests that in states which provide for greater protection of battered women through legislative reform, fewer battered women killed their assaultive partners following the changes than prior to them. The implication is that fewer women resort to homicide as a means of protection from further abuse when community resources for protection are available. Legislative change is thus one means of decreasing the external barriers to safety by creating a greater number of options for escaping from violence and abuse.

A FINAL NOTE ON CHOICE MAKING

An ultimate reality is that, regardless of her actions, her beliefs, or her coping strategies, a battered woman may not be successful in guaranteeing her safety or others' (e.g., children, family members, friends). Even when she has successfully engaged the cooperation of law enforcement, a parole board (e.g., when a batterer is returning to the community after incarceration), family, and friends, the battered woman may live with the uncertainty of not knowing when or where she may encounter her batterer or someone acting on his behalf. Failure to recognize this possibility is sufficient to falsely assure the mental health professional that danger is past. The battered woman needs not to be alone in her vigilance.

In the next chapter (Chapter 9) the discussion of intervention is shifted to a different emphasis. Once the danger of recurrent abuse is no longer the focal point of intervention, healing from the effects of the psychological trauma of battering, marital rape, psychological abuse, and their sometimes compounded effects can begin. The next chapter discusses interventions that facilitate this healing process.

9

Posttraumatic Therapy: Healing the Psychological Effects of Battering

Once the threat of violence has ceased or at least has been reduced substantially, the battered woman is often still left with multiple posttraumatic effects resulting from her exposure to chronic and/or severe abuse. Even when the actual physical assault was not severe, it can result in serious psychological damage. Until the violence has abated and the threat of recurrent violence has ceased, it may be difficult to separate ongoing traumatic stress from posttraumatic stress reactions. Figley (1985) defined traumatic stress reaction as a "set of conscious and unconscious actions and emotions associated with dealing with the stressors of the catastrophe and the period immediately afterwards" (p. xix). Posttraumatic stress reaction was defined as "a set of conscious and unconscious behaviors and emotions associated with dealing with the *memories* (emphasis mine) of the stressors of the catastrophe and immediately afterwards (Figley, 1985, p. xix). A battered woman who is exposed to repeated victimization may simultaneously experience traumatic and posttraumatic stress reactions. The experience of both traumatic and posttraumatic stress responses may be greater than either alone, although there currently exists no empirical data to address this issue.

Although some recovery and healing can occur when the focus of intervention is primarily of a protective (see Chapter 7) or choice-making nature (see Chapter 8), intensive focus on healing can only occur once abuse and ongoing threats of it have stopped. Survival and empowerment are powerful components of recovery and healing. Complete recovery and transformation from the trauma of battering may take a lifetime (Wilson, 1989), although specific symptoms may be alleviated effectively in much less time.

Although discussions of intervention with battered women often make reference to some of the psychological effects (cf. Campbell, 1986; Geffner & Pagelow, 1990; NiCarthy et al., 1984; Pressman, 1989), with few exceptions (cf. Stark & Flitcraft, 1988) posttraumatic therapies with battered women have not been widely described.

An important assumption for the clinician working therapeutically with battered women is to recognize the symptoms as explicitly related to exposure to the trauma of battering and abuse and that intervention should be focused accordingly. Failing to do so can lead the clinician to operate as though these symptoms were evidence of personality disorders or premorbid psychopathology. Where a pretrauma history indicates evidence of psychopathology, it is important to determine its possible relationship to prior victimization or traumatic history.

After having said that interventions toward healing and recovery can begin only after the threat of violence by the abusive partner has ceased, a caveat is necessary. Living in a world where violence toward women is prevalent, both from intimates and from strangers, it is virtually impossible ever to escape at least the implicit threat of violence from somewhere. Perhaps a more realistically stated prerequisite for posttraumatic therapy is that it is necessary to create a domain within which the battered woman can feel safe from further victimization, including revictimization by the helping professional or other institutional system. For some women that domain is relatively large, encompassing a social support network of family and friends. For others whose world is excessively dangerous, the domain may be as small as the therapeutic environment. The essential point is that a safe physical and emotional space is necessary in order to begin posttraumatic therapy.

The previous chapter addressed interventions that enable choice making to empower the battered woman to take action against her victimization. For some women, that process is a difficult or even impossible one without some recovery or healing from the effects of victimization. The psychic wounds may be so deep or so pervasive as to render the battered woman too vulnerable or too wounded to fight against even her own victimization. In this case, active work on posttraumatic recovery and healing may be required concurrent with other previously described interventions (i.e., protection, choice making). What is most essential is to recognize the needs of each individual woman and to begin the work of recovery and healing within that framework.

This chapter addresses posttraumatic interventions useful for helping women recover from the effects of battering and abuse when leaving in itself does not alleviate the effects. Healing requires therapist attention to the woman as a whole person.

THE NATURE OF HEALING

What is the nature of healing? Victims abused at the hands of their intimate partners suffer injury to all levels of the self: physical, mental, emotional, and spiritual. Spirituality—derived from the Latin origin *spiritus* meaning breath, life—refers to "being fully alive and open to the moment . . . it includes a sense of belonging and of having a place in the universe" (Merwin & Smith-Kurtz, 1988, p. 67). Recovery from symptoms is a component of the healing process, but healing moves beyond that point and involves the whole person. Together, healing and recovery refer to a process of restoring the whole person to a state of wholeness and health (Merwin & Smith-Kurtz, 1988), health being more than merely an absence of symptoms. A holistic perspective to posttraumatic therapy requires an integration of various therapeutic approaches. No single theory, technique, or therapeutic orientation is sufficiently broad in scope to accomplish the goal of healing the whole person, including the emotional, cognitive, physical, and spiritual aspects.

COMPOUNDED TRAUMA: WHEN BATTERING IS NOT THE ONLY TRAUMA

When working to heal the effects of trauma, it is difficult to separate the cumulative effects of other traumas (e.g., previous childhood victimization, previous battering in an adult relationship, or recent sexual assault by someone other than the intimate partner) from the effects of more recent battering and abuse by an intimate partner. For example, it is estimated that one in two females have been victims of sexual assault at some point in their lives (Wolfe, Wolfe, & Best, 1988), that 16% of women report an experience of intrafamilial sexual contact before the age of 18 years, 31% report that they had been victims of extrafamilial sexual abuse (Russell, 1983), and that 10.7% of children experience severe physical violence toward them by their parents (Straus & Gelles, 1990). Therefore, it is not uncommon to find a battered woman with a previous victimization history.

Intervention with women focusing on the effects of trauma necessarily involves assessment that should uncover other traumatic experiences. For example, one young woman who had an extensive history of battering by her husband also had experienced childhood physical abuse and had been raped by two men during the time her husband was in jail for his abuse of their child. Posttraumatic therapy in such cases involves dealing with the cumulative effects of all types of traumatic experience to which a woman was exposed (e.g., battering, rape, childhood abuse, abuse of her child by her husband). This is especially true when there has been little or no healing or recovery experience such as psychological intervention with previous traumas. Some aspects of the posttraumatic therapy may focus on symptoms that are clearly identified with one form of trauma or another (e.g., dreams about the rape versus her own child's abuse) or, alternatively, the expression of an emotional reaction (e.g., anger, depression, panic attacks) may be in response to several different traumatic experiences simultaneously. Thus, although referral for intervention may be for one particular trauma or another (e.g., on the rape in the above example), the course of posttraumatic therapy will typically involve addressing other traumatic events as well.

POSTTRAUMATIC THERAPY: STRATEGIES FOR INTERVENTION

Posttraumatic therapy with battered women has many of the same elements as posttraumatic therapy with other victims of intimate violence. However, as noted previously, when the trauma involves abuse from someone with whom there has been a loving and trusting relationship (e.g., intimate partner), when it occurs repeatedly over perhaps a long period of time, and when it includes multiple forms of abuse (e.g., physical, sexual, and psychological), posttraumatic therapy differs from that for other victim groups (Stark & Flitcraft, 1988) (e.g., natural disaster, combat) and even from therapies for victims of other forms of intimate violence (e.g., rape by a stranger). Further, the continued and explicit threat of abuse that remains for battered women long after they leave their abusive relationship or after the actual abuse has stopped, presents a somewhat unique therapeutic challenge for the clinician. In these cases, interventions focused on healing and recovery must accompany a continued focus on choice making or empowerment as well as on crisis issues.

Ochberg (1988) describes five clinical paradigms involved with posttraumatic therapy: bereavement, victimization, autonomic arousal, death imagery, and negative intimacy. Ochberg stresses that these paradigms for intervention with trauma victims assume no preexisting psychopathology. Even when evidence exists of prior psychopathology, the initial focus of intervention should be on posttraumatic stress reactions. Pretrauma problems or deficits may be incorporated into the therapy, not as the primary focus of intervention, but as factors that reduced the victim's ability to respond effectively to the trauma or to recover from its effects.

Stark and Flitcraft (1988) caution that a traumatization model of therapy is not adequate for working with battered women for several reasons: (1) the demarcation of the trauma is difficult due to the ongoing nature of battering, (2) symptoms are identified solely with the trauma, not with other forms of secondary victimization imposed by institutional response to battered women as victims, and (3) posttraumatic therapy can reinforce dependency, not autonomous choice making, by overfocusing on the "rescue" from victimization rather than on support of the victim's choices. Larsen (1992) described a framework within which the constellation of (1) chronicity, (2) intentionality by an intimate partner, and (3) secrecy within a (4) context of patriarchy is needed to both understand a woman's response to battering and to develop effective interventions for addressing them. Incorporating interventions with battered women that extend beyond the realm of post-traumatic therapy to include protective (see Chapter 7) and choice-making (see Chapter 8) interventions, begins to address these concerns. Further taking into account Stark and Flitcraft's caution, adequate interventions with battered women must incorporate current trauma (e.g., battering, marital rape, psychological abuse), prior trauma (e.g., childhood abuse), as well as secondary institutional victimization (Dutton-Douglas, 1988).

Following from the prior discussion, the description of posttraumatic therapy with battered women is organized as several overlapping therapeutic processes: (1) reexperiencing the trauma, (2) shame reduction, (3) rage reduction, (4) facilitating the grief reaction, (5) making meaning of the victimization, and (6) rebuilding a new life. These tasks incorporate attention to compounded trauma, including secondary victimization, and are addressed from a holistic perspective of the battered woman.

Reexperiencing the Trauma

Reexperiencing the trauma through recollection of the memories is a hallmark of posttraumatic therapy, including therapy with incest survivors (cf. Briere, 1989; Courtois, 1988), Vietnam veterans (cf. Foy, 1992; Wilson, 1989), and rape survivors (cf. Hartman & Burgess, 1988). An empirical basis for this process relies on the evidence that traumas are biologically encoded (van der Kolk, Brown, & van der Hart, 1989) and subsequently produce an array of cognitive, affective, and physiological responses that may not be overtly expressed for many weeks, months, or even years following the trauma. Without adequate integration or reconditioning of the trauma, unrelated situational cues may trigger responses inappropriate or excessive to the situation. Such is the case with Vietnam veterans who may become violent, look for cover, or hit the ground at a sudden loud noise. A helicopter can trigger a flashback with sufficient emotional intensity and feelings of being out of control that the veteran believes he is again in Vietnam.

For battered women, the cue may be a raised voice, a sudden movement, the smell of alcohol, or anything that triggers the "physiological preparedness for the return of the trauma" (van der Kolk et al., 1989, p. 372), which itself requires "enduring vigilance for and sensitivity to environmental threat" (p. 372). Promoting expression of the complex array of feelings associated with the trauma is necessary to the healing process. Also important is the cognitive integration of the trauma that is required to make meaning of the abusive experience. Often meaning cannot be found within existing cognitive structures, thus they need to be challenged and new structures developed. Finally, treatment is focused on reducing the physiological response to cues functionally relevant to the trauma.

Recollection of the battering may involve very detailed accounting of specific incidents or pieces of various incidents that may have spanned many years. Typically, it is not necessary for the victim to recall every detail of every incident, although some may feel a need to do so. At minimum, it is necessary to recall enough detail to elicit in the present the conditioned emotional and physiological reaction that is associated with the original trauma. Acknowledgment and recognition of the abuse is a process that may need to occur repeatedly. Spontaneous recollection of various types of traumatic experience (e.g., battering, childhood abuse, prior rape) may occur through dreams, spontaneous memory during therapy, journaling, or in other ways. While focusing in the therapeutic process on reexperiencing one form of abuse (e.g., marital rape), it is not uncommon for a client to begin reexperiencing a different abuse (e.g., battering episode, childhood sexual abuse). Alternatively, the therapy may progress from a primary focus on one type of abuse (e.g., battering) for an extended period of time before shifting the focus to another (e.g., childhood sexual abuse). This process of recollection is helpful for validating or naming the experience as abusive. Language that does not recognize the abuse and victimization (e.g., describing battering as "marital conflict" or forced sex as "having sex" or "making love") deflects the real nature of violence and abuse and serves to distort the experience for the battered woman, minimizing the significance of its impact on her.

It is often necessary for the therapist to facilitate a titration of recall and affect, allowing for a sufficient level of affect in order for the client to process and integrate the material, but without overwhelming the client with anxiety or pain. Helping the client to gain a sense of control over the pacing of recall also facilitates empowerment over the trauma.

Experiencing the magnitude of the fear during the time of each original abusive episode may have been too overwhelming for the battered woman to tolerate and, further, it may have interfered with her attempts to stay safe. During the reexperiencing process of therapy, naming her emotional responses to the abuse (e.g., terror, fear, anger), acknowledging their appropriateness, and validating them are critical. Preparing the client to understand that the reexperiencing of feelings may be as intense as if the abuse were happening for the first time is important so that she may anticipate the process as much as possible.

Facilitating the battered woman's reexperiencing of trauma and the affect associated with it, requires the clinician to ensure that the client has adequate skills for regulating the arousal so as not to become overwhelmed by it. Reexperiencing the trauma of abuse cannot be fully controlled to occur within the therapy hour nor is it necessary that it does. Reexperiencing may occur inadvertently through dreams, intrusive thoughts, or flashbacks even without efforts to elicit it (cf. Figley, 1985; Ochberg, 1988; Wilson, 1989). It may also occur outside the therapy session through more deliberate planning, such as journal writing or meditation. Training women to cope with and reduce arousal both within and outside the therapy session helps to facilitate personal control. Minimizing the likelihood that the reexperiencing process will be a revictimization experience and increasing the likelihood that it will be a healing one is of utmost importance.

Shame Reduction

Shame is the affect that is associated with negative self-image such as inferiority, low self-esteem, or self-hatred (Kaufman, 1989). Shame is an organizing principle used to refer to physiological or visceral response, cognitions or thoughts about self, feelings or emotion, and nonverbal behaviors, especially facial expression (Tomkins, 1987).

Shame, humiliation, low self-worth, or simply feeling diminished or inferior are normal reactions to intimate abuse or victimization (cf. Douglas, 1987; Ochberg, 1988; Walker, 1984). Having experienced repeated invasions of personal boundaries through battering and sexual abuse by an intimate partner, abused women often develop a sense of inferiority about themselves that reflects the manner in which they have been treated. This inferiority can be identified as negative thoughts about self, feelings of embarrassment, shame, being wrong or bad, interpersonal behavior that expresses or defends against the feelings of shame, and facial signs of shame (Kaufman, 1989). As is often the case, when the physical or sexual abuse is accompanied by chronic verbal degradation and humiliation, a woman may also eventually come to believe, or internalize, the ideas expressed by her abuser.

Shame and embarrassment resulting from victimization and exposure to the humiliation of abuse may have led some battered women to remain in an abusive situation. Perhaps she feels undeserving of a more loving partner. A battered woman may report that she believes she deserves to be loved and not to be abused, although she may have internalized a different set of feelings and beliefs and act from those instead. The shame of revealing the truth to others may keep such women in isolation even after having escaped the abusive situation. Having left, the battered woman may consciously or unconsciously attempt to avoid these feelings because they are so painful to experience. Efforts toward numbing may lead her to isolate herself from the support and companionship of others or to use drugs and alcohol (Stark et al., 1981).

The purpose of therapy focused on shame is to move the battered woman through the shame experience so that letting go of it is possible. By failing at some point either to acknowledge or to express the feeling of shame, it may function as an obstacle to healthy emotional functioning (Kaufman, 1989).

Sometimes shame associated with the victimization from a battering relationship is built on a foundation of shame from childhood sexual or physical abuse, prior rape, or other traumatic experience involving victimization. For example, repeated experiences of battering may trigger the shame of earlier abuse; the current experience is a combination of both abuse experiences. In these examples, more extensive work may be necessary to heal the shame from both the past and the present traumas. The therapist's expression of genuine acceptance of the battered woman, especially while she is most intensely experiencing shame, is a powerful intervention.

Reducing shame through the use of psychotherapy requires the context of a trusting therapeutic relationship with a therapist who has been able to confront and effectively respond to her/his own shame that is triggered both inside and outside the therapeutic relationship (Kaufman, 1989). Otherwise, the experience of exploring shame in a therapeutic relationship can exacerbate the shame reaction. Further discussion of therapist issues relevant for working with battered women as trauma victims can be found in Chapter 10.

Anger Work

Anger or rage is a common reaction to the experience of abuse and victimization (Ochberg, 1989). Facilitating the acknowledgment and safe expression of anger is the essential task of rage expression.

Although anger is a normal response to victimization, many women neither name nor directly express their feelings as anger. Overt expressions of anger generally are considered to be unacceptable for women (Ho, 1990; Miller, 1986; Rosewater, 1988) and thus are experienced negatively by them (Daugherty & Lees, 1989). As such, the first task in working with a female victim's anger and rage is to identify and name the feelings. Simply increasing the battered woman's awareness of her feelings of anger can have a surprisingly powerful effect. Having identified and named the response of anger and rage, the next step is to direct the expression of feelings in a manner that is not destructive.

Occasionally, the previously unacknowledged anger and rage can become ignited, with the battered woman reporting experiences of anger "all of the time." Small annoyances may trigger major rage reactions. Both guided experiences within the therapy session and well-planned exercises of expression outside of therapy can be used to direct the rage reactions. Encouraging any client to intentionally access and express intense emotions outside a therapy session should be done only after carefully considering the potential risks. In situations in which the client has access to few internal and external controls, the therapist may encourage her to limit her expression of rage to the therapy session until she builds the supports necessary for the safe release of feelings outside of therapy.

The emotional and physical energy accompanying feelings of anger can be directed toward expression in a variety of ways including journal keeping, physical exercise, creative expressions of art, and pounding pillows or a bed, for example. In addition, these feelings can be directed constructively toward involvement in social and political activism. Mobilizing anger toward action for self-protection (e.g., encouraging police officers to arrest batterer, leaving battering situation) and empowerment (Jones & Schechter, 1992; Hartman, 1987) has been a cornerstone of feminist therapy.

Separation of the processes involved in anger or rage reduction from those involved in problem solving is critical. Problem solving, including assertive communication, may follow from the energy that is mobilized by acknowledging feelings of anger. However, intense feelings of anger and rage often require expression separate from attempts to solve the problems on which these feelings are based.

Facilitating the Grief Process

The battered woman often does not recognize the losses she has endured. These may include loss of relationship with husband or partner, loss of home, loss of job, loss of economic security, loss of children, loss of friends and other sources of social support, loss of a positively valued self-identity, among others (See Chapter 4 for further discussion). Recognition of the losses that have occurred is the essential first step in facilitating the bereavement process.

Even when the battered woman is clear that she does not want to remain in an abusive situation, the attachment and love she feels for her partner may make her decision difficult or impossible. The potential losses may be many. Other emotional issues may complicate the situation further. For example, battered women who have previously experienced abandonment or severe loss in prior intimate relationships (e.g., childhood relationships with parents, deaths, divorce), may allow the positive aspects of the relationship in which abuse occurs to obfuscate the physical danger and emotional harm done by battering. The grieving process may be facilitated by helping the battered woman to experience the loss of positive aspects of her relationship, as well as attending to its negative components.

Attachment to a battering partner may be based on anger, rather than love. One battered woman was so angry at her batterer that she was willing to endure continued abuse in order not to let him "get off" without being accountable to her. Although this woman's anger at her batterer was alive and strong, she would not leave the relationship in order to protect herself from further abuse.

Thus, working through the grief process requires acknowledging and accepting the losses that have occurred. The *loss or betrayal of trust* is an inevitable loss for battered women. When the assumption that the person who loves you will not intentionally hurt you is shattered, the effect is significant. However, some women may not hold this assumption, perhaps because of childhood abuse or previous victimization that has taught them otherwise. Ironically, previously abused women often believe in the initial phases of the abusive relationship that they have found someone who is different from the others, someone who they believe will love them, not hurt them. When battering eventually occurs in these relationships, betrayal also occurs and trust is likewise shattered.

The *loss of relationship* is another major loss that the battered woman inevitably faces. She loses the relationship that may have held the promise of a happy future or which initially she may have experienced as loving and kind. It is not the loss of the abusive aspect of a relationship that battered women grieve, but the loss of the real or hoped for loving, caring relationship.

Some battered women do not acknowledge the relationship losses that confront them, whether they include a loss of trust, of intimacy, or of the relationship altogether. Denial of relationship losses or the unending hope that what was lost will return again in her relationship with the abuser, becomes an important therapeutic issue. Even when the battered woman holds onto the hope that the future will include a loving relationship, relationship losses have already occurred (e.g., trust, intimacy). Some women believe they need too much, perhaps attributing their need to childhood causes, so that when they experience loss within an adult intimate relationship, it is not recognized as legitimate. Loss in the abusive relationship requires considerable therapeutic attention.

The loss of relationship that many battered women fear the most is the relationship with their children. The fear of this loss is a common one for battered women; it often functions to keep women in abusive situations. Batterers threaten to kidnap children or to fight bitter custody battles. Battered women know that the batterer is capable of "winning" at both (Chesler, 1991). It is not uncommon for the batterer to present himself as a calm, responsible individual who is protecting his children from their "crazy" mother, often a woman who is affected by a long history of abuse by her partner. The loss of children may also mean that the children are at risk for physical and/or sexual abuse by the abusive partner.

Whether battered women actually lose custody of their children or not, they often lose the warmth and affection in their relationship with them.

Sometimes children, especially older male children, will identify with their fathers and begin to treat their mothers accordingly, including resorting to physical and/or sexual abuse. The battered woman's stepchildren (from the abuser's previous marriage) are especially at risk of being estranged from her.

The loss of relationships other than with the intimate partner or children may also occur. In-laws, parents, family members, and friends may distance themselves from the battered woman, indicating they can no longer provide shelter, support, or even social contact. When the abusive partner has actively isolated the battered woman from her support network, they may attribute the distance to her lack of interest, her greater loyalty to her abusive partner, or her disregard for them. Lack of support from others is sometimes a result of their blaming the battered woman for the partner's abuse. Fear of physical harm can lead previously supportive individuals to back away from the battered woman. Finally, discomfort or distress at knowing about details of the abuse causes some to distance themselves.

Loss of income or financial security may directly result from a battering relationship. A batterer's harassment of a woman at her place of employment may easily result in her being terminated from that job. If, due to repeated injuries and long nights of abuse, the battered woman is unable to maintain adequate work performance, she may lose her job and thus lose her source of income. Although some employers are sympathetic and helpful, a battered woman often cannot count on her employer to accommodate the unpredictable and intrusive behavior of her batterer insofar as it impacts on the workplace or her performance there. Sometimes an employer can fear for her/his own safety, especially if the employer has previously been a source of support for the battered woman.

Economic security may also be lost during the process of separation or divorce. Sometimes week-to-week existence depends on income produced by the abusive partner. Without that financial support, the battered woman and her children may find themselves without a home or food to eat, waiting weeks or months before the legal system is able to adequately address the problem (if at all). For women living middle or upper-middle class lifestyles, economic security may be, or appear to be, dependent on remaining in the abusive relationship. Access to a home and car, vacations, credit cards, and money to pay for children's private education may become unavailable if the battered woman were to leave the relationship. Some battered women know that their abusers can probably be successful in denying them access to these resources. One woman indicated that if she left her relationship, her total source of income would be cut off and, further, that she would be implicated in the fraudulent business practices of her husband. He had placed many of the official documents in her name and she felt as though she could not effectively challenge him without risking the loss of all her economic support. Some battered women realistically fear loss of access to the basic necessities: food, shelter, transportation, and medical care. Even when battered women remain in their abusive relationships, their economic support is very often based on the whim of their partners.

Loss of self is a central issue with battered women. The impact of repeated violent and abusive experiences to which one is exposed often results in the erosion of the victim's self-esteem. She may become a reflection of her batterer as her survival, and the survival of her children, may depend on her ability to anticipate the batterer's mood and behavior. Even when the battered woman is unable to avoid the abuse, her efforts to do so continue. By focusing her energy and attention on efforts to stay safe, the woman often has little energy left to direct toward herself or her children.

It is the therapist's task to facilitate the client's mourning of these losses, moving through the anger, depression, and acceptance characteristic of the mourning process (Sanders, 1989). As with the treatment of adult survivors of incest, it is also true for battered women that "grieving is likely to be one of the most painful parts of the therapy...the survivor must give up attempts to control that which she cannot and accept the losses involved" (Courtois, 1988, p. 181).

Making Meaning of the Victimization

An important component of posttraumatic therapy is to help the victim make meaning out of the abusive experience (Foa et al., 1989; Janoff-Bulman, 1985; McCann, Sakheim, & Abrahamson, 1988). According to Janoff-Bulman (1985), victimization involves the shattering of certain basic assumptions. These include (1) the "assumption of invulnerability" especially with regard to one's intimate partner, (2) "the world as meaningful," such that the victim questions how it makes sense that the abuse happened to her, that someone who loves her hurts her so badly, and (3) "positive self-perceptions" so that the victim has to cope with the lowered self-esteem and damaged self-image that result from victimization. Healing involves "coming to terms with these shattered assumptions and reestablishing a conceptual system that will allow the victim to once again function adequately" (Janoff-Bulman, 1985, p. 23).

Having integrated the abusive experience and come to terms with the shattered assumptions about oneself and the world, the battered woman can examine the meaning the victimization has for her present life. In defining meaning, it is important to identify both negative and positive aspects of the abuse and its sequelae. One battered woman commented that the end result of her abuse was that it required her to gain control over the direction of her own life; she had to develop a community for social support. Another woman who experienced severe physical and sexual abuse felt that her abuse had opened her eyes to the oppression and mistreatment that so many women in the world experience. She felt more connected to other people as a result of her experience. No battered woman or other victim of violence seeks out abuse experiences in order to attain these positive outcomes; the cost is simply too great. Meaning is derived from the series of life experience involving the abuse, the response to it, and the sequelae that followed.

Building a New Life

Perhaps a final step in the healing process is life rebuilding as a survivor of abuse, that is, no longer as a victim. The right not to be abused or victimized is the foundation of a new life regardless of whether the battered woman chooses to remain in the relationship with a previously abusive partner, to seek a new relationship, or to be in no intimate relationship at all.

Actively setting boundaries against exploitation, violence, and abuse within newly developed intimate relationships, in relationships with one's children or other family members, or in other relationships (e.g., friends, employers, neighbors) is a component of this final phase of intervention. For example, one woman's leaving her abusive partner was not enough to stop the violence; her adolescent drug-abusing son began to abuse her. Some women learn to identify clearly and object to the abuse against them by an intimate partner, but do not name the abusive behavior of nonintimates (e.g., sexual harassment by an employer). It is important to help the formerly battered woman recognize her right to live without the violation of personal boundaries not only by her intimate partner, but by others as well, including persons with greater authority. In this manner, the battered woman's vision is widened beyond the focus of her intimate relationship to include the perspective of dominance and oppression in the broader social context.

The development of new friendships, and in some cases, new intimate relationships is part of building a new life. Developing a social network for companionship and emotional and physical nurturance is a basic aspect of taking responsibility for one's own needs.

Finally, helping a formerly battered woman to identify and/or develop her life goals helps her experience her empowerment or control over her own life. Taking responsibility for future direction can be both liberating and overwhelming. It is necessary to work through both kinds of feelings to reach a greater sense of self-direction.

ADJUNCTIVE THERAPIES

Other forms of intervention may be very useful as adjunctive to the psychotherapeutic approach described above, or perhaps, in some cases, as alternatives sufficient to restore the victim to a state of wholeness. A holistic approach to healing may include interventions such as body work, self-help groups, and healing rituals.

Body Work

The use of body work with trauma victims, therapeutic techniques that facilitate the body's expression of affect (Hodgson, 1990; Turner, 1990) through movement, sound, or touch depends on a theory of mind-body integration (cf. Rossi, 1986). Direct intervention with the body is important for releasing emotions that may have been unexpressed for long periods of time (Hodgson, 1990). Because the mind and body are considered to be integrally related, the body is an important arena for identifying unexpressed emotions and for facilitating their expression. Sometimes these emotions are not as readily expressed verbally and can be more easily accessed through nonverbal methods.

The decision to use body work and the timing of it are both important considerations. Body work can facilitate the release of emotion at a point where avoidance by numbing and denial of feelings are extensive. However, the use of body work may create a flooding of emotion that may require considerable expertise and time to effectively work through. Under no circumstances should body work proceed without a client's full and informed consent. The client should be fully aware of what to expect and to have already recognized and dealt with intense emotion in the therapeutic work. Further, the client should have adequate coping skills and support to deal with the intense experience that body work is likely to facilitate. Confidence in using coping skills will increase the battered woman's sense of her ability to regain control when the intense release of emotion may lead her to feel out of control. Unless the psychotherapist is also adequately trained to engage in body-work techniques, the use of an adjunctive therapist is necessary. Ideally, consent for the psychotherapist to consult with the body-work therapist allows for better integration of the work. Also, working conjointly can allow immediate processing of the body work by the therapist with whom there is a trusted and knowledgeable relationship.

Having made a decision to include body work in the overall treatment package, careful consideration should be given to selecting the type. Some approaches involve physical pain; others may be routinely conducted while only partially clothed. It is of utmost importance that whatever approach is selected that every effort is made to avoid revictimizing the battered woman.

Self-Help Groups

Self-help groups, such as women's consciousness raising or support groups, 12-step programs (e.g., Alcoholics Anonymous, Narcotics Anonymous, Overeaters Anonymous, Incest Survivors Anonymous, Alanon and Adult Children of Alcoholics Alanon) also may prove to be useful adjuncts to psychotherapy.

Specific advantages of 12-step programs include (1) the availability of a network of supportive individuals on a 24-hour, 7-day a week, 365-day a year basis through the use of the tools in the program such as sponsorship, phone contacts, and meetings; (2) focus on spirituality which typically is lacking in psychotherapy approaches, thus incorporating an added dimension helpful in the healing process; (3) the program is offered at no cost, thus making it available to anyone regardless of economic resources; (4) the program is based on a self-help, peer-support model, with a focus on self-direction and self-responsibility, thus reducing the likelihood of exploitation by "experts" or persons in power positions; (5) the program is based on the notion that healing occurs over the course of a lifetime, thus providing an ongoing source of support and personal growth; and (6) the program places a strong emphasis on phenomenology, not on intellectual understanding, thus supporting validation of the individual's personal experience. Further, the use of 12-step programs lessens the dependency on the therapist and provides the client with an opportunity for informal contact with others who have been through and survived similar experiences.

Disadvantages of 12-step programs include the patriarchal orientation from which the literature is written, including a male-referenced god. There have been some attempts to rewrite the 12-steps from a perspective that empowers women (Kasl, 1990). Other problems include the risk that some women will perceive that they are being blamed for the behavior of their partner when they may be asked to examine the areas in which they can take responsibility for their own behavior. Further, because there are all kinds of people who participate in 12-step programs at all levels of recovery, vulnerable or naive clients may be at particular risk, for example, concerning boundary violations and other means of exploitation.

Healing Rituals

Few cultural rituals for healing, growth, and psychic integration exist in mainstream American culture today. There has been little discussion of formal healing rituals for battered women. However, rituals originating from specific cultural contexts have been suggested as effective in the healing process. For example, ritualistic dancing, singing, and sweatlodge healing ceremonies for incest survivors within a Native American community (Hodgson, 1990) and among Vietnam veterans (Wilson, 1989) have been reported. Developing group rituals around special events (e.g., holidays, birthdays, graduation, divorce, marriage) has been suggested for adult survivors of incest (Courtois, 1988). The use of healing rituals in various forms may provide an important arena for further development of methods of recovery from the trauma of victimization by intimate violence.

10

Issues for the Professional Working with Abuse

Working with victims requires not only a broad knowledge base and a wide variety of clinical and advocacy skills, but also an attention to oneself as a person involved in the therapeutic process. Ochberg (1988) states:

> Our work calls on us to confront, with our patients and within ourselves, extraordinary human experiences. This confrontation is profoundly humbling in that at all times these experiences challenge the limits of our humanity and our view of the world we live in. No matter how overwhelmingly tragic and painful, or how shocking and shameful, comprehending and integrating victimization are ultimately solidly grounding and thereby liberating both for our patients and for ourselves. (p. 293)

There is no professional experience more demanding than working with trauma victims. The focus must simultaneously be on the trauma victim's needs and on one's own reactions and responses to working in that situation.

Issues presented in this chapter extend beyond the traditional definition of the term countertransference, namely the unresolved or unconscious conflicts of the therapist, which are triggered in the therapy process. This chapter presents a range of issues for consideration by therapists and their supervisors when working with survivors of trauma and victimization. These issues include vicarious victimization of the therapist when working with trauma victims, attitudes and values of the therapist, and personal victimization history of the therapist.

VICARIOUS TRAUMATIZATION

Work within the victimization literature has focused on painful feelings, images, and thoughts that can accompany work with trauma victims

(McCann & Pearlman, 1990). Symptoms paralleling posttraumatic response (e.g., guilt, rage, dread and horror, grief and mourning, shame, inability to contain intense emotions, nightmares, alienation, irritability, psychophysiologic reactions) have been identified in therapists working with Holocaust survivors (Danieli, 1988), Vietnam veterans (Lindy, 1988), and adult survivors of incest (Briere, 1989; Courtois, 1988).

When working with trauma victims, two major categories of therapist countertransference issues include overidentification with the victim and emotionally distanced and detached reactions (Courtois, 1988; Herman, 1988; Wilson, 1989). Overidentification may lead to feelings of becoming overwhelmed, hopeless, and despairing, similar to the victim client's reactions. When these responses occur, the therapist may inadvertently adopt a role of rescuer or liberator (Courtois, 1988), setting an agenda for the client with whom she may or may not concur. Emotionally distanced and detached reactions to the victim client may originate from identification with the offender (Herman, 1988) or from a strong reaction of fear, anxiety, or empathic distress (Wilson, 1989). The therapist who experiences these responses may be at risk for revictimizing the battered woman through rigid, authoritarian, psychologically controlling, and abusive behavior.

Although these various emotional reactions are normal responses to the exposure to traumatic events presented by clients, they need to be carefully monitored to minimize their negative impact on the ongoing therapeutic process and therefore also on the client. At times, it may be quite useful to openly express an emotional response to the battered woman's report of violence and abuse; genuine empathy may have a powerful therapeutic effect (Jordan, 1984). However, at other times, the therapist's own emotional response may negatively interfere in the therapeutic process. For example, a therapist's expression of anger may frighten the battered woman, triggering her to defend her abusive partner. Alternatively, a therapist's tearfulness or response of overwhelming emotion may lead the battered woman to comfort and attempt to rescue the therapist, thereby deflecting the focus from herself as the client.

On the other hand, absolute neutrality or lack of emotional response is not an effective therapeutic option with battered women, or other victims of intimate violence. The professional, stoic, and aloof therapeutic stance communicates that the battered woman's experience of violence and abuse demands no response. Acknowledgement of the injustice done to her is essential (Fortune, 1987) and requires something more than a neutral stance in order to be effectively communicated. Holding to an emotionally distant and detached position with a battered client may simply be a therapist's attempt to cover her or his own difficulty in the situation and to give an appearance of competence and control.

The term vicarious traumatization (McCann & Pearlman, 1990, p. 133) has been used to refer to the "enduring psychological consequences for therapists of exposure to the traumatic experiences of victim clients." Accordingly, these effects are disruptive and painful and can persist for months or years. Based on constructivist self-development theory (McCann & Pearlman, 1990), therapists may experience disruptions in cognitive schemas, that is, cognitive manifestations of psychological needs that include beliefs, expectations, and assumptions about the world (McCann, Pearlman, Sakheim, & Abrahamson, 1988; McCann, Sakheim, & Abrahamson, 1988). The areas identified by McCann and Pearlman (1990) relevant to therapists' reactions when working with victims include dependency/trust, safety, power, independence, esteem, intimacy, and frame of reference. Shifts in these schemas resulting from work with victims, among other things, may be used to explain the emotional distress of therapists.

For example, therapists may develop some of the following perspectives: (1) all men batter or abuse their wives and girlfriends (trust), (2) there is never a safe place in the world (safety), (3) the therapist is helpless to take care of the self or to help others (power) or alternatively that she or he has great power to rescue victims and change others (power), (4) one's personal freedom is limited (independence), (5) all men are unworthy (esteem), (6) working with victims sets one apart from others (intimacy), or (7) the battered woman is to blame for her victimization or that speculating about the motives of the batterer is important when talking with the battered woman (frame of reference). These and other cognitive shifts that result from vicarious exposure to traumatic events may create emotional distress described earlier (e.g., rage, grief, guilt). Further, they interfere with effective functioning in the role of therapist. In some cases, the cognitive shifts may be from an overly naive view of the world (e.g., "people don't do such things to each other") to a more realistic one (e.g., "some intimate partners inflict serious, and sometimes lethal, harm) compared to an unrealistic belief (e.g., "all men hit their female intimate partners"). Recognizing naive beliefs and determining whether the shifts in cognitive schemata are dysfunctional for the battered woman is important.

RISK TO THE THERAPIST

Actual physical risk may exist for the therapist whose client's partner is angered, for example, by changes that the battered woman is making, including plans to leave the abusive relationship (Douglas, 1987). Explicit threats to harm the therapist must be taken seriously, as should any other indication that the batterer may actually do harm. Professionals who testify in court on behalf of a battered woman (e.g., for the prosecution in a criminal case against the batterer, for the defense when the battered woman has injured or killed her abusive partner, in a divorce case when the battered woman is fighting to remove child custody or visitation from her abusive partner) must also consider the risk of actual physical danger from the batterer or someone acting on his behalf.

Of course, it is essential that the therapist carefully consider the personal impact of actual threats and potential risks on oneself as well as the implications for working with the battered woman. The therapist who takes the stance of "I'm not afraid of anything," or "he can't hurt me" communicates an unrealistic image to the battered woman and models a position of denial and minimization of the potential danger. A battered woman's use of denial and minimization in similar circumstances could substantially increase her risk of physical injury or even death. In addition, such a position may also lead the therapist to avoid taking precautions necessary to remain safe. Conversely, the therapist who overreacts and appears out of control in response to a batterer's actions models a position of helplessness. The impact on the battered woman of the latter reaction could include withdrawal from therapy in order to protect the therapist and an increased sense of hopelessness, both of which could increase the danger to her. Some therapists may inadvertently blame battered women for the risks that result from their work in this area.

Other considerations of danger should be taken into account. Often it is difficult to protect the identity of the therapist and the office location when the battered woman is seen at a clinic or professional office setting. It is for this reason that some battered women's shelters do not reveal their location to the public. Explicit safety planning should be done for therapists as well as for clients and may include plans for going to and from the car, meeting clients in the waiting room, and dealing with the batterer's unexpected intrusion into the office. Care not to publicize one's telephone number or home address is important, although it is not particularly difficult for someone to obtain this information. Recently available caller-identification services offered by telephone companies place therapists at unusual risk. Active efforts to lobby against the availability of these services or the introduction of certain precautions has been made on behalf of professionals working in problem areas (e.g., domestic violence, sexual abuse) that incur potential physical risks.

ATTITUDES AND VALUES OF THE PROFESSIONAL

The attitudes and values of the professional working with the battered woman are important issues for examination. Attitudes concerning emotional intimacy and management of interpersonal power in relationships may impact heavily on the therapist's style; furthermore, these issues may be gender-related (Briere, 1989) or they may be formed through experiences other than those based solely on gender.

Given the inherently personal nature of physical, sexual, and psychological abuse and emotional responses to it, issues of intimacy in the therapeutic relationship are particularly important when working with battered women and other victims of intimate violence. The therapist's tolerance for emotional intimacy will influence the level of self-disclosure and emotional expression available to the client. For example, a client's reluctance to discuss marital rape or severe psychological abuse may be influenced by the therapist's inadvertent communication that the intimacy level that such a discussion entails is not acceptable or is too uncomfortable. It is also important that the therapist not push for disclosure (e.g., of marital rape or degrading verbal abuse) or emotional expression (e.g., of vulnerability, anger, pain) at too intimate a level before the client is comfortable with it. Monitoring the therapeutic relationship is paramount to guard against the therapist's use of it for meeting her or his own intimacy needs. While attending to the potential for exploiting the client is essential when working with all clients, it is especially important with a client who comes with the vulnerabilities inherent to a victimization history. Issues of emotional intimacy may be viewed quite differently by male and female therapists (Briere, 1989) working with battered and sexually abused women and should be addressed accordingly in the supervision process.

The therapist may need to feel in control at all times. This may result in the use of controlling tactics that mimic those of the batterer. For example, the overcontrolling therapist may dictate the agenda for the therapy session rather than allowing interventions to be guided by the client's own needs. In other areas, the therapist may assume more control and authority than is necessary or useful, due simply to the therapist's need to feel a sense of (illusory) competence. I have been told by battered women about former therapists who refused to see them as long as they remained with the battering partner. Although the intent of such a therapist response may be to help, the effect is to coerce the client into certain behavior by threatening withdrawal of support and alliance if she fails to comply. The process of using power in this way undermines self-determination by the battered woman and potentially creates an unhealthy dependency on the therapist who may be seen as the one who knows what she should do. The parallel to the batterer's use of power and control in the abusive relationship is remarkable.

Beliefs about the acceptability of violence in intimate relationships and about violence toward women in general are basic areas of importance for the therapist to examine in terms of the therapist's role (Douglas & Strom, 1987). Some therapists miss the problem of abuse in relationships altogether because they fail to regard the client's mention of a slap, hit, their partner's wild temper, or even more subtle cues as possible indicators of abuse. Of particular concern is the failure to recognize sexual abuse in intimate relationships. Attitudes that condone a woman's role in intimate relationships as less than equal to that of her partner's form the foundation for acceptance of violence or abuse on some level.

The belief that behavior (i.e., violent or abusive behavior) is caused by the interaction between two parties, a major tenet of systems theory, blames the victim for her partner's abuse rather than attributing responsibility for the use of violence to the batterer (Bograd, 1984; Douglas & Strom, 1987). Questions to the battered woman such as, "What were you doing that led him to hit you?" or "Did you provoke him in some way?" clearly, even if inadvertently, communicate that the battered woman is at least partially responsible. Therapists whose values condone violence are not effective in working with battered women or other victims of violence. Violence initiated by women (e.g., toward partners or children) is equally unacceptable to that initiated by men. Self-defense against the threat of physical harm is, of course, an exception.

Use of language that minimizes or neutralizes violence or abuse also communicates an attitude of condoning violence against the woman client. Referring to a severe beating as "an argument" or forced sex as "having sex" or "making love," for example, grossly distorts the abusive experience and may further strengthen the battered woman's own denial and minimization. Use of clear, overtly explicit language that accurately describes the abuse can be an important intervention. It requires the therapist's ability to recognize the abuse and to introduce it to the client in tolerable doses. Doing so provides the client with a vocabulary as well.

The therapist's belief about the course of therapy with battered women plays an important role in determining her or his expectations about it. Recognition of progress at the client's own pace, not based on the therapist's idea of how fast a battered woman should act to leave her abusive partner, obtain a job to establish economic security, or attain some other goal is essential. Change is a process, not an event. Recognition that each step a client takes toward change in a given direction may be followed by two steps backward helps prevent undue frustration or rejection of the client when she "fails" to make progress according to the therapist's timetable.

VICTIMIZATION HISTORY OF THE PROFESSIONAL

The therapist working with battered women or other victims (or offenders) of intimate abuse may have a personal victimization history that has led to the development of certain attitudes and beliefs such as those stated above. Vicarious traumatization, which may be considered normal, can be exacerbated in a therapist with a victimization history. The previously traumatized therapist may experience the battered woman's account of her physical, sexual, and psychological abuse as revictimization.

Finally, the therapist's conscious or unconscious motivation for selecting the mental health profession, and specifically the specialty of traumatization, may be grounded in a personal victimization history. Such a personal history may serve as an important foundation from which to establish genuine empathy with the battered woman, although this information is not always shared with a client. One battered woman seeking therapy was adamant about not wanting a formerly battered woman as a therapist. By processing this issue later in therapy, it became apparent that she did not believe that another battered woman would have anything useful to offer her. She clearly saw a victimization history as an indication of failure on the part of the victim and hence the therapist. Other battered women prefer to work with someone whose personal history of battering allows her to feel greater empathy.

It is imperative that the therapist's issues about her or his own victimization are well understood and adequately resolved. The therapist who wants to be a good model for other victims, to "show them how it can be done," may be overly invested in their client's "getting better" in the ways that the therapist, not the client, decides. The therapist may be too identified with an image of "having it all together" to allow human vulnerability to show to the client.

The therapist who has not examined her or his own victimization history, or believes that it is unimportant, is particularly at risk for harming the battered woman client, probably without even recognizing it. The therapist who has not adequately dealt with her or his own victimization history in the course of personal therapy is not in a position to offer effective help.

Supervision is another arena in which dealing with a therapist's abuse history may surface. However, supervision alone is not generally an adequate substitute for personal therapy as the scope of supervision is typically too narrow to adequately address the variety of issues that result from a victimization history. A further consideration is the dual relationship inherent in a supervisory and a therapeutic relationship. Although there can be considerable overlap between the two types of relationships, they are distinct. However, the supervisory context can provide an arena in which issues of power and control between the therapist and battered woman client, as well as between the therapist and supervisor, can be addressed. Identifying power and control issues as they emerge in the therapy or supervision process is one strategy for dealing with these issues. A more direct method of addressing these issues is through the therapist's use of her or his own genogram. By constructing and interpreting a genogram (McGoldrick & Gerson, 1985), patterns of abuse throughout the several generations can be made more obvious. This strategy is often very useful for identifying the therapist's issues of power and control and for discovering how they were developed within her or his own family of origin.

THERAPIST'S SELF-CARE

Therapists working with victims of violence need to make special efforts to protect themselves, for their own benefit and for their client's. This section describes some ways in which this care may be taken.

Supervision

Supervision of work with victims allows for the perspective of another professional to help identify areas of difficulty the therapist may be experiencing, but not necessarily recognizing. For students in training, relatively inexperienced therapists, or therapists whose experience has not been focused on work with victims, supervision by someone with expertise in the field is essential. Traditional psychology training programs typically do not provide adequate preparation for work with victimization. Notably absent is training that helps students examine, and establish a precedent for examining, their personal issues as they influence the therapy process and each individual's role as therapist.

The supervisory relationship is an arena within which power and control issues, gender-role expectations, and attitudes and beliefs will be played out and can be openly explored, given the acceptability of doing so with both the supervisor and therapist. This approach requires the supervisor's willingness to share the self with the therapist supervisee (Dutton, 1991; Dutton-Douglas & Rave, 1990). An emotionally distant and detached stance is as equally ineffective for supervisors working with their supervisees as it is for therapists working with their battered women clients because it does not allow for an exploration of necessary issues. An effective examination of power and control issues within the supervisory relationship demands that the supervisor, as well as the supervisee, be willing to share the interaction process in the relationship. Further, discussion of the supervisor's own therapy failures, as well as successes, requires her or his willingness for disclosure. Of course, establishing appropriate boundaries is an important task in the supervisory, as well as the therapeutic relationship.

Self-Nurturance

Work with victims demands considerable emotional energy. The needs of battered women may sometimes be overwhelming. Self-nurturing activities are critical for the therapist to remain able to work effectively. Self-nurturing can take many forms. Peer support and networking with others working in the field are ways to sustain the ability to work effectively. Support from family and friends is important, of course, but it cannot provide the same validation, feedback, and understanding that is possible from someone who understands the demands of the work.

Self-nurturance for the student therapist is equally important. The supervisor's role includes helping student therapists to develop peer support, this is as important as developing knowledge and skill, especially when working with victims.

Another important self-nurturing activity is providing time for the experiencing and expressing feelings. Activities such as meditating, journal-keeping, or simply reflective thinking allow time for the therapist to become aware of potentially distressing emotions that may have arisen from the work with battered women as clients. Recognizing defenses against vicarious traumatization and developing effective coping strategies requires an awareness of one's emotions.

Finally, basic self-care activities such as adequate rest, nutrition, and exercise are necessary to maintain a healthy mental and physical self. Time for play is equally important in maintaining a balance in one's life. Without such a balance, the therapist is at greater risk for burnout (Deutsch, 1984; Farber & Heifetz, 1982) and decreased effectiveness in working with victim clients.

Personal Therapy

Personal therapy for the therapist, especially during the early years of training, is recommended or required by some doctoral psychology training programs (Council of University Directors of Clinical Psychology, 1990). Personal therapy or personal growth activities (e.g., experiential workshops, retreats) may be helpful throughout one's professional career as a means of sorting through and monitoring personal reactions to clinical material. Personal therapy for therapists with a history of personal victimization is absolutely essential. Otherwise, the therapist can find her\himself helping a client through the course of post-traumatic therapy without ever having traveled that path personally. Understanding the client role based on one's personal experience in it broadens the therapist's ability to develop genuine empathy for the battered woman.

Diverse Professional Responsibilities

An important way to regulate the inevitable emotional reactions that come from working with battered women is to diversify professional responsibilities. This can be accomplished by developing a caseload that includes nontrauma victims. A caseload consisting only of survivors of battering, incest, rape, or other intimate violence demands a level of emotional energy that is difficult to maintain.

Diversity in professional responsibility can be attained by engaging in a variety of professional activities that differ in the nature of the emotional demand they exact. For example, combining therapy with teaching, research, or consultation allows for different levels of interaction with other people at different levels of emotional intensity.

Political Action

Political activism has been a central tenet of interventions rooted in feminist theory (Pence & Shephard, 1988; Rosewater & Walker, 1985; Sturdivant, 1980). Political and social action is required to change the very sources of social oppression that create the victimization from which battered woman suffer (Rosewater & Walker, 1985; Sturdivant, 1980). Further, political action by the therapist helps create a balance between efforts to transform an oppressive society and efforts directed toward transforming the psychological trauma of the individual woman. Balancing energy directed toward both societal and individual concerns helps one to maintain a perspective on the origin of the difficulties that battered women face. Further, social action provides an opportunity to translate the therapist's emotional tension resulting from repeated exposure to intense psychological trauma into potentially productive channels.

The maintenance of well-being for the therapist is as important as the healing of the client in physical, mental, emotional, and spiritual areas. Further, both are not events; they are lifelong processes.

> Learn to trust what is happening. If there is silence, let it grow; something will emerge. If there is a storm, let it rage; it will resolve into calm . . . The wise [therapist] knows how to facilitate the unfolding . . . process, because the [therapist] is also a process. The [client's] process and the [therapist's] process unfold in the same way, according to the same principle. (Heider, 1985, p. 115, substitutions by author.)

Appendix A

Abusive Behavior Observation Checklist (ABOC)

Abusive Observation Checklist (ABOC)

Please indicate how often the following behaviors (1) were done to you <u>by</u> your partner, (2) were done by your <u>to</u> your partner, and (3) were done <u>to</u> you by <u>any</u> previous partner at any time.

	You did to your partner					Partner did to you					Previous partner did to you ever	
	0	1-3	3-10	10-49	>50	0	1-3	3-10	10-49	>50	Yes	No
PHYSICAL ABUSE												
* Threw something at you/him/her												
* Pushed, grabbed, or shoved you/him/her												
Scratched you/him/her												
* Slapped you/him/her												
** Kicked, bit, or hit you/him/her												
** Hit or tried to hit you/him/her with something												
Wrestled you/him/her												
Punched you/him/her somewhere on the body (not face)												
Punched you/him/her in the face												
** Beat you/him/her up												
** Threatened you/him/her with a knife or gun												
** Used a knife or fired a gun												
Pinched you/him/her												
Pulled your/his/her hair												
Attempted to smother, strangle or hang you/him/her with an object												
Put dangerous substance (e.g., gasoline, acid) on your/his/her body												

	You did to your partner					Partner did to you					Previous partner did to you ever	
	0	1-3	3-10	10-49	>50	0	1-3	3-10	10-49	>50	Yes	No
PHYSICAL ABUSE												
Burned your/his/her body												
Physically restrained you/him/her by holding												
Physically restrained by tying you/him/her up												
Dragged or pulled you/him/her												
Used force or threat of force to get you/him/her to eat/drink something												
Used force or threat of force to get you/him/her to take/ingest drugs/alcohol												
Used force or threat of force to restrict you/him/her from eating food/drinking												
Used force or threat of force to restrict you/him/her from using toilet, shower, bath or otherwise attending to hygiene												
Restricted you/him/her from taking prescribed medication												
Restricted you/him/her from obtaining needed medical treatment												
Threw hot liquid on you/him/her												
Used car to attempt to run over you/him/her												
Put excrement on your/his/her body												
INJURY												
Lost hair												
Minor cuts												

	You did to your partner					Partner did to you					Previous partner did to you ever	
	0	1-3	3-10	10-49	>50	0	1-3	3-10	10-49	>50	Yes	No
INJURY												
Severe cuts												
Minor burns												
Severe burns												
Minor bruises												
Severe bruises												
Black eye(s)												
Sprains/strains												
Lost teeth												
Human bite												
Broken eardrum												
Joint or spinal cord injury												
Broken nose or jaw												
Other broken bones, including ribs												
Concussion												
Internal injury												
Permanent injury (blindness, loss of hearing, disfigurement, chronic pain)												
You/He/She required no medical treatment												
You/He/She required medical treatment, but received none												
You/He/She required medical treatment/ outpatient or clinic												

	You did to your partner					Partner did to you					Previous partner did to you ever	
	0	1-3	3-10	10-49	>50	0	1-3	3-10	10-49	>50	Yes	No
INJURY												
You/He/She required medical treatment/EMR												
You/He/She required hospitalization												
SEXUAL ABUSE												
Type of unwanted sexual behavior												
Vaginal intercourse												
Fellatio												
Cunnilingus												
Anal intercourse												
Sexual behavior with another adult (not partner)												
Sexual behavior with a child (below 18 years)												
Watched nudity or sexual behavior involving another												
Viewed pornographic film, photographs												
Filmed you/him/her during sexual activity												
Others watched you/him/her while engaging in sexual activity												
Forced nudity												
Required to dress in sexually provocative clothing												
Unwanted objects were inserted into your/his/her vagina/rectum												

	You did to your partner					Partner did to you					Previous partner did to you ever	
	0	1-3	3-10	10-49	>50	0	1-3	3-10	10-49	>50	Yes	No
Type of unwanted sexual behavior												
Required to be involved with an animal in a sexual way												
Type of force/coercion used to gain compliance												
Actual physical force												
Threat of physical force to you/him/her or another person												
Threat of negative consequences (other than physical)												
Social pressure to comply sexually (expectations of self/others)												
PSYCHOLOGICAL ABUSE* **												
Coercion and threats												
Made or carried out threats to do something to hurt you/him/her or someone else												
Threatened to kill you/him/her or someone else												
Threatened to leave relationship												
He/She threatened to commit suicide												
Threatened to report you/him/her to welfare, social services, police												
Attempted to get you/him/her to drop charges against the abuser												
Attempted to get/got you/him/her to engage in illegal activities												

	You did to your partner					Partner did to you					Previous partner did to you ever	
	0	1-3	3-10	10-49	>50	0	1-3	3-10	10-49	>50	Yes	No
Intimidation												
Instilled fear in you/him/her by looks, gestures, actions												
Smashed objects												
Destroyed your/his/her property												
Abused your/his/her family pets												
Displayed weapons												
Emotional abuse												
Insulted you/him/her or used "put downs"												
Called you/him/her names												
Attempted to make you/him/her feel crazy												
Humiliated you/him/her with words or gestures												
Attempted to make you/him/her feel guilty												
Verbally raged at you/him/her												
Engaged in extramarital affairs												
Withheld sex from you/him/her												
Isolation												
Attempted to control what you/he/she did												
Attempted to control what you/he/she read/ watched on TV or listened to												

	You did to your partner					Partner did to you					Previous partner did to you ever	
	0	1-3	3-10	10-49	>50	0	1-3	3-10	10-49	>50	Yes	No
Isolation												
Attempted to limit your/his/her involvement with others												
Used jealousy to justify actions against you/him/her												
Restricted your/his/her use of the phone												
Restricted your/his/her leaving the house												
Minimization, denial and blaming												
Minimized abuse and not take your/his/her concerns about it seriously												
Denied that the abuse happened												
Blamed you/him/her for the abuse												
Shifted responsibility for abusive behavior onto someone else												
Use of children to control you												
Attempted to make you/him/her feel guilty about children												
Used children to relay messages to you/him/her												
Used visitation to harass you/him/her												
Threatened to take children away (e.g., custody, kidnapping) from you/him/her												
Threatened to abuse children												
Use of male privilege												
Treated you/him/her like a "servant"												

	You did to your partner					Partner did to you					Previous partner did to you ever	
	0	1-3	3-10	10-49	>50	0	1-3	3-10	10-49	>50	Yes	No
Use of male privilege												
Made major decisions without your/his/her equal participation												
Acted like the "master of the castle"												
Unilaterally defined male/female roles												
Economic/Resource Abuse												
Attempted to prevent you/him/her from getting/keeping job												
Attempted to prevent you/him/her from going to school												
Required you/him/her to ask for money												
Controlled the money by giving you an allowance												
Took money from you/him/her												
Controlled your use of money												
Withheld information about/access to family resources												
Abandoned you/him/her from car during travel												
Restricted your/his/her access to transportation												
Locked you/him/her out of house												

*Overall Violence and **Severe Violence index items from the Conflict Tactics Scale (Straus, 1979). See Straus and Gelles (1990) for scoring instructions.

***Categories of psychological abuse taken from the Power and Control Wheel (Pence & Paymar, 1985).

	You did to your partner					Partner did to you					Previous partner did to you ever	
	0	1-3	3-10	10-49	>50	0	1-3	3-10	10-49	>50	Yes	No
Other Violence/Abuse												

Appendix B

Questionnaires for Assessing Battered Woman's Cognitions about Violence

ATTRIBUTION QUESTIONNAIRE

Name ____

(First Name and Last Initial Only)

Please read each item carefully. Write your answer in the space provided for #1 and #9. For each question make a mark on the line closest to the answer that most fits you or your circumstances.

(1) What is the major cause of the violence, abuse and control in your relationship? __________

____

(2) Is the cause of the violence due to something about you or something about your partner? (circle one)

Totally due to partner — Totally due to me

1---------- 2------------ 3----------- 4----------- 5----------- 6------------7

(3) In the future, will this cause continue to be present?

Never again be present — Always will be present

1---------- 2------------ 3----------- 4----------- 5----------- 6------------7

(4) Does the cause of the violence just influence the occurrence of violence or does it also influence other areas of your life?

Just the violence — All situations

1---------- 2------------ 3----------- 4----------- 5----------- 6------------7

(5) Is changing the violent or abuse behavior something which is

Totally my partner's job — Totally my job

1---------- 2------------ 3----------- 4----------- 5----------- 6------------7

(6) How likely do you believe that some behavior of yours will be effective in stopping future violence with your partner?

Not at all likely — Totally likely

1---------- 2------------ 3----------- 4----------- 5----------- 6------------7

(7) How likely do you think it is that the violence with this partner will occur again at any point in the future?

Not at all likely — Totally likely

1---------- 2------------ 3----------- 4----------- 5----------- 6------------7

(8) How able do you feel you are to make yourself happy?

Not at all able — Totally able

1---------- 2------------ 3----------- 4----------- 5----------- 6------------7

(9) What could you do to make yourself happy ______________________________

____

____

APPRAISAL OF VIOLENT SITUATION

Name ____
(First Name and Last Initial Only)

Please read each item carefully and circle your answer, responding as honestly as you can.

(1) How severe would you rate the violence which has occurred toward you by your partner/spouse?

Mild	Moderate	Severe
1	2	3

(2) How severe would you rate the violence which has occurred toward your partner/spouse by you?

Mild	Moderate	Severe
1	2	3

(3) How able by any means do you see yourself being able to stop the violence against you by your partner/spouse in the future?

Little or No Ability	Some Ability	Very Much Able
1	2	3

How? ____

____

(4) How able do you see yourself being able to control your violence against your partner/spouse in the future?

Little or No Ability	Some Ability	Very Much Able
1	2	3

How? ____

____

(5) How likely do you believe that the violence between you and your partner/spouse might lead to serious physical harm or possible death for you?

Not at all Likely	Somewhat Likely	Very Likely
1	2	3

(6) How likely do you believe that the violence between you and your partner/spouse might lead to serious physical harm or possible death for your partner?

Not at all Likely	Somewhat Likely	Very Likely
1	2	3

(7) Other Comments about how you see the violence in your family.

____

____

Appendix C

Response to Violence Inventory: Strategies to Escape, Avoid, and Survive Abuse

Response to Violence Inventory: Strategies to Escape, Avoid, and Survive Abuse

Name ______________________________ Date ________________________

Instructions: Ask the victim the frequency with which she has used each particular strategy. Then ask her what happened as a result of having used that strategy. Next ask her to rate the effectiveness of the strategy for protecting herself from violence. Finally, if the woman did *not* use the strategy, ask why she did not chose to do so.

Frequency	Effectiveness ratings	
0	-2	Very much worse
1-2	-1	Somewhat worse
3-10	0	No effect
11-20	+1	Somewhat helpful
>20	+2	Very much helpful

Frequency Effectiveness

_____ 1. Calling police _____

What happened?

If not used, why not?

_____ 2. Initiating contact/cooperating with state attorney to criminally prosecute batterer _____

What happened?

If not used, why not?

____ 3. Seek protective injunction order ____

What happened?

If not used, why not?

____ 4. Seek divorce action ____

What happened?

If not used, why not?

____ 5. Go to shelter ____

What happened?

If not used, why not?

____ 6. Seek help mental health professional ____

What happened?

If not used, why not?

____ 7. Seek help clergy or spiritual leader ____

What happened?

If not used, why not?

____ 8. Seek help–social services ____

What happened?

If not used, why not?

____ 9. Seek help-women's support group ____

What happened?

If not used, why not?

____ 10. Seek help-self-help or other group ____

What happened?

If not used, why not?

____ 11. Tell others about abuse/seek help to intervene ____

What happened?

If not used, why not?

____ 12. Escaping threatening/violent situation ____

What happened?

If not used, why not?

____ 13. Separation ____

What happened?

If not used, why not?

____ 14. Hiding/Disguising ____

What happened?

If not used, why not?

____ 15. Compliance with demands/anticipation of demands ____

What happened?

If not used, why not?

____ 16. Fighting back ____

What happened?

If not used, why not?

____ 17. Use children to protect/escape ____

What happened?

If not used, why not?

____ 18. Other strategies to escape, avoid, protect against abuse or violence ____

What specific strategies?

What happened?

Appendix D

Normative Data from a Sample of Battered Women on Measures of Psychological Effects of Trauma

TABLE D.1 Normative Mean Scores and SD on the Impact of Event Scale for Sample of Battered Women

	Partner abuse		Prior history of sexual abuse		Total sample
Measure	Physical abuse only (*n* = 88)	Physical and sexual abuse (*n* = 50)	No prior abuse (*n* = 51)	Prior abuse (*n* = 87)	(*n* = 162)
Impact of Event scale					
Total score	28.12 (19.01)	44.40 (15.96)	24.00 (19.23)	39.90 (17.32)	34.75 (19.52)
Avoidance subscale	15.19 (10.69)	23.04 (9.63)	13.71 (11.46)	20.55 (9.86)	18.46 (11.04)
Intrusion subscale	12.84 (9.96)	21.56 (8.67)	10.08 (8.71)	19.44 (9.72)	16.29 (10.21)

TABLE D.2 Normative T-score Mean and SD on the MMPI for Sample of Battered Women

Measure	Partner abuse $n = 143$		Prior history of sexual abuse $n = 143$		Total sample $n = 143$
	Physical abuse only ($n = 93$)	Physical and sexual abuse ($n = 50$)	No prior abuse ($n = 50$)	Prior abuse ($n = 93$)	
Validity scales					
L	53.45 (8.46)	52.64 (8.25)	53.54 (9.02)	52.97 (8.04)	53.17 (8.37)
F	60.92 (11.83)	64.98 (15.51)	59.12 (11.35)	64.08 (14.02)	62.34 (13.32)
K	53.02 (8.95)	51.67 (9.14)	52.80 (8.28)	52.41 (9.42)	52.54 (9.01)
Clinical scales					
Sc 1	57.74 (13.23)	66.10 (14.27)	54.12 (10.68)	64.18 (14.56)	60.66 (14.14)
Sc 2	65.12 (14.39)	72.68 (17.15)	63.24 (13.31)	70.19 (16.50)	67.76 (15.77)
Sc 3	62.99 (12.62)	68.94 (12.36)	59.04 (10.01)	68.31 (13.02)	65.07 (12.81)
Sc 4	70.70 (12.67)	75.50 (11.66)	68.86 (11.44)	74.27 (12.70)	72.38 (12.50)
Sc 5	49.15 (9.93)	47.84 (8.08)	50.18 (9.32)	47.89 (9.07)	48.69 (9.32)
Sc 6	62.96 (12.26)	70.20 (16.30)	61.74 (11.86)	67.50 (11.96)	65.49 (14.18)
Sc 7	60.18 (12.25)	67.12 (16.04)	57.60 (11.95)	65.30 (14.39)	62.61 (14.04)
Sc 8	62.89 (14.59)	73.22 (20.05)	59.64 (12.58)	70.19 (18.47)	66.50 (17.35)
Sc 9	61.71 (10.22)	60.56 (12.04)	59.70 (9.45)	62.17 (11.50)	61.31 (10.86)
Sc 0	56.57 (10.66)	62.06 (12.30)	57.36 (11.72)	59.10 (11.43)	58.49 (11.52)
Supplementary scales					
Keane PTSD	20.32 (7.88)	24.47 (10.37)	19.48 (7.47)	23.03 (9.57)	21.77 (9.02)
TR index	1.55 (1.90)	2.02 (1.98)	1.34 (1.89)	1.91 (1.94)	1.71 (1.93)
Carelessness	2.39 (1.50)	2.40 (1.40)	2.26 (1.60)	2.46 (1.39)	2.39 (1.46)
Cannot say	2.15 (3.78)	3.14 (4.61)	1.64 (3.12)	2.96 (4.45)	2.50 (4.07)
Gough dissimulation	57.86 (13.52)	64.58 (16.39)	55.66 (13.40)	62.66 (15.13)	60.21 (14.88)

TABLE D.2 (continued)

Measure	Partner abuse $n = 143$: Physical abuse only ($n = 93$)	Partner abuse $n = 143$: Physical and sexual abuse ($n = 50$)	Prior history of sexual abuse $n = 143$: No prior abuse ($n = 50$)	Prior history of sexual abuse $n = 143$: Prior abuse ($n = 93$)	Total sample $n = 143$
Positive	51.65	48.72	52.10	49.83	50.62
malingering	(11.54)	(10.87)	(12.97)	(10.38)	(11.35)
	52.28	57.96	51.72	55.63	54.27
Welsh anxiety	(11.74)	(13.37)	(12.21)	(12.63)	(12.58)
Welsh	68.11	68.68	68.12	68.41	68.31
repression	(11.69)	(11.23)	(11.94)	(11.31)	(11.49)
	53.53	49.02	53.44	51.15	51.95
Dominance	(10.45)	(11.58)	(9.24)	(11.85)	(11.03)
	53.86	59.32	52.90	57.31	55.77
Dependency	(11.59)	(12.76)	(12.34)	(11.98)	(12.25)
	64.03	61.50	63.76	62.82	63.15
McAndrews	(11.62)	(13.19)	(11.66)	(12.54)	(12.21)
	57.55	47.98	59.60	51.30	54.20
Ego strength	(11.93)	(15.94)	(11.30)	(14.79)	(14.20)

TABLE D.3 Normative Raw Mean Scores and SD on the SCL-90-R for a Sample of Battered Women

	Partner abuse		Prior history of sexual abuse		Total sample
Measure	Physical abuse only (*n* = 98)	Physical and sexual abuse (*n* = 53)	No prior abuse (*n* = 58)	Prior abuse (*n* = 93)	(*n* = 151)
Global measures					
GSI*	1.04	1.59	.87	1.46	1.23
	(.70)	(.78)	(.62)	(.77)	(.77)
PSDI	1.89	2.30	1.79	2.18	2.03
	(.60)	(.61)	(.60)	(.61)	(.63)
PST	44.85	59.53	39.02	56.85	50
	(21.84)	(18.92)	(20.82)	(19.84)	(21.95)
PTSD**	1.00	1.61	.81	1.46	1.21
	(.74)	(.87)	(.66)	(.84)	(.84)
Dissoc***	.55	1.32	.29	1.12	.70
	(.68)	(.74)	(.58)	(.67)	(.74)
Clinical subscales					
SOM	.91	1.38	.78	1.26	1.08
	(.76)	(.87)	(.71)	(.84)	(.83)
OC	1.16	1.76	1.01	1.60	1.38
	(.89)	(.96)	(.86)	(.94)	(.96)
INT	1.10	1.70	.94	1.54	1.31
	(.85)	(1.02)	(.82)	(.96)	(.95)
DEP	1.48	2.11	1.27	1.97	1.70
	(.94)	(.91)	(.91)	(.92)	(.98)
ANX	1.04	1.76	.87	1.54	1.29
	(.76)	(.99)	(.74)	(.92)	(.92)
HOS	1.09	1.45	.87	1.43	1.22
	(.94)	(.82)	(.81)	(.90)	(.91)
PHOB	.47	.88	.37	.77	.62
	(.59)	(.89)	(.45)	(.83)	(.73)
PAR	1.09	1.59	.91	1.49	1.27
	(.78)	(.84)	(.75)	(.82)	(.84)
PSY	.75	1.14	.57	1.08	.88
	(.74)	(.85)	(.64)	(.83)	(.80)

* The table abbreviations stand for the following: GSI = Global Symptom Index; PSDI = Positive Symptom Distress Index; PST = Positive Symptom Total; PTSD = Crime-related Post-Traumatic Stress Disorder Index; Dissoc = Dissociative Index; SOM = Somatization; OC = Obsessive-Compulsive; INT = Interpersonal Sensitivity; DEP = Depression; ANX = Anxiety; HOS = Hostility; PHOB = Phobic Anxiety; PAR = Paranoid Ideation; PSY = Psychoticism.

**Saunders et al., 1990.

***Briere, J., & Runtz, M. (1988). Symptomology associated with childhood sexual victimization in a nonclinical adult sample. *Child Abuse and Neglect*, *12*, 51–59.

TABLE D.4 Normative Raw Score Mean and SD on the Modified Fear Survey III for a Sample of Battered Women

	Partner abuse		Prior history of sexual abuse		Total sample
	Physical abuse only ($n = 107$)	Physical and sexual abuse ($n = 68$)	No prior abuse ($n = 64$)	Prior abuse ($n = 111$)	($n = 175$)
Modified Fear Survey—	235.	300.07	232.33	276.40	260.28
total score	(68.19)	(72.17)	(69.89)	(75.76)	(76.48)
Animal	16.13	20.00	16.56	18.25	17.63
	(6.14)	(7.30)	(6.46)	(7.04)	(6.86)
Tissues	41.42	49.97	41.17	46.80	44.74
	(13.42)	(13.83)	(13.74)	(14.07)	(14.17)
Classic	27.56	34.68	27.55	31.93	30.33
	(10.17)	(11.18)	(10.51)	(11.16)	(11.10)
Social	38.48	51.40	37.41	47.01	43.50
	(13.40)	(14.19)	(13.66)	(14.76)	(15.06)
Misc.	24.08	30.60	23.53	28.40	26.62
	(8.23)	(8.57)	(8.46)	(8.74)	(8.93)
Failures	39.28	51.98	37.30	48.21	44.22
	(14.94)	(14.33)	(15.11)	(15.07)	(15.94)
Rape	86.07	112.72	85.69	102.62	96.43
	(25.81)	(30.07)	(25.44)	(31.38)	(30.39)

TABLE D.5 Normative Mean and SD on the Interpersonal Support Evaluation List for a Sample of Battered Women

	Partner abuse		Prior history of sexual abuse		Total sample
	Physical abuse only ($n = 88$)	Physical and sexual abuse ($n = 48$)	No prior abuse ($n = 50$)	Prior abuse ($n = 86$)	($n = 136$)
Interpersonal support	28.73	24.77	29.52	26.06	27.33
evaluation list—total	(8.58)	(9.84)	(8.51)	(9.41)	(9.21)
Appraisal	6.57	5.92	6.69	6.13	6.34
	(1.29)	(2.84)	(2.48)	(2.80)	(2.69)
Belonging	7.17	5.79	7.48	6.22	6.68
	(2.63)	(3.50)	(2.48)	(3.22)	(3.03)
Tangible	7.91	7.21	7.98	7.48	7.67
	(2.45)	(2.78)	(2.41)	(2.67)	(2.58)
Self-esteem	7.17	5.96	7.42	6.34	6.75
	(2.58)	(2.69)	(2.61)	(2.64)	(2.67)

TABLE D.6 Normative Mean and SD on Battered Women's Cognition Related to Battery

Measure	Partner abuse: Physical abuse only	Partner abuse: Physical and sexual abuse	Prior history of sexual abuse: No prior abuse	Prior history of sexual abuse: Prior abuse	Total sample
Appraisal of Violence Questionnaire					
Appraisal severity of partner's violence	2.18 (.75) (n = 158)	2.50 (.62) (n = 89)	2.17 (.72) (n = 96)	2.38 (.71) (n = 151)	2.30 (.72) (n = 247)
Appraisal Severity of own violence	1.44 (.69) (n = 113)	1.26 (.55) (n = 57)	1.48 (.71) (n = 71)	1.31 (.60) (n = 99)	1.38 (.65) (n = 170)
Appraisal ability to stop partner's violence	2.10 (.73) (n = 154)	1.88 (.73) (n = 88)	2.13 (.76) (n = 92)	1.96 (.72) (n = 150)	2.02 (.74) (n = 242)
Violence likely to be lethal for client	1.76 (.76) (n = 62)	2.38 (.67) (n = 21)	1.68 (.83) (n = 35)	2.08 (.71) (n = 48)	1.92 (.78) (n = 83)
Violence likely to be lethal to partner	1.40 (.71) (n = 55)	1.95 (.82) (n = 20)	1.35 (.75) (n = 31)	1.68 (.77) (n = 44)	1.55 (.78) (n = 75)
Attribution of Violence Questionnaire					
Internal attribution of violence	3.02 (1.58) (n = 160)	2.94 (1.94) (n = 86)	2.95 (1.52) (n = 96)	3.02 (1.83) (n = 150)	2.99 (1.71) (n = 246)
Stable attribution of violence	3.78 (2.21) (n = 153)	4.47 (2.28) (n = 87)	3.66 (2.26) (n = 93)	4.39 (2.24) (n = 147)	4.10 (2.27) (n = 240)
Global attribution of violence	4.80 (2.19) (n = 157)	5.80 (1.61) (n = 83)	4.37 (2.39) (n = 92)	5.62 (1.67) (n = 148)	5.14 (2.07) (n = 240)
Belief that violence will recur	4.21 (2.34) (n = 163)	5.10 (2.07) (n = 89)	3.96 (2.41) (n = 98)	4.88 (2.14) (n = 154)	4.52 (2.29) (n = 252)

Appendix E

Psychological Evaluation Report

Identifying Information
Name
Date of Birth
Date of Evaluation
Case No: [Applicable if court case]

REFERRAL

Make a statement indicating that [client name] was referred for psychological evaluation by [referring source] for the purpose of [state reason for evaluation] *or* indicate that evaluation was performed as part of the standard assessment procedure of [identify treatment program or clinic]. Reasons for evaluation may include (1) treatment planning or (2) for use in court (e.g., divorce or custody hearing, criminal trial, civil tort action). If possible, state specific referral question to be answered by evaluation. Also indicate the date(s), total time required, and location of the evaluation.

EVALUATION METHODS

List the evaluation methods used, for example:

Clinical interview
Minnesota Multiphasic Personality Inventory (MMPI-2)

Symptom Checklist (SCL-90-R)
Impact of Events Scale (IES)

If other materials or documents were reviewed as part of the evaluation, list them as additional, for example:

Review of Documents

[City name] Police Report, Date, Officer name
Hospital], Emergency Room Intake Report/ Date, Physician
Psychotherapy Progress Notes, Date, [Name prior therapist]

DESCRIPTION AND BACKGROUND

Provide a brief description of client including age, gender, race, ethnic/cultural status, current marital status, parental status, living arrangement, current employment status, highest educational level, current physical disabilities or medical complications.

Provide historical description of *family of origin and childhood/adolescence* beginning from birth, including description of birth parents (age, occupation, any other relevant information such as medical status, drug/alcohol addiction, mental illness), whether they are currently living or deceased (date and cause of death if deceased), siblings (date and cause of death if deceased), description of childhood home (including primary caretakers; presence or absence of others living in the childhood home; social class; ethnic, cultural, or religious influence; nature of familial relationships including history of abuse between parents; emotional climate in home; extended family network), school performance, peer and dating relationships, childhood or adolescent drug and alcohol use, legal involvement, employment history; significant personal/familial medical history; personal/familial history of psychotherapy or counseling. Indicate significant life events during childhood and adolescence (dates of births, deaths, marital separations or divorce by parents, graduation from school), including traumatic or stressful events (e.g., accidents, illnesses, physical and/or sexual abuse, early pregnancies, loss of parent or sibling, frequent moves).

Provide historical description of *adulthood* including chronology of significant intimate relationships (e.g., dating, engagements, marriages, love affairs) separations, divorces, chronology of employment and/or adult education history, nature of adulthood relationships with family of origin, peer and social support network, adulthood medical history (including illicit and prescription drug and alcohol use, surgeries, illnesses, pregnancies, births, abortions), adulthood criminal history, adulthood history of psychotherapy or counseling. Include a chronology of significant adulthood life events, including births, deaths, illnesses, traumatic events such as battering and marital rape, sexual harassment, sexual or other criminal assault, major accidents or natural disasters.

Describe nature of victimization history in current/target relationship beginning with a summary statement of prior history (above-described). Provide *overall description* of current/target abuse including the nature of abuse (physical, sexual, psychological), duration in time (from onset to most recent event), date of onset and stage of relationship (e.g., during courtship, prior to marriage while living together, during first pregnancy) of first identifiable event, all specific abusive behaviors (e.g., punch, choke, kick, hold gun to head, use of physical force to engage in fellatio, locked out of house), physical injuries (e.g., black eye, broken nose, bruises, concussion, headache, marks on neck), patterning or frequency of discrete abusive episodes (e.g., weekly, periods of frequent and severe abuse followed by long periods of relatively minor and infrequent abuse; abuse occurred primarily in evening and at night; abuse typically following perpetrator's heavy use of alcohol; abuse escalated during pregnancies), client's efforts to protect self or children from abuse or violence (e.g., call police, hold a knife threateningly, run to neighbor's house, stay quiet) and outcome of those efforts (e.g., abuser stopped when police called, police arrived and arrested client for assault on police officer, police arrived and talked to abuser outside, sexual abuse typically occurred but resulted in no physical injury when client did not physically resist), client's cognitions about the violence (e.g., minimizes it, attributes its cause to self, relates tolerance for some levels of violence).

Provide description of selected *specific or particularly relevant episodes* (e.g., most recent, worst, incident for which criminal charges pending). Provide same information above for specific episode (e.g., specific abusive behaviors, physical injuries, client's effort to protect self or children, outcome of efforts) as well as setting or context for this particular episode (e.g., after birthday party for youngest child in evening, following client's return home later than scheduled, during family gathering at Thanksgiving) and any other relevant information.

TEST RESULTS

Provide an easily understandable statement of the results of each test, questionnaire, or psychological assessment instrument administered. DO NOT USE PSYCHOLOGICAL JARGON AND DO NOT REFER TO SPECIFIC TEST SCORES HERE. USE SEPARATE ATTACHMENT TO SUMMARIZE RAW AND/OR STANDARDIZED TEST SCORES FOR EACH INSTRUMENT. State the results as suggested indications based on the testing data and available normative information, for example:

SCL-90-R

Results of the SCL-90-R suggest that [client's name] is currently feeling depressed and anxious and is experiencing somatic symptoms. Further, results suggest positive screening for Post-Traumatic Stress Disorder. BASE STATEMENTS OF COMPARISONS ON NORMATIVE DATA FOR NON-PATIENT SAMPLE. PERCENTILE SCORES IN COMPARISON TO OTHER NORMATIVE GROUPS (E.G., OUTPATIENT CLINIC SAMPLE, BATTERED WOMEN) SHOULD BE INCLUDED IN SEPARATE ATTACHMENT.

CONCLUSIONS AND FORMULATION

State conclusions and your formulation (e.g. theoretically and empirically-based explanation) of each referral question(s) specifically, for example, (1) Is [client] a battered woman? (2) What are the psychological effects of having been abused? (3) How did [client] protect self and children by using [specific protection, avoidance, escape strategies: e.g., use lethal weapon to protect self; staying in relationship, keeping the abuse a secret; fleeing home leaving children with abuser]? How is the nonuse of particular strategies (e.g., not calling police, not telling family or friends, not leaving relationship) explained? (4) What risk would joint custody following divorce present for [client] and what recommendations are suggested to the court to decrease such risk? (5) What are treatment recommendations? (if applicable).

The formulations should provide a rationale and evidence to support the veracity of each conclusion. The rationale should include a theoretically derived and/or empirically-based formulation to support the conclusions made.

____________________ ________

Name Date

Title

Profession License

References

American Psychiatric Association. (1980). *Diagnostic and statistical manual of mental disorders* (3rd Ed.). Washington, DC: Author.

American Psychiatric Association. (1987). *Diagnostic and statistical manual of mental disorders* (3rd Ed., Revised). Washington, DC: Author.

American Psychiatric Association Task Force. (1991). *DSM-IV options.* Washington, DC: American Psychiatric Press.

American Psychological Association. (1987). *General guidelines for described providers of services.* Washington, DC: Author.

American Psychological Association. (1990). Ethical principles of psychologists (Amended June 2, 1989). *American Psychologist, 45*(3), 390-395.

Arias, I., Samios, M., & O'Leary, K. D. (1987). Prevalence and correlates of physical aggression during courtship. *Journal of Interpersonal Violence,* 2, 82-90.

Bates, C. M., & Brodsky, A. M. (1989). *Sex in the therapy hour: A case of professional incest.* New York: Guilford Press.

Beck, A. (1967). *Depression: Clinical, experimental and theoretical aspects.* New York: Harper & Row.

Bennett, T. L. (1987). Post-traumatic epilepsy: Its nature and implications for head injury recovery. *Cognitive Rehabilitation,* Sept/Oct, 14-18.

Berk, R., Newton, P., & Berk, S. (1986). What a difference a day makes: An empirical study of the impact of shelters for battered women. *Journal of Marriage and the Family, 48,* 481-490.

Bernard, G., Vera, H., Vera, M., & Newman, G. (1982). Till death do us part. *Bulletin of the American Academy of Psychiatry and the Law, 10*(4), 271-280.

Blackman, J. (1989). *Intimate violence: A study of injustice.* New York: Columbia University Press.

Bograd, M. (1984). Family systems approaches to wife battering: A feminist critique. *American Journal of the Orthopsychiatric Association, 54*(4), 558-568.

Bograd, M. (1986). Holding the line: Confronting an abusive partner. *Networker, 10*(4), 44-47.

Bowker, L. (1983). Marital rape: A distinct syndrome? *Social Casework: The Journal of Contemporary Social Work, 64, June*, 347-352.

Bowker, L., & Maurer, L. (1986). The effectiveness of counseling services utilized by battered women. *Women and Therapy, 5*(4), 65-82.

Brickman, P., Rabinowitz, V. C., Karuza, J., Coates, D., Cohen, E., & Kidder, L. (1982). Models for helping and coping. *American Psychologist, 37*,(4), 368-384.

Briere, J. (1989). *The effects of childhood sexual abuse on later psychological functioning: Defining a "post-sexual-abuse syndrome."* Paper presented at the Third National Conference on Sexual Victimization of Children. Washington, DC.

Brodsky, A. (1977). Countertransference issues and the female therapist: Sex and the student therapist. *Clinical Psychologist, 30*, 12-14.

Brody, C. (Ed.). (1987). *Women's therapy group*. New York: Springer Publishing Co.

Brown, L. S., & Root, M. P. P. (Eds.) (1990). *Diversity and complexity in feminist therapy*. New York: Harrington Park Press.

Browne, A. (1987). *When battered women kill*. New York: The Free Press-MacMillian.

Browne, A., & Finkelhor, D. (1986). The impact of child sexual abuse: A review of the research. *Psychological Bulletin, 99*(1), 66-77.

Browne, A., & Flewelling, R. (1986, October). *Women as victims or perpetrators of homicide*. Paper presented at the Annual Meeting of the American Society of Criminology, Atlanta, GA.

Browne, A., & Williams, K. R. (1989). Exploring the effect of resource availability and the likelihood of female-perpetrated homicides. *Law and Society Review, 23*(1), 75-94.

Brownmiller, S. (1975). *Against our will: Men, women and rape*. New York: Bantom Books.

Burgess, A. W. (Ed.). (1985). *Rape and sexual assault: A research handbook*. New York: Garland Publishing.

Campbell, J. (1986). Nursing assessment for risk of homicide with battered women. *Advances in Nursing Science, 8*(4), 36-51.

Chesler, P. (1991). *Mothers on trial*. New York: Harcourt Brace.

Chodorow, N. J. (1989). *Feminism and psychoanalytic theory*. New Haven, CT: Yale University Press.

Cotton, D. H. G. (1990). *Stress management: An integrated approach to therapy*. New York: Brunner/Mazel.

Council of University Directors of Clinical Psychology. (1980). *Summary of annual questionnaire*. Unpublished manuscript.

Courtois, C. A. (1988). *Healing the incest wound: Adult survivors in therapy*. New York: W. W. Norton.

Danieli, Y. (1988). Confronting the unimaginable: Psychotherapists' reactions to victims of the Nazi Holocaust. In J. P. Wilson, A. Harel, & B. Kahan (Eds.), *Human adaptation in extreme stress*. (pp. 219-238). New York: Plenum.

Daugherty, C., & Lees, M. (1989). Feminist psychodynamic therapies. In M. A. Dutton-Douglas & L. E. A. Walker (Eds.), *Feminist psychotherapies: Integration of therapeutic and feminist systems*. Norwood, NJ: Ablex Publishing Co.

Derogatis, L. (1977). *SCL-90R Manual-L*. Towson, MD: Clinical Psychometric Research.

Deutsch, C. J. (1984). Self-reported sources of stress among psychotherapists. *Professional Psychology: Research and Practice, 15*, 833-845.

Douglas, M. A. (1987). The battered woman syndrome. In D. Sonkin (Ed.), *Domestic violence on trial: Psychological and legal dimensions of family violence.* New York: Springer Publishing Co.

Douglas, M. A., & Strom, J. (1988). Cognitive therapy with battered women. *Journal of Rational-Emotive and Cognitive Behavioral Therapy, 6,* (1/2), 33-49.

Dutton, D. (1985). An ecologically nested theory of male violence towards intimates. *International Journal of Women's Studies, 8*(4), 404-413.

Dutton, D. (1988). *The domestic assault of women.* Boston: Alyn & Bacon.

Dutton, D., & Painter, S. (1981). Traumatic bonding: The development of emotional attachments in battered women and other relationships of intermittent abuse. *Victimology: An International Journal, 6,* 139-155.

Dutton, M. A. (1991, January). *Training issues in violence and victimization: Focus on gender.* Invited presentation at the Conference of the National Council of Schools of Professional Psychology. Tucson, AR.

Dutton, M. A. (1992). Assessment and treatment of PTSD among battered women. In D. Foy (Ed.), *Treating PTSD: Procedure for combat veterans, battered women, adult and child sexual assaults.* New York: Guilford Press.

Dutton, M. A., Perrin, S., Chrestman, K., & Halle, P. (1990). *MMPI trauma profiles for battered women.* Paper presented at the annual convention of the APA. Boston, MA.

Dutton, M. A., Perrin, S., Chrestman, K., Halle, P., & Burghardt, K. (1991). *Post-traumatic stress disorder in battered women: Concurrent validity.* Poster presented at the annual convention of the APA. San Francisco, CA.

Dutton-Douglas, M. A. (1988). Victimization and empowerment: The judicial process. In L. Rosewater (Chair), *Battered women who kill: Policy issues.* Symposium conducted at the Annual Conference of the American Psychological Association. Atlanta, GA.

Dutton-Douglas, M. A., & Dionne, D. (1991). Counseling and shelter services for battered women. In M. Steinman (Ed.), *Redefining crime: Responses to spouse abuse.* Anderson Press.

Dutton-Douglas, M. A., & Rave, L. (1990). Feminist ethical issues in psychotherapy training and supervision. In H. Lerman & N. Porter (Eds.), *Feminist ethics in psychotherapy.* New York: Springer Publishing Co.

Dutton-Douglas, M., & Walker, L. (Eds.). (1988). *Feminist psychotherapies: Integration of therapeutic and feminist systems.* Norwood, NJ: Ablex Publishing Co.

D'Zurilla, T. J. (1986). *Problem solving therapy: A social competence approach to clinical intervention.* New York: Springer Publishing Co.

Ellis, E. (1983). A review of empirical rape research: Victim reactions and response to treatment. *Clinical Psychology Review, 3,* 473-490.

Ewing, C. P. (1987). *Battered women who kill: Psychological self-defense as legal justification.* Lexington, MA: Lexington Books.

Farber, B. A., & Heifetz, L. J. (1982). The process and dimensions of burnout in psychotherapists. *Professional Psychology, 13*(2), 293-301.

Feminist Therapy Institute, Inc. (1987). *Ethical guidelines for feminist therapists and code of ethics.* Denver, CO: same.

Figley, C. R. (Ed.). (1985). Trauma and its wake: The study and treatment of post-traumatic stress disorder. New York: Brunner/Mazel.

Figley, C. R. (Ed.). (1986). *Trauma and its wake.* (Vol 2): *Traumatic stress theory, research, and intervention.* New York: Brunner/Mazel.

Figley, C. R. (1988). Post-traumatic family therapy. In F. M. Ochberg (Ed.), *Post-traumatic therapy and victims of violence.* New York: Brunner/Mazel.

Figley, C. R. (1989). *Helping traumatized families.* San Francisco: Jossey-Bass Inc., Publishers.

Finkelhor, D. (1979). *Sexually victimized children.* New York: Free Press.

Finkelhor, D., & Yllo, K. (1983). *License to rape: Sexual violence against wives.* New York: Holt & Rinehart.

Foa, E., & Kozak, M. (1986). Emotional processing of fear: Exposure to corrective information. *Psychology Bulletin, 99*(1), 20-35.

Foa, E., Stetekee, G, & Rothbaum, B. (1989). Behavioral/cognitive conceptualization of post-traumatic stress disorder. *Behavior Therapy, 20,* 155-176.

Fodor, I. G. (1988). Cognitive behavior therapy: Evaluation of theory and practice for addressing women's issues. In M. A. Dutton-Douglas & L. E. A. Walker (Eds), *Feminist psychotherapies: Integration of therapeutic and feminist systems.* Norwood, NJ: Ablex Publishing Corp.

Fortune, M. (1987). Epilogue: Justice-making in the aftermath of women battering. In D. Sonkin (Ed.), *Domestic violence on trial, psychological and legal dimensions of family violence.* New York: Springer Publishing Co.

Foy, D. (Ed.). (1992). *Treating PTSD: Procedure for combat veterans, battered women, adult and child sexual assaults.* New York: Guilford Press.

Freeman, A., Simon, K., Beutler, L., & Arkowitz, H. (Eds.). (1989). *Comprehensive handbook of cognitive therapy.* New York: Plenum Press.

Freeman, A., & White, D. (1989). Cognitive therapy of suicide. In A. Freeman, K. M. Simon, H. Arkowitz, & L. Beutler (Eds.), *Handbook of cognitive therapy.* New York: Plenum Press.

Freud, S. (1958). Remembering, repeating and working through. *Standard edition* (Vol 12, pp. 145-150). London: Hogarth Press. (Original work published in 1914)

Friedman, M. J. (1991). Biological approaches to the diagnosis and treatment of post-traumatic stress disorder. *Journal of Traumatic Stress,* 4(1), 67-91.

Frieze, I. (1980). *Causes and consequences of marital rape.* Paper presented at the American Psychological Association. Montreal.

Frieze, I. H., Knoble, J., Washburn, C., & Zomnir, G. (1980). *Characteristics of battered women and their marriages.* Part of the Final Report of Grant #1 R01 MN30193 to the National Institute of Mental Health. Rockville, MD.

Ganley, A. (1981). *Court mandated treatment for men who batter.* Washington, DC: Center for Women Policy Studies.

Ganley, A. (1987). Perpetrators of domestic violence: An overview of counseling the court-mandated client. In D. Sonkin (Ed.), *Domestic violence on trial.* New York: Springer Publishing Co.

Ganley, A. (1989). Integrating feminist and social learning analyses of aggression: Creating multiple models for intervention with men who battered. In P. Caesar & L. Hamberger (Eds.), *Treating men who batter.* New York: Springer Publishing Co.

Geffner, R., & Pagelow, M. D. (1990). Victims of spouse abuse. In R. T. Ammerman & M. Hersen (Eds.), *Treatment of family violence: A sourcebook.* New York: John Wiley.

Gelles, R. (1974). *The violent home: A study of physical aggression between husbands and wives.* Beverly Hills, CA: Sage Publications.

George, L. K., & Winfield-Laird, J. (1986). Sexual assault: Prevalence and mental health consequences. Final report submitted to the National Institute of Mental Health. Rockville, MD.

Giles-Sims, J. (1983). *Wife battering: A systems theory approach.* New York: Guilford Press.

Gilligan, C. (1982). *In a different voice: Psychological theory and women's development.* Cambridge, MA: Harvard University Press.

Gleser, G., Green, B., & Winget, C. (1981). *Buffalo Creek revisited: Prolonged psychosocial effects of disaster.* New York: Simon & Schuster.

Goldberg, H. (1982). Dynamics of rage between the sexes in a bonded relationship. In L. R. Barnhill (Ed.), *Clinical approaches to family violence.* Rockville, MD: Aspen Systems Corp.

Gondolf, E. (1988). The effect of batterer counseling on shelter outcome. *Journal of Interpersonal Violence,* 3(3), 275-289.

Goodrich, T. J., Rampage, C., Ellman, B., & Halstead, K. (1988). *Feminist family therapy: A casebook.* New York: Norton & Company.

Gordon, N. (1989). Migraine, epilepsy, post-traumatic syndromes, and spreading depression. *Developmental Medicine and Child Neurology, 31,* 682-689.

Graham, D., Rawlings, E., & Rimini, N. (1988). *Battered women as survivors: An alternative to treating learned helplessness.* Lexington, MA: Lexington Books.

Gurly, D. (1989). *Understanding the mixed roles of social support and social obstruction in recovery from child abuse.* Presentation to the Responses to Family Violence Research Conference. Purdue University, Indiana.

Hammond, D. C. (Ed.) (1990). Handbook of hypnotic suggestions and metaphors. New York: W. W. Norton & Co.

Hartman, A. (1987). Family violence: Multiple levels of assessment and intervention. *Journal of Social Work Practice,* 2(4), 62-78.

Hartman, C. R., & Burgess, A. W. (1988). Rape trauma and treatment of the victim. In F. M. Ochberg (Ed.), *Post-traumatic therapy and victims of violence.* New York: Brunner/Mazel.

Heider, J. 1985. *The Tao of leadership.* Atlanta: Humanics Limited.

Herman, J. L. (1988). Father-daughter incest. In F. M. Ochberg (Ed.), *Post-traumatic therapy and victims of violence.* NY: Brunner/Mazel.

Herman, J., Perry, C., & van der Kolk, B. A. (1989). Childhood trauma and borderline personality disorder. *American Journal of Psychiatry, 146*(4), 490-495.

Hilberman, E. (1980). Overview: The "wife-beater's wife" reconsidered. *American Journal of Psychiatry, 137*(11), 1336-1347.

Hilberman, E., & Munson, K. (1978). Sixty battered women. *Victimology,* 2, 460-470.

Ho, C. K. (1990). An analysis of domestic violence in Asian American communities: A multicultural approach to counseling. In L. S. Brown & M. P. P. Root (Eds.), *Diversity and complexity in feminist therapy.* New York: Harrington Park Press.

Hodgson, M. (1990). Shattering the silence: Working with violence in Native communities. In Laidlaw, T. A., Malmo, C., & Assoc. (Eds.), *Healing voices: Feminist approaches to therapy with women.* San Francisco: Jossey-Bass.

Holmes, T., & Rahe, R. (1967). The social readjustment rating scale. *Journal of Psychosomatic Research, 11*, 213-218.

Holtzworth-Monroe, A. (1988). Causal attributions in marital violence: Theoretical and methodological issues. *Clinical Psychology Review, 8*, 331-344.

Horowitz, M. (1976). *Stress response syndromes.* Northvale, NJ: Jason Aronson.

Horowitz, M. (1979). Psychological responses to serious life events. In V. Hamilton & D. Warburton (Eds.), *Human stress and cognition.* New York: Wiley.

Horowitz, M. (1986). *Stress response syndromes* (2nd ed.). Northvale, NJ: Jason Aronson.

Horowitz, M., Wilner, N., & Alverez W. (1979). Impact of event scale: A measure of subjective stress. *Psychosomatic Medicine, 41*, 209-218.

Janoff-Bulman, R. (1985). Criminal vs. non-criminal victimization: Victim's reactions. *Victimology: An International Journal, 10*, 498-511.

Janoff-Bulman, R. (1989). Assumptive worlds and the stress of traumatic events: Applications of the schema construct. *Social Cognition, 7*(2), 133-136.

Janoff-Bulman, R. (1992). *Shattered assumptions: Toward a new psychology of trauma.* New York: The Free Press.

Jones, J., & Barlow, D. (1990). The etiology of posttraumatic stress disorder. *Clinical Psychology Review, 10*, 299-328.

Jordan, J. V. (1984). *Empathy and self boundaries.* (Working paper no. 16). Wellesley, MA: Wellesley College. The Stone Center.

Kahana, B., Harel, Z., & Kahana, E. (1988). Predictors of psychological well-being among survivors of the Holocaust. In J. P. Wilson, Z. Harel, & B. Kahana (Eds.), *Human adaptation to extreme stress. From the Holocaust to Vietnam.* New York: Plenum Press.

Kalmuss, D., & Straus, M. (1982). Wife's marital dependency and wife abuse. *Journal of Marriage and the Family, 44*(2), 277-286.

Kasl, S. V. (1990). Some considerations in the study of traumatic stress. Special issue: Traumatic stress: New perspectives in theory, measurement, and research. *Journal of Applied Social Psychology, 20*(20, Part 2), 1655-1665.

Kaufman, G. (1989). *The psychology of shame: Theory and treatment of shame-based syndromes.* New York: Springer Publishing Co.

Keane, T., Malloy P., & Fairbank, J. (1984). Empirical development of an MMPI subscale for the assessment of combat-related stress disorder. *Journal of Consulting and Clinical Psychology, 52*(5), 888-891.

Keane, T., Zimering, R., & Caddell, J. (1985). A behavioral formulation of posttraumatic stress disorder in Vietnam Veterans. *The Behavior Therapist, 8*, 9-12.

Kilpatrick, D. G., & Veronen, L. J. (1983). *The aftermath of rape: A three-year follow-up.* Paper presented at the 17th Annual Convention of the Association for Advancement of Behavior Therapy. Washington, D.C.

Kilpatrick, D. G., Veronen, L. J., & Best, C. (1985). Factors predicting psychological distress among rape victims. In C. Figley (Ed.), *Trauma and its wake.* New York: Brunner/Mazel.

Korb, M. P., Gorrell, J., & Van De Riet, V. (1989). *Gestalt therapy: Practice and theory* (2nd ed.). New York: Pergamon Press.

Koss, M. P. (1989). *Is there a rape epidemic?* Paper presented at the Annual Meeting of the American Association for the Advancement of Science. San Francisco, CA.

Koss, M. P. (1990). The women's mental health research agenda: Violence against women. *American Psychologist, 45*(3), 374-380.

Koss, M. P., & Burkhart, B. (1989). A conceptual analysis of rape victimization: Long-term effects and implications for treatment. Psychology of Women Quarterly, 13, 27-40.

Lang, P. (1977). Imagery in therapy: An information processing analysis of fear. *Behavior Therapy, 8*, 862-886.

Lang, P. (1979). A bio-informational theory of emotional imagery. *Psychophysiology, 16*, 495-512.

Larsen, B. (1992). *The traumatic effects of battering: A conceptualization*. Unpublished manuscript. Nova University.

Lewinsohn, P. M. (1975). The behavioral study and treatment of depression. In M. Hersen, R. Eisler, & P. Miller (Eds.), *Progress in behavior modification*. New York: Academic Press.

Lindsey, K. (1978). When battered women strike back: Murder or self-defense. *Viva*, 58-74.

Lindy, J. D. (1988). *Vietnam: A casebook*. NY: Brunner/Mazel.

Lobel, K. (Ed.). (1986). *Naming the violence: Speaking out about lesbian battering*. Seattle: Seal Press.

Mahoney, M. R. (October, 1991). Legal images of battered women: Redefining the issue of separation. *Michigan Law Review, 90*(1), 1-94.

Malmo, C. (1990). Recreating equality: A feminist approach to ego-state therapy. In T. A. Laidlaw, C. Malmo & Assoc., *Healing voices: Feminist approaches to therapy with women*. San Francisco: Jossey-Bass.

Mantooth, C., Geffner, R., Franks, D., & Patrick, J. (1987). *Family preservation: A treatment manual for reducing couple violence*. Tyler, TX: University of Texas at Tyler Press.

Marshall, L. L., & Rose, P. (1987). Gender, stress and violence in adult relationships of a sample of college students. *Journal of Social and Personal Relationships, 4*, 299-316.

McCann, I. L., & Pearlman, L. A. (1990a). Vicarious traumatization: A framework for nderstanding the psychological effects of working with victims. *Journal of Traumatic Stress, 3*(1), 131-149.

McCann, I. L., & Pearlman, L. A. (1990b). *Psychological trauma and the adult survivor: Theory, therapy, and transformation*. New York: Brunner/Mazel Publishers.

McCann, I. L., Pearlman, L. A., Sakheim, D. K., & Abrahamson, D. J. (1988). Assessment and treatment of the adult survivor of childhood sexual abuse within a schema framework. In S. M. Sgroi (Ed.), *Vulnerable populations: Evaluation and treatment of sexually abused children and adult survivors* (Vol. 1, pp. 77-101). Lexington, MA: Lexington Books.

McCann, I. L., Sakheim, D. K., & Abrahamson, D. J. (1988). Trauma and victimization: A model of psychological adaptation. *The Counseling Psychologist, 16*(4), 531-594.

McGoldrick, M., & Gerson, R. (1985). *Genograms in family assessment*. New York: W. W. Norton.

McMullin, R. (1986). *Handbook of Cognitive Therapy Techniques*. New York: W. W. Norton.

Merwin, M., & Smith-Kurtz, B. (1988). Healing the whole person. In Ochberg, F. (Ed.), *Post-traumatic Therapy and Victims of Violence*. New York: Brunner/Mazel.

Miller, J. B. (1986). *Toward a new psychology of women* (2nd ed.). Boston: Beacon Press.

Miller, D. T., & Porter, C. A. (1983). Self-blame in victims of violence. *Journal of Social Issues, 39*(2), 139-152.

Morgan, P. (1982). Alcohol and family violence: A review of the literature. National Institute of Alcoholism and Alcohol Abuse, Alcohol consumption and related problems. *Alcohol and Health Monograph 1*. Washington, DC: USDHHS.

Morganstern, K. P. (1988). Behavioral interviewing. In A. S. Bellack, & M. Hersen (Eds.), *Behavioral assessment: A practical handbook*. New York: Plenum Press.

The National Center on Women and Family Law. (1988). Battered Women's Litigation Packet, Item #24. New York, NY.

Nezu, A. M., Nezu, C. M., & Perri, M. G. (1989). Psychotherapy for adults within a problem-solving framework: Focus on depression. Special issue: Problem-solving and cognitive therapy. *Journal of Cognitive Psychotherapy*, *4*(3), 247-256.

NiCarthy, G., Merriam, K., & Coffman, S. (1984). *Talking it out: A guide to groups for abused women*. Seattle: Seal Press.

Ochberg, F. M. (1980). Victims of terrorism. *Journal of Clinical Psychiatry*, *41*, 72-74.

Ochberg, F. M. (1988). *Post-traumatic therapy and victims of violence*. New York: Brunner/Mazel.

Ochberg, F. M. (1989). Cruelty, culture, and coping: Comment on the Westermeyer paper. *Journal of Traumatic Stress*, *2*(4), 537-541.

Pagelow, M. (1981). Factors affecting women's decisions to leave violent relationships. *Journal of Family Issues*, *2*(4), 391-414.

Pence, A. R. (1990). Worlds apart? Integrating research and practice in professional child and youth care training. *Child and Youth Services*, *13*(2), 235-241.

Pence, E. (1987). *In our best interest*. Duluth, MN: Minnesota Program Development, Inc.

Pence, E., & Paymar, M. (1985). *Criminal justice response to domestic assault cases: A guide for policy development*. Duluth, MN: Minnesota Program Development, Inc.

Pence, E., & Paymar, M. (1986). *Power and control: Tactics of men who batter: An educational curriculum*. Duluth, MN: Minnesota Program Development, Inc.

Pence, E., & Shephard, M. (1988). Integrating feminist theory and practice: The challenge of the battered women's movement. In K. Yllo & M. Bograd (Eds.), *Feminist approaches on wife abuse* (pp. 282-298). Newbury Park, CA: Sage Publications.

Perls, F. S. (1969). *Gestalt therapy verbatim*. Lafayette, CA: Real People Press.

Peterson, C., & Seligman, M. (1983). Learned helplessness and victimization. *Journal of Social Issues*, 2, 103-116.

Peterson, C., Semmel, A., von Baeyer, C., Abramson, L. Y., Metalsky, G. I., & Seligman, M. P. E. (1982). The Attributional Style Questionnaire. *Cognitive Therapy and Research*, *6*, 287-299.

Pirog-Good, M., & Stets, J. (1989). Recidivism in programs for abusers. *Victimology: An International Journal*.

Pope, K., & Bohoustous, J. (1986). *Sexual intimacy between therapists and patients*. New York: Praeger.

Pressman, B. (1989). Wife-abused couples: The need for comprehensive theoretical perspectives and integrated treatment models. *Journal of Feminist Family Therapy, 1*(1), 23-43.

Rachley, S. F. (1990). *An investigation of social support and sexual abuse history in victims of childhood sexual abuse.* Dissertation presented at Nova University. Ft. Lauderdale, FL.

Renzetti, C. (1988). Violence in lesbian relationships. *Journal of Interpersonal Violence, 3*(4), 381-399.

Renzetti, C. (1989). Building a second closet: Third party responses to victims of lesbian partner abuse. *Family Relations, 38,* 157-163.

Renzetti, C. M. (1992). *Violent betrayal: Partner abuse in lesbian relationships.* Newbury Park: Sage Publications.

Report of the Florida Supreme Court Gender Bias Study Commission. (1990). Tallahassee, FL: The Florida Supreme Court.

Rosenthal, R. H., & Akiskal, H. S. (1985). Mental status examination. In M. Hersen & S. M. Turner (Eds.), *Diagnostic interviewing.* New York: Plenum Press.

Rosewater, L. (1987). A critical analysis of the proposed self-defeating personality disorder. *Journal of Personality Disorders, 1*(2), 190-195.

Rosewater, L. (1988). Battered or schizophrenic: Psychological tests can't tell. In K. Yllo & M. Bograd (Eds.), *Feminist perspectives on wife abuse.* Beverly Hills, CA: Sage Publications.

Rosewater, L., & Walker, L. (Eds.). (1985). *Handbook of feminist therapy: Women's issues in psychotherapy.* New York: Springer Publishing Co.

Rossi, E. L. (1986). *The psychobiology of mind-body healing: New concepts of the therapeutic hypnosis.* New York: W. W. Norton.

Ruch, L., & Leon, J. (1983). Sexual assault trauma and trauma change. *Women and Health, 8,* 5-21.

Russell, D. (1982). *Rape in marriage.* New York: MacMillan.

Russell, D. (1984). The prevalence and seriousness of incestuous abuse: Stepfathers vs. biological fathers. *Child Abuse and Neglect, 8,* 15-22.

Sales, E., Baum, M., & Shore, B. (1984). Victim readjustment following assault. *Journal of Social Issues, 40*(1), 117-136.

Saunders, C. M. (1989). *Grief: The mourning after.* New York: Wiley.

Saunders, D. (1986). Wife abuse, husband abuse, or mutual combat? A feminist perspective. In K. Yllo & M. Bograd, (Eds.), *Feminist perspectives on wife abuse.* Beverly Hills, CA: Sage Publications.

Saunders, D. (1989). *Who hits first and who hurts most? Evidence for the greater victimization of women in intimate relationships.* Paper presented at the 41st Annual Meeting of the American Society of Criminology. Reno, NV.

Saunders, D. (1990). Post-traumatic stress disorder: A label that does not blame? *Wisconsin Coalition Against Domestic Violence, 9*(1), 5-6.

Saunders, D., Arata, C., & Kilpatrick D. (1990). Development of a crime-related post-traumatic stress disorder scale for women within the Symptom Checklist-90-Revised. *Journal of Traumatic Stress, 3*(3), 439-448.

Schechter, S. (1987). Guidelines of mental health practitioners in domestic violence cases. National Coalition Against Domestic Violence. Washington, DC.

Schutte, N., Bouleige, L., & Malouff, J. (1986). Returning to partner after leaving a crisis shelter: A decision faced by battered women. *Journal of Social Behavior and Personality, 1*(2), 295-298.

Scrignar, C. B. (1988). *Post-traumatic stress disorder: Diagnosis, treatment, and legal issues* (2nd ed.). New Orleans: Bruno Press.

Selgiman, M. (1975). *On depression, development and death.* San Francisco: Freeman.

Sgroi, S. M. (1988). *Vulnerable populations: Evaluation and treatment of sexually abused children and adult survivors* (Vol 1). Lexington, MA: Lexington Books.

Sherman L., & Berk, R. (1984). The Minneapolis Domestic Violence Experiment. *Police Foundation Reports, 1,* 1-8.

Shields, N. M., Resick, P. A., & Hanneke, C. R. (1990). Victims of marital rape. In R. T. Ammerman & M. Hersen (Eds.), *Treatment of family violence: A sourcebook.* NY: Wiley.

Slagle, D. A. (1990). Psychiatric disorders following closed head injury: An overview of biopsychosocial factors in their etiology and management. *International Journal of Psychiatry in Medicine, 21*(1), 1-35.

Snyder, D., & Fruchtman, L. (1981). Differential patters of wife abuse: A databased typology. *Journal of Consulting and Clinical Psychology, 49,* 848-885.

Snyder, D., & Scheer, N. (1981). Predicting disposition following brief residence at a shelter for battered women. *American Journal of Community Psychology, 9*(5), 556-566.

Stark, E., & Flitcraft, A. (1988). Personal power and institutional victimization: Treating the dual trauma of woman battering. In F. M. Ochberg (Ed.), *Post-traumatic therapy and victims of violence.* New York: Brunner/Mazel.

Stark, E., Flitcraft, A., Zuckerman, D., Grey, A., Robison, J., & Frazier, W. (1981). Wife abuse in the medical setting: An introduction for health personnel. *Domestic Violence, 7,* 1-54.

Steketee, G., & Foa, E. (1987). Rape Victims: Post-traumatic stress responses and their treatment: A review of the literature. *Journal of Anxiety Disorders, 1,* 69-86.

Stets, J., & Straus, M. (1990). Gender differences in reporting marital violence and its medical and psychological consequences. In M. Strauss & R. Gelles, (Eds.), *Physical violence in American families.* New Brunswick, NJ: Transatlantic Publishers.

Stone, L. (1984). Shelters for battered women: A temporary escape from danger or the first step toward divorce? *Victimology: An International Journal, 9*(2), 284-289.

Straus, M. A. (1979). Measuring family conflict and violence: The conflict tactics scale. *Journal of Marriage and the Family, 41,* 75-88.

Straus, M. A. (1990). The Conflict Tactics Scales and its critics: An evaluation and new data on validity and reliability. In M. A. Straus & R. J. Gelles (Eds.), *Physical violence in American families.* New Brunswick: Transaction Publishers.

Straus, M. A., & Gelles, R. J. (Eds.). (1990). *Physical violence in American families. Risk factors and adaptations in 8,145 families.* New Brunswick, NJ: Transatlantic Publishers.

Strube, M., & Barbour, L. (1983). The decision to leave an abusive relationship: Economic dependence and psychological commitment. *Journal of Marriage and the Family, 45,* 785-793.

Sturdivant, S. (1980). *Therapy with women: A feminist philosophy of treatment.* New York: Springer Publishing Co.

Thurman v. City of Torrington. 595 F. Supp. 1521 (D. Conn. 1984).

Tolman, R. (1989). The development of a measure of psychological maltreatment of women by their male partners. *Violence and Victims*, 4(3), 159-177.

Tomkins, S. S. (1987). Shame. In D. L. Nathanson (Ed.), *The many faces of shame.* New York: Guilford Press.

Totman, J. (1978). *The murderess: A psychosocial study of criminal homicide.* San Francisco: R & E Research Associates.

Trimble, M. R. (1985). Post-traumatic stress disorder: History of a concept. In C. R. Figley (Ed.), *Trauma and its wake: The study and treatment of post-traumatic stress disorder.* New York: Brunner/Mazel.

Truesdell, D., McNeil, J., & Deschner, J. (1986). Incidence of wife abuse in incestuous families. *National Association of Social Workers–Briefly Stated*, 138-140.

Turner, J. (1990). Let my soul soar: Touch therapy. In Laidlaw, T. A., Malmo, C., & Assoc. (Eds.), *Healing voices: Feminist approaches to therapy with women.* San Francisco: Jossey-Bass.

van der Kolk, B. A. (Ed.). (1987). *Psychological trauma.* Washington, DC: American Psychiatric Press.

van der Kolk, B. A. (1988). The trauma spectrum: The interaction of biological and social events in the genesis of the trauma response. *Journal of Traumatic Stress, 1*(3), 273-290.

van der Kolk, B. A., Brown, P., & van der Hart, O. (1989). Pierre Janet on post-traumatic stress. *Journal of Traumatic Stress*, 2(4), 365-378.

Walker, L. E. A. (1979). *The battered woman.* New York: Harper & Row.

Walker, L. E. A. (1984). *The battered woman syndrome.* New York: Springer Publishing Co.

Walker, L. E. A. (1989). *Terrifying love.* Glenview, IL: Harper Collins.

Walker, L. E. A., & Edwall, G. E. (1987). Domestic violence and determination of visitation and custody. In D. J. Sonkin (Ed.), *Domestic violence on trial* (pp. 127-152). New York: Springer Publishing Co.

Watson, C. (1990). Psychometric posttraumatic stress disorder measurement techniques: A review. *Psychological Assessment*, 2(4), 460-469.

Watson v. Kansas City. 57 LW 1049 (Oct. 4, 1988).

Watson v. Kansas City, 857 F.2d 690 (10th Cir. 1988).

Wilson, J. P. (1989). *Trauma, transformation, and healing: An integrative approach to theory, research, and post-traumatic therapy.* New York: Brunner/Mazel.

Wilson, J., & Walker, A. (1990). Toward an MMPI trauma profile. *Journal of Traumatic Stress*, 3(1), 151-169.

Wolfe, D. A., Wolfe, W., & Best, C. L. (1988). Child victims of sexual abuse. In V. B. Van Hassett, R. L. Morrison, A. S. Bellack, & M. Hersen (Eds.), *Handbook of family violence.* New York: Plenum Press.

Wolfgang, M. E. (Ed.). (1967). *Studies in homicide.* New York: Harper & Row.

Yllo, K. (1988). Political and methodological debates in wife abuse research. In M. Bograd & K. Yllo (Eds.), *Feminist perspectives on wife abuse.* Beverly Hills, CA: Sage.

Index